# MARCO ⊕ POLO

# MEDITERRANEAN

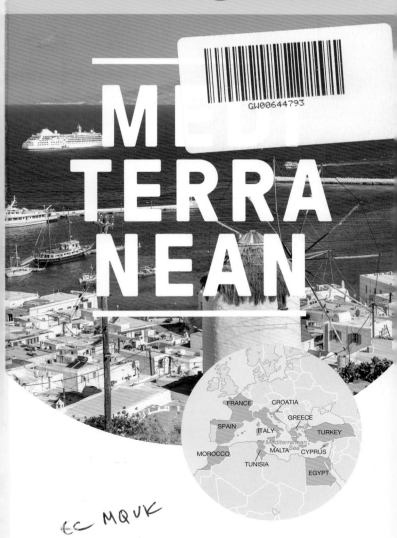

GW00644793

FRANCE    CROATIA
          GREECE
SPAIN   ITALY
               TURKEY
          Mediterranean
MOROCCO   MALTA Sea CYPRUS
     TUNISIA
               EGYPT

EC MQUK

Arriving on the cruise ship is already something special, because seen from the sea everything looks quite different.

Much to see, art and culture, the country and its people –a cruise offers you a multifaceted experience. And there's more: modern liners also offer you entertainment and recreation on board.

**So, bon voyage and ship ahoy on your tour around the Mediterranean Sea!**

**SYMBOLS**

INSIDER TIP  Insider Tip

★  Highlight

☆  Scenic View

🍃  Green & fair: for ecological or fair trade practices

**PRICE CATEGORIES RESTAURANTS**

| | |
|---|---|
| *Expensive* | over 12 euros |
| *Moderate* | 6–12 euros |
| *Budget* | under 6 euros |

Prices for a main dish and one non-alcoholic drink

**DID YOU KNOW?**
Timeline → p. 8,
Animal kingdom for families → p. 17, Cataspanish → p. 20, Travel with kids→ p. 25, White or blue → p. 34, Watery fun → p. 36, Beaches for sun lovers → p. 38, P as in prominence → p. 44, Fragrant fields → p. 52, Strength in peace and calm → p. 55,

# CONTENTS

Fontana di euros → p. 61, Vatican curiosities → p. 64, Mafia → p. 69, Pizza Napoletana → p. 70, Time to chill → p. 72, Island of towers → p. 80, Puppet shows → p. 82, Volcanoes & earthquakes → p. 85, Devil's time → p. 90, Backstage → p. 104, Building instead of saving → p. 111, Beach Life on

Mykonos → p. 117, The donkeys of Santorini → p. 119, White-blue → p. 121, Animal welfare → p. 126, Oh, you juicy melon! → p. 140, Ramadan → p. 148, Travel with kids → p. 151, Veils → p. 165, Oriental wellness → p. 163, Veils → p. 156,

**MAPS IN THE GUIDEBOOK**
(📖 1/A3) refers to the pull-out maps

**INSIDE FRONT COVER:**
The best highlights

**INSIDE BACK COVER:**
General map

# The best MARCO POLO Insider Tips

## Our top 15 Insider Tips

**INSIDER TIP** **Medieval skyscrapers**
Marvel in the evening sun at the wonderful sight of the *Plaça del Rei* (King's Square) and the fascinating silhouette of the historic royal palace → p. 17

**INSIDER TIP** **Catalan snacks at delicatessen shop**
Savour delectable refreshments: tapas, sausages and wine at the grocery of *La Pineda* → p. 20

**INSIDER TIP** **Mixed, not shaken**
Enjoy freshly made tiger-nut milk, *horchata*, at Valencia's *Horchatería El Siglo* on the *Plaça Santa Catalina* → p. 24

**INSIDER TIP** **City exotics**
A modern zoo of the 21st century, maintaining high standards and animal habitats designed in a true-to-life way: Valencia's *Bioparc in the Parque de Cabecera* → p. 25

**INSIDER TIP** **Eat globally**
In Palma's trendy neighbourhood, *Santa Catalina*, you can sample all the foods of the world – in more than 80 international restaurants and bars → p. 36

**INSIDER TIP** **Japan on the Mediterranean**
Would you have expected so much greenery within Monaco's concrete jungle? Here it is – the *Jardin Japonais.* The Shinto garden is a natural work of art made of water, stone and plants → p. 44

**INSIDER TIP** **Magnificent view of the port**
Throughout the centuries, only a few initiates could enjoy this view. Generally accessible since 2013, the fortress tower of *Roi René* at the Fort *Saint-Jean* in Marseille offers an exceptional view of the port (photo above) → p. 52

CAST OFF

# DISCOVER THE MEDITERRANEAN!

It is time to take a deep breath! You are probably feeling somewhat relieved and pleased that you have not forgotten your passport and that you and your luggage are now safely aboard. The prospect that this very ship is going to be your floating home for the next days or weeks – even though, most of the time, you will not even notice that the ground below you is moving – is certainly a dream come true.

Now, as we are about to see the mooring lines being cast off, we can at last set sail! Leaving the port of embarkation is always a very special and enthralling experience, not only for first-time travellers on a cruise. Time after time, this very moment sends even the most seasoned travellers into rapture: as the ship moves further and further away from the quay, and the coastline gradually disappears in a haze, you will sense the embrace of the wide, seemingly infinite sea.

*So let's go and enjoy the thrilling exploration of new shores*, the quest for exciting experiences and the discovery of fascinating cultures. You might very well imagine yourself as an adventurous seafarer of bygone times. Fortunately, and contrary to the old seafaring explorers on the high seas, you do not have to worry about anything. On modern ships, every care is taken to ensure your well-being, and especially your

Photo: Full steam ahead to new shores and fascinating experiences safety. Mariners of old would no doubt have wished for similar conditions on their ships.

As the ship is softly gliding on its course, your mind is perhaps wandering back to the days when you pored and mulled over travel catalogues and compared tours. You might have considered various destination options in remote and far-away places, or maybe even a big world tour, but you selected the *Mediterranean*. Congratulations, you have chosen well! A very good choice indeed, because you will be served a whole menu of travel delicacies: *art* and *architecture*; *foreign cultures* and *history* encompassing thousands of years; *beautiful nature* and *exotic specialities*. We leave it to you to determine the menu items you would like to have

as starters, main courses and desserts. Without a doubt, your voyage on the Mediterranean, the mare nostrum of the ancient Romans, will not disappoint you with any boring moments.

Discover the most popular summer travel destinations within Europe, such as Spain and Italy, from a very different perspective. Experience a Mediterranean holiday filled

> **Eclectic: the Mediterranean flourishes on its rich variety**

with adventure, relaxation, solitude, conviviality and much more. Explore the rich culinary variety on the shores of the Mediterranean. The enticing palette ranges from Mediterranean to Oriental cuisine. Right from the outset, many diverse and novel dishes will tantalize your palate and delight your senses.

Across borders, you will be visiting fascinating cities with a history dating back centuries, even thousands of years. Although you may have experienced history as a

**Around 4000 BC**
Beginning of advanced Egyptian civilization

**Around 3000 BC**
Beginning of Minoan culture on Crete

**From approximately 2600 to 2500 BC**
Construction of the pyramids of Giza

**From 1000 BC**
Highly advanced Etruscan art and technology

**700–480 BC**
Beginning of the Greek city-states

**4th–1st century BC**
Rome rules the entire Mediterranean area

Fabulous destinations and a floating hotel – good reasons for a cruise

set of dull figures at school, you may rest assured that this tour will be awesome and fascinating. You will experience the cradles of culture such as *Greece*, *Egypt* or *Italy*, stroll through medieval cities like *Dubrovnik* in Croatia, admire the *cathedrals of Valencia and Barcelona* or delight in the *Hagia Sophia* in Istanbul. You will be amazed at the extraordinary architectural craftsmanship of the 6th century and stunning domes as high as eighteen storeys. On *France's southern coast* and in the *Principality of Monaco*, you may reminisce about Grace Kelly and Cary Grant, and indulge in the entrancing stylish luxury, as if you were a celebrity yourself. Of course, you can also trace Humphrey Bogart's footsteps in Casablanca, and immerse yourself in the colours and fragrances of "One Thousand and One Nights" in northern African countries like *Morocco*, *Tunisia* and *Egypt*.

Just a reminder: you will definitely also visit islands on your trip, although there might not always be much time ashore for extended sea- and sunbathing. *Cyprus* and *Malta*, *Rhodes* and *Crete*, *Ibiza* and *Mallorca* will pleasantly surprise you with culture and nature.

**5th century**
Teutons, Lombards, Vandals and Huns invade Italy; fall of the Roman Empire

**From 722**
Reconquista, re-conquest of Muslim spheres of influence on the Iberian Peninsula

**From the 13th century**
The seaport republics of Venice, Genoa and Pisa control the maritime trade

**1870**
Unification of Italy

**From 1951**
Decolonization of North Africa

# AROUND THE MEDITERRANEAN

## DEEP, DEEPER DEEPEST

The *Calypso Deep*, south-west of the Greek Peloponnese peninsula, is the deepest point in the Mediterranean Sea, with a maximum depth of 5267 m/17,280 ft. The average depth of the water is around 1430 m/4690 ft. Thus, the seventh largest ocean of the world (2.5 million sq km/965,255 sq mi) is comparatively shallow. On average, the world's oceans have a depth of 4000 to 5000 m/13,000 to 16,000 ft.

## FIRE AND WATER

There are two active volcanoes in the Mediterranean: Stromboli, approx. 916 m/3000 ft high, on the island of Stromboli (part of the Lipari Islands); and Etna, approx. 3323 m/10,900 ft high, situated on Sicily near Catania and Messina. In Naples, Mount Vesuvius is also still active, though its last eruption was in 1944. Nonetheless, new eruptions cannot be ruled out. Vesuvius' cataclysmic eruption on 24th August AD 79 led to the total destruction of the towns of Pompeii, Herculaneum, Oplontis and Stabiae, burying them under molten lava and cinders. It was a catastrophe for the inhabitants. In later times, when excavations began, scientists discovered beneath the thick layer of volcanic matter magnificent relics and evidence of Roman culture.

## THE MIDDLE OF THE EARTH

The Romans called it "Our Sea" (mare nostrum) to demonstrate their power.

## Dive into the depths of the Mediterranean: from impressive underwater worlds to onshore places steeped in history

The Turks regard it as the "White Sea" and the ancient Egyptians referred to it as the "Great Green". The word "Mediterranean" derives from the Latin mediterraneus, which means the middle of the earth. According to the world-view of ancient civilizations, the Mediterranean constituted the centre of the world, as they knew it.

## LIONS EMBODY VENETIAN POWER

Around the Mediterranean Sea, the winged Lion of St Mark prominently and resplendently graces city entrances, churches and squares. It symbolizes the long predominance of the Venetian Republic and its colonies in the *eastern Mediterranean* and the *Adriatic Sea*. From the 7th/8th century until 1797, the "Lion's Republic" was the strongest maritime and economic power, stretching from *northern Italy* to *Crete* and occasionally to the *Crimea* and to *Cyprus*. The winged lion usually stands with a raised paw and an open book with the inscription (in Latin): "Peace be with you, Mark, my evangelist."

World-famous cultural monuments: the pyramids of Giza with sphinx

Sometimes the lion also wields a sword, symbolizing Venetian naval power.

# EVERYTHING HERE IS INCREDIBLY OLD

In antiquity, advanced civilizations inhabited areas around the Mediterranean Sea. Human settlements there actually date back to prehistoric times. Around 2500 BC, at about the same time when the Egyptians erected the pyramids, the Minoan culture developed on Crete. The Romans started to expand their power in the 1st century BC. The Migration Period ultimately spelt the end of the vast Roman Empire. Although the ancient empires and kingdoms belong to the realms of history, plenty of evidence and countless relics of their cultures have survived throughout the ages. Today we can still admire them, notably the pyramids of Giza, the Acropolis in Athens and the Colosseum in Rome.

# FLOWERING BEAUTIES

The tube anemone has no fragrance, but millions of divers and snorkelers admire it for its stunning flowery crown of tentacles and its many different species. It lives on the Mediterranean seabed, at a depth of 5 to 40 m/15 to 130 ft. True anemones use a pedal disc foot to attach to stones, rocks, shells or other objects. Other species deflate and condense their cone-like bodies to drive into sand or mud; others have long tube structures and retract into their tube to protect them from attacks.

# TALES OF FISH MOTHERS AND SEA GODS

The sea is of great significance in ancient Greek mythology. Pontus, one of the primordial deities, personified the Mediterranean Sea. He is the father of many sea gods. Somewhat later, the sea goddess Thalassa made her appearance in stories. According to mythology, she mingled with Pontus and produced all fish and marine living creatures. There are various depictions of her: sometimes as a transparent woman formed of seawater; or as a woman with crab-claws in her hair; or dressed with bands of seaweed; or with a ship's oar in her hand.

## SALTY MEDITERRANEAN

Through the Strait of Gibraltar, the Atlantic Ocean feeds water with low salinity values into the salty Mediterranean, thereby preventing the latter from eventually drying out. More Mediterranean water is constantly evaporating than can be replenished by precipitation alone, which causes a continuous salinity increase. Fortunately, the exchange of high- and low-salinity water between the Mediterranean and the Atlantic offsets the high evaporation, and the Mediterranean will probably not dry out soon.

## SHARKNADO – SHARK ALARM IN THE MEDITERRANEAN?

Are there any shark alarms in the Mediterranean? About one-tenth of the worldwide 500 shark species are present in the Mediterranean, and 15 of those species are so large that they could perhaps pose a danger to humans. In all probability, nothing will happen though, given the decreasing numbers of the very large ones. Smaller species abound, and species from tropical regions are on the increase. Large sharks endemic to the Mediterranean include the blue shark, with a length of 3.50 m/11 ft and the thresher shark, which can be as long as 6 m/20 ft.

## TO FISH OR NOT TO FISH...

Since time immemorial, fishing has been an integral part of the lives of people living on seashores. In modern times, and on a global scale, fisheries are suffering from the negative effects of commercialization. In the Mediterranean, unrestricted fishing activities have led to overfishing of 90 percent of fish stocks and some species are in danger of becoming extinct. Small-scale indigenous fishing people are battling to survive. A programme drafted and agreed upon by 13 Mediterranean states contains measures to protect fish stocks and to advance sustainable small-scale fishing.

## KNIGHTS OF TIMES GONE BY

Who were the legendary knights of the Middle Ages who engaged in battles around the Mediterranean? They were Crusaders who waged bitter wars against Muslims in a quest to conquer the Holy Land. In the end, they suffered defeat. They came from all over Europe. Since some were not first-borns and had to forego family inheritances, they sought their bliss in foreign spheres. Distinct traces of the knights have remained, notably on Malta, the origin of the Order of Malta. The Knights Templar and the Knights of the Order of St John also traversed the Mediterranean.

## THE STONE OF THE KITCHEN

*Olea europea* – this is the rather dry botanical name of the indigenous tree that grows in the entire Mediterranean region. Gnarled olive trees, with their silvery-green leaves, bestow the famed special charm on Mediterranean landscapes. Yet their fruit, also referred to as stone fruit or drupes, has much greater significance: it is the source of olive oil. Foodies and all proud cookery enthusiasts have at least one bottle of good olive oil in their kitchen. The highest quality is always the best, and the label should indicate that it is cold-pressed extra virgin olive oil. Sustainability-conscious consumers will naturally prefer organically certified olive oil. Olivewood, widely appreciated for its lovely grain, is used for furniture making and other products. The olive tree also features in religion: as a sign of peace, a dove brings Noah an olive branch.

# SPAIN

**Fiesta or siesta? This question should actually bear no relevance to your onshore excursions on the Spanish Mediterranean coast.**

Lavishly celebrate the rich cultural treasures of this region. Exciting and atmospheric Barcelona with Gaudí's architectural work and vibrant La Rambla promenade will fill you with exuberant enthusiasm. Admire the cathedrals of Palma, Valencia, Cadiz or Malaga, which represent a celebration of religious faith expressed by architects of earlier centuries. Speaking of celebrating: the islands of Ibiza and Mallorca are famous, though sometimes also notorious, for their rambunctious party-beaches.

Yet, the image is deceiving. In fact, these islands offer a host of possibilities to celebrate and feast in the realms of history, art and culture, which will regale you. In this sense, "it's party time"!

# BARCELONA

**The capital of Catalonia (pop. 1.6 million) is one of the most pulsating and fascinating metropolitan areas in Europe.**

Barcelona's history dates back to Roman times. It is captivatingly attractive because of its many different features and diverse traits. There are parks and promenades, the old town and trendy hotspots, the harbour and La Ramblas, plenty of museums and art nouveau buildings of Antoni Gaudí.

Photo: Summer, sun, Mallorca – Port de Sóller on the north-west coast

A classic holiday destination: bays, beaches and vibrant cities on the coastline between the French border and Andalucía

One of the contemporary architectural highlights is the Torre Glòries (formerly known as *Torre Agbar*), a skyscraper designed by the French architect Jean Nouvel. At night, it is spectacularly illuminated. Barcelona extends between the foothills of the Serra de Collserola mountain range and the Mediterranean Sea. Its 13 km/8 mi shoreline features many beaches. In the city, ⚅ *Montjuic Hill* (173 m/567 ft), close to the port, and ⚅ *Tibidabo Mountain* (532 m/1745 ft), in the north-west, offer splendid views.

## SIGHTSEEING

### BARRI GÒTIC ⭐ (*𝄞 1/D2*)

The Gothic Quarter is the heartbeat of Barcelona's old town. Here life pulsates between the Rambla and the *cathedral*. In the cloister of this imposing religious edifice, one will always find a gaggle of 13 white geese in honour of St Eulàlia, the young patron saint of Barcelona, who suffered martyrdom. The *Pla de la Seu*, the *Plaça del Pi*, the *Plaça de Sant Jaume* and the town hall are just a few of Barcelona's showpieces. Other points of attraction are the *Royal Palace* and the *Barcelona City History Museum* (MUHBA). Equally lovely is a walk through the narrow alleys. In the Middle Ages, the *Carrer del Call* enclosed the Jewish Quarter. A particular highlight is the *Plaça Reial* and its arcades, from where you can walk to the nearby Rambla.

### CATEDRAL (CATHEDRAL) ⭐ (📖 1/D2)

The impressive and enormous religious edifice was built over a long period. In the 11th century, it was erected on the foundations of the early Christian basilica, which the Moorish invaders had earlier destroyed. Only between 1298 and 1448, the magnificent church nave took on its present form, whereas the completion of the neo-Gothic main facade only occurred in 1890. The choir stalls in the centre of the interior are beautiful – a special feature of Spanish churches that were not exclusively designed for liturgical purposes. One of the 29 side chapels that date mainly from the16th and 17th centuries contains a cross that allegedly has miraculous qualities. It apparently helped to defeat the Turkish

Cathedral of Barcelona

fleet in the great Battle of Lepanto. The cathedral's function was not only to spread the glory of God, but also earthly fame. It is dedicated to the martyr St Eulàlia, the patron saint of the city, who suffered martyrdom in Roman times. The saint is buried in an alabaster sarcophagus in the crypt beneath the high altar.

It is worthwhile visiting the enchanting cloister and its small chapels, garden, Gothic fountain and flock of geese. The cloister leads to the cathedral's small museum (Mon–Sat 1pm–5pm, Sun 2pm–5pm | admission 7 euros), displaying cult objects, archaeological finds and Gothic altar pictures. *Admission free | 7 euros | Plaça de la Seu | Info & opening hours at: www.catedralbcn.org | Metro L4: Jaume I*

### PALAU DE LA MÚSICA CATALANA ⭐ (📖 1/D1)

Between 1905 and 1908, Lluís Domènech i Montaner built this music palace in the most opulent art nouveau-style. The columns of the ornately decorated street facades, facing the Carrer Sant Pere Més Alt, are covered with mosaics and crowned with the busts of Bach, Beethoven, Wagner and Palestrina. The centre of the auditorium features an exceptionally beautiful multi-coloured, stained-glass skylight, in the form of an inverted dome. Ornamental flowers and tendrils, dragonheads and other sculptures decorate the ceilings, walls and columns in the hall. No reservation; buy tickets well in advance! *Admission 18 euros | C/ de Sant Pere Més Alt | Info & opening hours at: www.palaumusica. cat | Metro L1, L4: Urquinaona*

### PLAÇA DEL REI (📖 1/D2)

A monumental architectural ensemble! The Palau Reial Mayor, the Grand Royal Palace, with its large Gothic ceremonial hall, Saló del Tinell, and the impressive watchtower, Mirador del Rei Martí (a kind

# ANIMAL KINGDOM FOR FAMILIES

## AQUÀRIUM (🗺 1/D3)

The main attraction is a large transparent tunnel, offering underwater views of sharks and ocean sunfish. In an interactive area, children can discover the marine world. *July/Aug daily 9.30am–11pm, Sept–June Mon–Fri 9.30am–9pm, Sat/Sun 9.30am–9.30pm | admission 20 euros (online 17 euros), children 15 euros (online 12.75 euros) | Moll d'Espanya del Port Vell | www.aquariumbcn.com | Metro L4: Barceloneta*

## PARC ZOOLÒGIC (🗺 1/E2)

The zoo, with its open-air enclosures, dolphin shows and pony rides, is in the Parc de la Ciutadella, where you can rent bicycle rickshaws or boats. *Winter daily 10am–6pm, mid-May–mid-Sept daily 10am–8pm, otherwise daily 10am–7pm | admission 19.90 euros, children (3–12 years) 11.95 euros (online 10 percent discount) | Parc de la Ciutadella | www.zoobarcelona.cat | Metro L1: Marina or Arc de Triomf*

of medieval high-rise building), together with the adjacent Palau del Lloctinent (Lieutenant's Palace, with Gothic facade and Renaissance-style inner courtyard) and the small Gothic chapel of Santa Agata (14th century) form a INSIDER TIP splendid setting, especially at sunset. Interesting concerts take place in summer, taking full advantage of the especially good acoustics. In the Saló del Tinell, the ceremonial banqueting hall of the Royal Palace, Spanish kings received Christopher Columbus after his return from America. In the 15th century, the Spanish Inquisition held its court proceedings there. Convicted heretics were burnt on the square outside. Access the palace interior from the Barcelona City History Museum (MUHBA), at the other end of the Plaça del Rei. *Metro L4: Jaume I*

## MUSEU PICASSO (PICASSO MUSEUM) ⭐ (🗺 1/D2)

Among Barcelona's museums, this museum boasts the highest number of visitors. It mainly displays Pablo Picasso's work from his early creative phase, the "Blue Period". This phase dates from 1895 to 1904, the time when the painter lived in Barcelona. He had a lifelong connection with Barcelona. From the 1930s onwards, Picasso donated paintings to the city, including the famous "Harlequin". In 1963, all the scattered works eventually found their way into one single museum. Picasso gave the museum his famous "Las Meninas"-series and all the early works that he had created in the family residence in Barcelona. In addition, his widow Jacqueline donated valuable ceramics to the museum. *Tue–Sun 9am–7pm, Thu until 9.30pm | admission 11 euros, every 1st Sun of month and every Sun from 3pm free | C/ de Montcada 15–23 | www.museupicasso.bcn.cat | Metro L4: Jaume*

## CASA BATLLÓ

The fantasy building has a roof simulating a dragon spine, columns like elephant feet, balconies reminiscent of skeletal bones, an undulating facade and glittering tiles resembling fish-scales. When Antoni Gaudí created it between 1904 and 1906, the tale of the dragon killer Sant Jordi (Saint George), the patron saint of Barcelona, inspired him. Like the

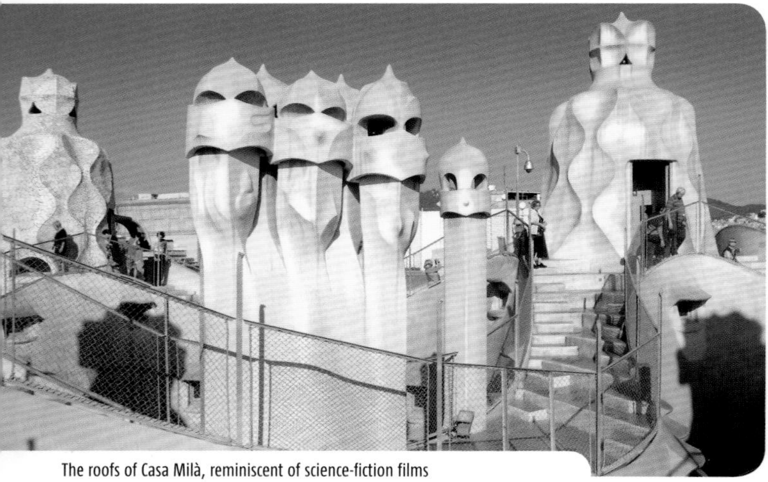

The roofs of Casa Milà, reminiscent of science-fiction films

Casa Amatller, the Casa Batlló is part of the Manzana de la Discòrdia (Block of Discord) and a Unesco world heritage site. *Daily 9am–8pm | admission 23.50 euros (including audio guide) | Passeig de Gràcia 43 | www.casabatllo.es | Metro L2, L3, L4: Passeig de Gràcia*

## CASA MILÀ ★

The undulating facade of Gaudí's most famous building is reminiscent of plastic modelling material. The facade is self-supporting, free of load-bearing walls. The columns resemble knobbly tree trunks. The rough-hewn appearance of the Casa Milà, built with limestone blocks, stuns visitors with its creator's ingenuity and architectural idiosyncrasy. Head to the rooftop with its innovative skylights, staircase exits and an assembly of unusual, curiously quirky chimneys, also known as the "garden of warriors". Apart from the roof terrace, you can view an apartment and visit the multimedia Espai Gaudí for information on the master's life and work. Of special note are guided tours by night, with sparkling wine, video projections and live music on the roof terrace. *March–Oct daily 9am–8pm, Nov–Feb daily 9am–6pm | admission 22 euros | Passeig de Gràcia 92 | www.lapedrera.com | Metro L3, L5: Diagonal*

## SAGRADA FAMÍLIA ★

Antoni Gaudí worked for four decades on his major masterpiece, which is still incomplete. He devoted the last twelve years of his life exclusively to this project. When he died in 1926, he had completed only one-tenth of the building: the apse, one of the 18 envisaged spires, the neo-Gothic crypt, and the east-facing facade (Christmas facade) that is dedicated to the birth of Christ.

Since then, work has resumed, financed by donations and entrance fees. Optimists predict that it will be completed in 2026, the 100th commemoration of Gaudí's death. Meanwhile, the roof construction is complete and the pope has consecrated the basilica. The roof of the spectacular nave rests on enormous columns stretching towards the sky, like soaring trees.

Gaudí considered the mammoth edifice in the tradition of medieval cathedrals, which took generations to complete. He regarded his project as "sermon in stone". *April–Sept daily 9am–8pm, Oct and March daily 9am–7pm, Nov–Feb 9am–6pm | admission 15 euros, lift 4.50 euros | Plaça de la Sagrada Família | www.sagradafamilia.org | Metro L2, L5: Sagrada Família*

### LA RAMBLA ★ (*ɱ 1/D1–2*)

Strolling on this first-class promenade is an amazing experience, whether by day or by night. From the Plaça de Catalunya, the Rambla runs for 1200 m/3937 ft in the direction of the monument of Christopher Columbus and the port, passing cafes, hotels, the *Mercat de la Boqueria* (the legendary vibrant covered marketplace) and the opera house, the *Gran Teatre del Liceu*. Street-artists, musicians, caricaturists and flower-sellers contribute to the buzz and overall vivacity. Note: beware of pickpockets!

### YACHT HARBOUR AND BEACH ☼ (*ɱ 1/C4–F3*)

Preparations for the 1992 Olympic Games and an urban-renewal project gave Barcelona an opening to the seafront. The revitalization of a run-down area, and the construction of a new beachfront of 4.5 km/2.5 mi, led to the removal of an old railway. The beach stretches from the old fishing district of Barceloneta to the Olympic Village, featuring a modern yacht harbour, the Port Olímpic, restaurants, nightclubs, pubs and Frank O. Gehry's bronze fish sculpture (50 m/164 ft long). In the direction of Barceloneta, the beach promenade leads up to the Parc de la Barceloneta. On the beach a little more to the south, Rebecca Horn's sculpture of four stacked cubes evokes memories of shacks that once stood here until the 1980s. *Metro L4: Barceloneta*

### MONTJUÏC (*ɱ 1/A3*)

The well-known hill (173 m/567 ft) is inextricably linked to Barcelona's history, culture and leisure activities. During the Battle of Barcelona and the Castilian siege, it was of strategic importance. The fortress castle was built in the 17th century. During the Franco dictatorship, the castle was a dreaded prison. Today the hill is one of Barcelona's most attractive recreational areas. From the Parallel (L3) metro station, a cable car (*Funicular de Montjuic*) takes you to Avinguda de Miramar, from where the cableway *Telefèric de Montjuïc (daily from 10am | 9 euros one way, 12.50 euros return)* takes you to the fortress. From the Old Harbour, the cableway Transbordador del Port takes visitors to Montjuïc *(daily from 11am | 11 euros one way, 17 euros return)*.

## TAPAS

### BAR LEO (*ɱ 1/D3*)

Unusual tapas bar, always packed. The old songs emanating from the jukebox are great fun. Enjoy wine or beer, paired with mussels, croquettes and more. *Daily | C/ de Sant Carles 34 | Tel. 9 32 24 20 71 | Metro L4: Barceloneta*

### CERVECERIA CATALANA

Popular and classic tapas: huge piles of tantalizing appetizers and tempting snacks, around the clock. Avoid long queues at noon and grab a bite between meals. *Daily | C/ de Mallorca 236 | Metro L3, L5: Diagonal*

### EL XAMPANYET (*ɱ 1/D2*)

This rustic spot offers *cava* (Catalonian sparkling wine), wine and delicious tapas; a charming, wildly popular and quintessential tapas bar. *Closed Sun evenings, Mon, and Aug | C/ Montcada 22 | Tel. 9 33 19 70 03 | Metro L4: Jaume*

## SHOPPING

### INSIDER TIP ▶ LA PINEDA (⌖ 1/D1)

Tapas, sausages and wine: sample sumptuous Catalonian delicatessen at tasting tables in this marvellous old grocery store. *Mon–Sat 9am–3pm and 6pm–9.30pm, Sun 11am–3pm | C/ del Pi 16 | Metro L3: Liceu*

### OLD TOWN ★ (⌖ 1/C–D 2–3)

Enjoy the pleasant atmosphere of Barcelona's old town. Browse and shop around at leisure. If antiques fascinate you, check out the antique dealers in the medieval alleys in the former Jewish Quarter of El Call. The most interesting shops are in the Carrer de la Palla and in the alleyway of Carrer dels Banys Nous.

### MERCAT DE SANT JOSEP ★ (⌖ 1/C1)

Visit Barcelona's famous marketplace on the Rambla, aptly called "La Boqueria" or "Stomach of Barcelona". Mesmerizing and enticing displays of finely filigreed piles of fish and other seafood, mushrooms, pepperoni, nuts or truffles will overwhelm you. Almost everybody buys here, Catalonian homemakers and top-class chefs alike. Enjoy a bite at one of the food stalls, but preferably not at lunchtime, when crowds flock to the market. Avoid the overpriced stands at the entrance. *Closed Sun | La Rambla 91 | Metro L3: Liceu*

### INSIDER TIP ▶ HAPP BARCELONA (⌖ 1/E2)

Happ derives from the word "happening" and that is the motto of this concept store. Pop-up retail, exhibitions, and events: the slogan "be happ-y" covers innovative fashion ranges and accessories, lifestyle design products, jewellery and cosmetics, all featuring young labels. Sustainably produced in small Spanish artisanal centres, most items come at fair prices. *Tue–Sat 11.30am–2.30pm and 4.30pm–8.30pm | C/ Comercial 3 | Metro L4: Jaume I*

### LA MANUAL ALPARGATERA ★ (⌖ 1/D2)

For many generations, this traditional and popular enterprise has been making *espardenyes* (Catalan for espadrilles), customized and tailor-made, even for prominent Hollywood stars like Michael Douglas. The popular canvas shoes have natural-fibre soles made of bast, jute rope or braids. Almost all materials are sustainably sourced and recyclable. The shoes fit easily into any luggage! *C/ Avinyó 7 | Metro L3: Liceu*

# CATASPANISH

Officially, Catalonia is bilingual. Theoretically, all notices, forms, signposts, and so on are supposed to be in both Spanish and Catalan. However, in everyday life, Catalonians prefer their own language to Spanish, which can sometimes cause a bit of confusion. When you respond in Spanish to a question or a greeting, Catalan speakers usually switch automatically to Spanish. Approximately 6 million people speak Catalan. They are geographically located along the Mediterranean coast between Perpignan and Alicante, on the Balearic Islands, in Andorra and in the Sardinian city of Alghero.

# FOOD & DRINK

## In tapas paradise: Spain's delectable appetizers and mini-snacks

**When it comes to eating and drinking, genuine hedonism prevails in Spain. The mere act of nourishing oneself is never an insipid daily routine, but always a long, pleasant, convivial and sumptuous ritual.**

The *rhythm of Spanish everyday life* differs from other countries. Days start relatively late, with a small breakfast *(desayuno)* at around 8am or 8.30am (some Spaniards skip breakfast when going to work). It is a rather meagre affair to start the day with nothing but strong *coffee with milk (café con leche)* and a sweet bread-roll *(bollo suizo)* or a croissant. Therefore, it is customary to have a more nourishing light meal around noon or at 12.30pm, when bars start serving tapas and all kinds of *appetizers* and snacks. Many bars are regarded as tapas paradises because of their tempting and delicious variety of tapas, copiously ranging from marinated anchovies *(boquerones)* to small meatballs *(albóndigas)* to a Russian salad *(ensaladilla rusa)* made of potatoes, eggs and mayonnaise. A good choice for a snack between meals would be a mixed salad *(ensalada mixta)* or a vegetable stew *(menestra)*. Sumptuous lunches *(comida)* are available from 2pm/2.30pm. *Dinner (cena)* is usually taken later in the evening, from around 9pm/9.30pm, often even as late as 10pm. Dinners usually start with tapas. Alternatively, you can enjoy a full dinner and opt for an exciting *tapas-tour*, hopping from bar to bar.

### LOCAL SPECIALITIES

**chorizo** – countrywide available salami with paprika and garlic

**churros** – fried-dough pastry, served with thick chocolate sauce

**gazpacho** – cold Andalucían soup, made of a mixed purée of white bread, tomatoes, cucumber, garlic, onions, bell peppers, oil and vinegar

**jamón serrano** – air-dried ham; especially good if originating from the Andalucían mountain towns of Jabugo and Trevélez

**paella** – originally from Valencia, this rice dish has countless variations; basic ingredients are saffron rice and vegetables

# VALENCIA

There is a special atmosphere in Valencia, a touch of something exotic. The Romans and Moors also felt magnetically drawn to the city and left their mark on the Mediterranean metropolis.

In 1094, the Spanish national hero El Cid advanced on the city and wrested it from the Muslims for the first time. However, it was not until 1238 that King Jaume I completed the Christian reconquest. The catastrophic flooding of the Turia river in 1957 led to the 'Plan Sur' and the diversion of the river to the south. The drained river bed was turned into a magnificent garden complex. Life is traditional in the Barri del Carmen, the thousand-year-old city district where narrow streets alternate with impressive monuments such as the El Carmen Church. The 'City of the Arts and Sciences' has become an international architectural landmark. The splendid Old Town and many of the promenades were spruced up, the harbour and seafront area changed completely.

SIGHTSEEING

### CATEDRAL ⭐

The cathedral shows a heady mix of styles ranging from Gothic to neo-Classicism. The forerunners of the mediaeval house of worship (13th century) were a Roman temple and the main mosque from the Moorish period. The *Puerta de Palau*, one of the three portals of the cathedral, dates from this early period. On the exterior, the Baroque *Puerta de los Hierros* and the Gothic *Apostle Gateway* with its numerous figures are well worth seeing. The highlights in the interior: the Santo Cáliz Chapel with the 'Holy Grail', the Borgia Chapel with Goya's masterful painting 'San Francisco y el Moribundo Impenitente', the high altar, the arm relic of Saint Vincent Martyr in the Capilla de la Resurrección, and the museum with its exhibits of sacred art. You should also take the time to climb up the almost 51 m/167.3 ft-high ⚜ bell tower *El Miguelete (Mon–Sat 10am–7pm, Sun 10am–1pm and 5pm–7pm)*. *Cathedral Mon–Sat 10am–6.30pm, Sun 2pm–6.30pm (in winter on every day*

The Ciutat de les Arts i les Ciències is an architectural masterpiece

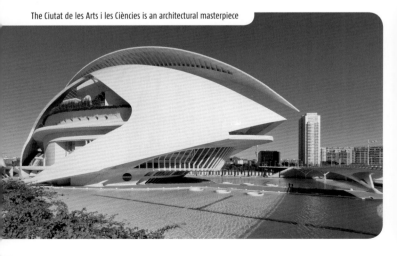

until 5pm) | audio guide | www.catedralde valencia.es | Plaza de la Reina

## CIUTAT DE LES ARTS I LES CIÈNCIES ⭐ (*2/A4*)

Dazzling white, curving forms, inlaid work of broken tiles, buildings like monumental sculptures – the modern 'City of the Arts and Sciences', which combines the fascinating architectural concepts of Santiago Calatrava and Félix Candela, offers both culture and leisure activities. The series of buildings in the complex include the *Palau de les Arts Reina Sofía* (concert hall and opera house), the *Hemisfèric* (Imax cinema), which resembles a gigantic eye, the *Umbracle* (the verdant 'foyer' of the complex), the events hall *Ágora*, the *Museu de les Ciències Príncipe Felipe (science museum) (open daily 10am–9pm)* and the *Oceanogràfic* aquarium (*Sun–Fri 10am–6pm, Sat 10am–8pm*). The exhibits in the Science Museum are there to be touched and experimented with. The highlight of the excellently planned *Oceanogràfic* is the underwater glass tunnel in the 'Oceans' section where sharks and rays float above the heads of the visitors. You will be able to save money if you buy the INSIDER TIP ▶ combined ticket (ask for *conjunta*) for the *Hemisfèric*, Science Museum and *Oceanogràfic*. Av. del Professor López Piñero 3–7 | www.cac.es

## INSTITUT VALENCIÀ D'ART MODERN (IVAM) ⭐

Temporary exhibitions of works by contemporary artists are held in the modern main building of the Institute for Modern Art. The IVAM has an enormous art collection and regularly exchanges works with museums from all over the world. The Hall of the *Great Wall (Sala de la Muralla)*, in which a section of the mediaeval city wall runs between modern columns, is unusual and makes a particularly interesting setting for exhibitions. *Tue–Sun 11am–7.30pm | Sun free admission | Guillem de Castro 118 | www.ivam.es/en*

## JARDINS/JARDINES DEL TURIA ⭐ (*2/A4*)

After the catastrophic flood in the middle of the 20th century, the River Turia was diverted to the south far away from the city; the dried-out riverbed was then used to create large new gardens and parks. Today, there are countless palms and orange trees, as well as fountains and even football grounds. The city inhabitants have become very fond of the 7.5 km/4.7 mi strip of green that runs through the city all the way to the *Ciutat de les Arts I les Ciències*. Near the Old Town, the Jardines del Turia pass close by the *Torres de Serrans/Serranos* the massive remains of the mediaeval city walls.

## LLOTJA/LONJA DE LA SEDA ⭐

Starting in the late 15th century, merchants went about their business in Valencia's Silk Exchange, which is now one of the Unesco World Heritage Sites. The towering building with its spiral columns combines Gothic with early-Renaissance elements. Sundays, the Lonja is the site of a coin and stamp market. *Mon–Sat 9.30am–7pm (in winter until 6pm), Sun 9.30am–3pm | Plaza del Mercat*

## MUSEU DE BELLES ARTS ⭐

The scope of the exhibits in the Museum of Fine Arts ranges from Roman objects and magnificent altar paintings to 20th-century artworks. There are works by all of the famous names in Spanish painting, including Diego de Velázquez, Alonso Cano, Juan Ribalta, Francisco de Goya and Joaquín Sorolla, in addition to an interesting choice of temporary exhibitions. The museum's café and restaurant are

Bell tower in the Plaza Santa Catalina

also a nice place to relax. *Tue–Sun 10am–8pm | free admission | C/ San Pio V 9 | museo-bellasartesvalencia.gva.es*

### MUSEU FALLER

Anyone truly interested in the tradition of the *Fallas* festivities in Valencia should visit this museum housed in what used to be a military hospital. You will be able to admire Falla figures that were 'pardoned' at the wish of the people and saved from the flames. *Tue–Sat 9.30am–7pm (in winter until 6pm), Sun 10am–3pm | Plaza Monteolivete 4*

### MUSEU NACIONAL DE CERÀMICA

The museum houses halls with precious furniture and porcelain as well as a replica of a Valencian kitchen from the 18th century. *Tue–Sat 10am–2pm and 4pm–8pm, Sun 10am–2pm, Sat afternoon and Sun free admission | C/ del Poeta Querol 2 | mnceramica.mcu.es*

### EL PATRIARCA

Valencia's most beautiful Baroque church simply overflows with an abundance of decoration. A very special atmosphere is created with the INSIDER TIP Gregorian chants sung by a 20-member choir on Thursday evening at 6.30pm and Tue–Sun during Lauds at 9.30am. The choral tradition dates back to the year 1604. *C/ de la Nau 1*

### PLAÇA/PLAZA SANTA CATALINA

Lively inner-city square with the Baroque bell tower of the Santa Catalina Church. The cool tigernut milk horchata is stirred fresh every day in the INSIDER TIP *Horchatería El Siglo*. You can visit the Gothic *Santa Catalina Church* on the adjacent *Plaza Lope de Vega* and buy embroidery and lace on the renovated 'Round Square' *Plaça/Plaza Redonda*.

### PLAÇA/PLAZA DE LA VIRGEN

Terrace cafés and orange trees create the very special atmosphere of this square at the back of the Cathedral. This was the site of the forum in Roman days. The most important building is the *Basílica de la Mare de Déu dels Desamparats* where the picture of the 'Holy Virgin of the Defenceless' is revered.

### TORRES DE SERRANS/SERRANOS

The defence towers of old Valencia overlook the river bed of the Turia. They were built at the end of the 14th century and are an interesting work from the Gothic period by Pere Balaguer. The towers, which were also used as a prison for the nobility, have stood free since the surrounding city walls were demolished in the 19th century. *Mon–Sat 9.30am–7pm (in winter until 6pm), Sun 9.30am–3pm / Plaça dels Furs*

## TAPAS

Typical tapas bars in the Old Town include INSIDER TIP *El Molinón (Calle Bosseria/Bolsería 40)*, offering a selection of over 50 different snacks, and *El Pilar (C/ del Moro 13)*. The vibrant area around the Gran Via Marquès del Turia, with restaurants such as *Aquarium (Gran Via Marquès del Turia 57)*, is another pop-ular place to enjoy oneself; all Budget.

## SHOPPING

The experts have still not made up their minds. Is Barcelona's Boquería or the ★ *Mercat Central (Mercado Central | Mo–Sa 7–15 Uhr | Plaza del Mercat 6 | www.mercadocentralvalencia.es)* in Valencia Spain's most beautiful market? The stalls on the 86,000 ft² of this Art Nouveau building overflow with sausages, fruit, vegetables, fish and meat. There is an elegant shopping area near another historical building, the *Mercat Colón (Mercado Colón)* on *C/ Jorge Juan*. This is where you will find many exclusive shoe shops. The *C/ de las Cestas* is famous for its handcrafted goods made of willow basketwork. In the Barri del Carmen around the *C/ Bolsería, C/ Quart* and *Pl. del Tossal*, you will find unusual fashion shops. There are several branches of the *El Corte Inglés* department store chain on *C/ Pintor Sorolla, Avenida Pio XII, C/ Colón* and at other locations. The markets selling all kinds of wares (*mercadillos*), e.g. on Tue at the *Mercadillo Jerusalén-Pelayo (Convento Jerusalén)* and on Wed at the *Mercadillo Mosén Sorell (Plaza Mossén Sorrell)*, are always full of life.

## BEACHES

Valencia has more than 7 km/4.4 mi of beaches. The best section starts north of the port with the connecting *Las Arenas* and *Malvarossa* beaches; they are lined with beautiful promenades.

# TRAVEL WITH KIDS

INSIDER TIP BIOPARC ✪

A little piece of Africa and even more – that is what the Bioparc offers. An innovative zoo that meets all the demands of the 21st century, Bioparc makes it possible for visitors to view the animals in authentically recreated habitats in which they have as much space as possible. Rhinoceros, lions, giraffes, elephants, lemurs and monkeys are just some of the animals. *Daily from 10am to 9pm, April–Jun until to 8pm, at other times 6/7pm depending on the month | admission 23.80, children (4–12 years) 18 euros, under 4 years free | Av. Pío Baroja 3 | www.bioparcvalencia.es*

**PARQUE GULLIVER (JARDINES DEL TURIA)**

Popular are the Jardines del Turia, a park area that was developed over a 7.5 km-/4.7 mi-area, also includes the *Parque Gulliver* between the Palace of Music and 'City of the Arts and Sciences'. There you can see an enormous model of the legendary giant lying tied to the ground. His clothes form other playground facilities. What is also nice is that INSIDER TIP no admission is charged for the playground. It is shut if the weather is bad. *July/Aug daily 10am–2pm and 5pm–9pm, at other times daily 10am–8pm*

# SHOPPING

Craftworks, wine and olive oil are a good buy – either from traditional *mercadillos* or supermarkets. But beware of cheesy bric-a-brac

Tiny flamenco dolls, pilgrims' sets including fedoras and cloaks or porcelain figures of the Virgin Mary – trashy goods and kitsch is ten a penny in Spain. But don't worry, you will find plenty to take your fancy if you make sure to keep your eyes open for the quality products. Authentic local handicrafts and delicacies make nice souvenirs for your loved ones at home.

## CULINARY ITEMS

You should definitely buy some high-quality Serrano ham or Manchego cheese – it is two to three times less expensive than at home. An even better idea is to have sausages and cheese shrink-wrapped *(envasar al vacío)* for a small additional fee. Other specialities are marinated and pickled peppers *(pimientos)* and olives *(aceitunas)*. Águilas in the region of Murcia is famous for its preserved capers *(alcaparras)*. Cold-pressed olive oil *(aceite de oliva virginextra)* is always good value for money.

## ARTISANSHIP

Ceramics have always been a popular souvenir. Thanks to tourism demand the pottery craft still florishes today, escpecially in the Andalucían cities of Granada and Seville. Pottery shops that sell handmade jugs, dishes, bowls and vases with unique designs. At first glance these may seem a little rustic and tacky, but there's no escaping their charm. The pottery makers will pack your souvenirs carefully to ensure they won't break in transit. But beare in mind that handmade ceramics are only rarely dishwasher-safe.

## WINE & SCHNAPPS

The wine-growing country Spain offers a variety of quality wines. Selected cultivation areas have a protected designation of origin (Denominación de Origen, or DO for short). Brandy or sherry are not really worth buying as the prices are similar to those at home.

# ALACANT/ ALICANTE

**From the sea, whether by road or by air – Alicante (pop. 330,000) is a hub of plane and car travel, as well as a port for cruise ships and yachts. However, the sprawling city is much more than just a way station.**

Visitors can experience the lively character of a Mediterranean city in the area around the marina and Explanada d'Espanya; the Sant Joan beach area makes an attractive holiday destination. The Romans were the first to enthuse about the special quality of the light that today shines over faceless high-rise buildings as well as pleasant promenades and parks such as Monte Tossal and El Palmeral. The highlight of the city's rich heritage is the *Santa Bárbara* Castle.

## SIGHTSEEING

### OLD TOWN

This compact area is north of the Explanada de Espanya and east of the bustling Rambla de Méndez Núñez with the small pedestrian precinct C/ Mayor (bars, restaurants), the Baroque Town Hall (18th century) and the 17th-century *San Nicolás Cathedral* with its 45 m/147.6 ft) blue dome.

### CASTELL/CASTILLO DE SANTA BÁRBARA ★ ⛅

The castle complex on the steep Monte Benacantil dominates the scene from an altitude of 166 m/545 ft above the city. The origins of the Castillo can be traced back to the early Middle Ages. There is a lift *(ascensor) (April–Sept daily 10am– 10pm, at other times 10am–8pm)* up to the castle from behind the Playa del Postiguet. The view is absolutely spectacular!

### EXPLANADA DE ESPANYA

Somebody once counted them: the ground of Alicante's showpiece promenade is covered with 6.6 million pieces of marble in black and white and red tones. This is where everybody meets to indulge in their favourite activity of promenading in the shade of the palm trees. The marina is located on the other side of the coastal road.

### MUSEU ARQUEOLÒGIC PROVINCIAL

Take a walk through the past from prehistoric times to the middle ages. There is a special atmosphere when you INSIDER TIP visit in the middle of summer when the museum stays open until midnight *Plaza del Doctor Gómez Ulla 6 | Information & opening hours: www.marqalicante.com*

## SHOPPING

The well-stocked markets attract everyone eager to buy or just take a look round, including the *Mercat Central (Mon–Sat mornings and Sat afternoons | Av. Alfonso X El Sabio 8)* and the *Mercat Babel (same opening hours | C/ Asilo)*. There are additional markets on some mornings until around 1.30pm–2pm (*mercadillos*), e.g. on Thu and Sat the *Mercadillo Teula* and around the C/ Gran Vía and C/ Teulada. There is also an *arts and crafts market* well worth visiting in the summer on Fri–Sun 7pm until midnight (otherwise Sun 10am– 2pm) on the Plaza de Santa Faz.

## BEACHES

The best beaches are to the north-east, beginning with the 900 m/2953 ft long *Playa del Postiguet*. The small bays (*calas*) around *Cabo de las Huertas* have a great deal of charm. Far and away the most popular and longest beach is the *Platja de San Juan/Playa de San Juan*, a 3 km/1.9 mi sandy dream.

The coastal city of Cartagena has a rich history

## WHERE TO GO

### GUADALEST ⭐ ☀

When one considers that only about 200 people live here, Guadalest is subject to one of the largest touristic onslaughts in Spain, receiving around 2 million visitors every year. The historical centre is over-looked by a castle. The views of the sur-rounding countryside are fantastic: the rugged mountains above and the Guadal-est reservoir below in the valley. Museums to visit include the folkloric *Casa Orduña* and the *Museo de Instrumentos de Tortura (in the summer open daily 10.30am–9pm, otherwise until 6pm)*, which focuses on the themes of the Inquisition and a collection of torture instruments. A curious museum is the *Museo de Microminiaturas (open dai-ly July 10am–7pm, Aug. 10am–9pm, other-wise 10am–6pm)*, which displays miniature works – such as Goya's 'Naked Maya' on the wing of a fly – by the artist Manuel Ussá. More miniatures can also be found in the *Museo de Microgigante (same opening hours)*. Guadalest is about 60 km/37 miles

northeast of Alicante. *information: Oficina de Turismo (Av. de Alicante | tel. 9 65 88 52 98 | www.guadalest.es)*

### ELX/ELCHE

Palms, palms – nothing but palms! There are almost as many palm trees as residents in Elche (pop. 227,000). ⭐ *Palmerar (El Palmeral)*, the grove of palm trees that was laid out under Moorish rule is considered the largest of its kind in Europe and is on Unesco's World Heritage List. During their occupation, the Moors not only created verdant gardens but, as experts in oasis cultivation, they were able to develop ag-riculture by using sophisticated irrigation methods. The famous statue of the 'Lady from Elche' was created 2500 years ago when the city was called Heliké. Besides the architecture that bears witness to the time of the Moors, such as the castle *Palau d'Altamira,* also known as *Alcàsser de la Senyoria* (with the Archaeological Museum) and the chunky *La Calaforra/Calahorra* tower, modern architecture has started occupying the cityscape.

# CARTAGENA

**The harbour city, situated 30 km/18.6 mi in the south-west (pop. 218,000), looks back on over 2000 years of history.**

Discover the remains of a *Punic city wall (Muralla Púnica) (open daily Juli–mid-Sept. 10am–20pm, in winter Tue–Sun 10am–5.30pm, otherwise Tue–Sun 10am–7pm | C/ San Diego 25)* with an information centre and an entrance into a monastery crypt dating from the 18th century and the field of destroyed buildings on the *Cerro Molinete*. Follow the traces of the Romans in the *Casa de la Fortuna (Tue–Sun 10.30am–3.30pm | entrance at the Plaza del Risueño)*, the *Augusteum (Information about opening times in the Casa de la Fortuna | C/ Caballero)*, the *Archeological Museum (C/ Ramón y Cajal 45 | www.museoarqueologicocartagena.es)* and the *Teatro Romano (Plaza del Ayuntamiento 9 | next to the Muralla Bizantina)*. The ☆ castle hill with the *Castillo de la Concepción* offers the best views of the theatre, docks and surrounding mountains and can be easily reached by a ☆ panoramic lift. At the bottom of the station, you will see the entrance to a former bunker from the Spanish Civil War – now a museum *(Refugio-Museo de la Guerra (July–mid-Sept daily 10am–8pm, Nov–March Tue–Sun 10am–5.30pm, at other times Tue–Sun 10am–7pm | C/ Gisbert 10). Info: Oficina de Turismo (Palacio Consistorial | Plaza del Ayuntamiento 1 | Tel. 9 68 12 89 55 | www.cartagenaturismo.es | www.cartagenapuertodeculturas.com)*

## WHERE TO GO

**MURCIA**

The regional capital, 75 km/46.6 mi. north-west of La Manga del Mar Menor on the Rio Segura, can look back on 1200 years of eventful history. Its first rulers were the Moors, who enclosed the settlement within a massive mantle of walls, named it *Mursiya* and were in control until well into the 13th century. The Christians then moved in and, in 1394, began construction of the magnificent ☆ *Cathedral*, which is still Murcia's most important architectural monument. Its 90 m/295.3 ft-high tower is the visible symbol of the city from afar. Anyone interested in art should also pay a visit to the *Cathedral Museum (Museo de la Catedral | from 10am)* and the interesting *Museo de Santa Clara (from 10am | Av. Alfonso X el Sabio I)*. There are attractive gardens towards the river near the Cathedral. A visit to the *Museo Salzillo (from 10am | Plaza de San Agustín 3/C/ Doctor Quesada | www.museosalzillo.es)* with an exhibition from the oeuvre of the local Baroque sculptor Francisco Salzillo (1707–1783) is especially worthwhile. The *Museum of Fine Arts (Museo de Bellas Artes) (C/ Obispo Frutos 12 | entrance free)* focuses on paintings from the Renaissance and Baroque periods.

# MALAGA

**Malaga is Andalucía's second largest city (pop. 570,000). With its fascinating museums, lively Old Town, enchanting parks and new harbour area, the city is always fun to explore.**

Malaga is no longer just a transfer point for holidaymakers on the Costa del Sol. Ever since the Picasso Museum opened in 2003, the culture in this harbour city has been flourishing. Malaga now offers a variety of new museums, such as the *Museo Carmen Thyssen* and the *Museo Automovilístico*. An elegant harbour area has even been built for the guests arriving on cruise ships. Apart from the city's old tapas bars, the entire Old Town has been given a new shine. Some of the Malagueños' beloved rituals include the Easter processions, strolling down the Calle Marqués de Larios, hopping between tapas bars and visiting one of the chiringuitos on Sunday. At these beach bars, sardines are grilled on wooden skewers over an open fire. In short, Malaga is a city you'll quickly fall in love with!

## SIGHTSEEING

### ALCAZABA ✂️

At one point in time, this 11th-century Moorish fortification was supposedly even more beautiful than the Alhambra in Granada. It now boasts tranquil gardens with relaxing water features and romantic corners with beautiful views. *Daily 9am–6pm, April–Oct til 8pm | admission 2.20 euros, Alcazaba and Gibralfaro 3.55 euros*

### CASTILLO DE GIBRALFARO ✂️

Malaga's second Moorish fortress towers over the city from its hilltop site. It's linked to the Alcazaba by a walled-in footpath that leads up the hill. It's worth visiting the Gibralfaro just to get a view over Malaga and its harbour. *Daily 9am–6pm, April–Oct til 8pm | admission 2.20 euros, Gibralfaro and Alcazaba 3.55 euros, free on Sun after 2pm*

### CATHEDRAL DE LA ENCARNACIÓN

The Malagueños call their cathedral *La Manquita*, 'the one-armed lady'. Its construction dragged on for more than 250 years (1528–1783). With the locals no longer wanting to pay a special tax to finance all the pomp, its second tower was never completed. Especially noteworthy are the 17th-century choir stalls carved by Pedro de Mena and the 4000-pipe organ. *Mon–Fri 10am–6pm, Sat 10am–5pm | admission 5 euros*

### MUELLE UNO

Malaga's modern harbour is decked out in white. From its promenade, you can casually walk towards the lighthouse. In the evening, there are plenty of bars where you can enjoy a drink. You can also view some exciting art at the Parisian ⭐ *Centre Pompidou (daily 9.30am–8pm | admission 7 euros | centrepompidou-malaga.eu)*. Here, in the Spanish branch, you find changing exhibitions of contemporary art.

### MUSEO CARMEN THYSSEN

It took four years to construct the Palacio Villalón in the Old Town of Malaga. This cultural highlight cost 25 million euros and is now home to 230 works of art. This famous, first-class collection belongs to the Baroness Carmen Thyssen-Bornemisza. Among the works are 19th-century paintings with mostly Andalucían motifs. The artists include Joaquín Sorolla, Mariano Fortuny and Julio Romero de Torres. *Tue–Sun 10am–8pm | admission 6 euros | C/ Compañía 10 | www.carmenthyssenmalaga.org*

The Alcazaba: a fortification relic dating from the Moorish period

### MUSEO PICASSO MALAGA ⭐

The Picasso Museum in Malaga is a must for all Picasso fans – and for those who have not yet formed an opinion about the artist. Picasso's daughter-in-law and her son, Bernard, have given the museum more than 200 works – or lent them as permanent loans. *From 10am | admission 7 euros | C/ de San Agustín 8 | www.museopicassomalaga.org*

### TABACALERA

He checks out the cars while she observes the art? Not really the best plan. Why not look at them both together? Located in the old tobacco factory south of the centre, the *Museo Automovilístico y de la Moda (Tue–Sun 10am–7pm | admission 8.50 euros | www.museoautomovilma laga.com)* and the *Colección del Museo Ruso (Tue–Sun 9.30am–8pm | 8 euros | www.coleccionmuseoruso.es)* has some truly impressive exhibitions. 'Cars are art' is the message proclaimed at the car museum, where roughly 100 beautifully designed automobiles, stemming from all decades,

are placed in halls alongside 200 haute couture clothing articles by Chanel, Dior and many others. At the Russian National Museum, Museo Ruso, a portion of their giant art collection is on display. You may know the works by the Russian artist Marc Chagall, a Constructivist from the 1920s. The giant paintings stemming from the 19th centruy are truly impressive. *Av. Sor Teresa Prat 15*

### BEACH BARS

*Chiringuitos* is the name given to the popular beach bars and restaurants in Andalucía. In Malaga, they're a culinary staple. In summer, the fish is grilled over an open flame. You can taste it, e.g. on the beaches of Malagueta and Pedregalejo.

### WHERE TO GO

#### GRANADA

The attraction of this Spanish top-notch destination (pop. 240,000) emanates from the once religious enemies, the Moors, who created a wonder of the world with their "red castle" (the meaning of the Arabic al-hambra). Due to the daily deluge of visitors to the ⭐ *Alhambra*, admission numbers are limited. It is therefore advisable that you make an early advance reservation, using your credit card. The relevant link is available on the official Alhambra homepage *www.alhambra-patronato.es*. The district of ⭐ *Albaicín* has retained the character of a medina. Very narrow alleyways wind up the steep hill, lined with Arabian tea rooms and souvenir shops.

# GIBRALTAR (U.K.)

Gibraltar (pop. 29,000) is a very English area. The Rock of Gibralter has been a British Overseas Territory since 1713. Some 7 million visitors come here every year to explore the massive Rock that is home to the famous apes and to shop in the *Main Street* with its duty-free shopping (they do accept euros). It is well worth visiting the ☽ *Upper Rock Nature Reserve*. Here you'll find the limestone caves of *St Michael's Cave*, the *Great Siege Tunnels* (a defence system from the end of the 18th century) and the *Apes' Den* (where the famous Barbary macaques leap around), which offers a beautiful view. The reserve is best reached by cable car *(daily 9.30am–5.15pm, April–Oct till 7.15pm | roundtrip 14 pounds, incl. the nature reserve 22 pounds)*. Dolphin watching *(approx. 30 euros/ person)* is also very popular. There are several companies operating, mostly out of Marina Bay.
Information: *Gibraltar Tourist Board (Cathedral Square | Tel. 00350 20 074 9 50 | www.visitgibraltar.gi)*

# CADIZ

**In the evenings on the Campo del Sur and on the Alameda de Apodaca, the people in ⭐ Cadiz (pop. 120,000) enjoy breathing in the salty air and soaking in the last rays of sun as it sets over the sea.** Europe's oldest city (founded by the Phoenicians in the 11th century BC) is flanked by the Atlantic on three sides. Apart from the small beach in the west, a city wall separates the land and ocean. Within the city wall, Baroque townhouses, some with tall lookout towers, dominate the scene. Merchants used to keep watch here to see their ships approaching the harbour. In 1717, Cadiz was granted a monopoly to trade with Latin America, which had previously brought wealth to Seville. Known for its many tiny squares, this lovely city is home to the *Gaditanos*, the Cadiz people.

## SIGHTSEEING

### CATEDRAL
When gleaming in the sun, the cathedral sparkles of sandstone, jasper and marble décor (1722–1838, with Baroque and neo-Classical elements). One of Spain's most important 20th-century composers, Manuel de Falla (1876–1946), was born in Cadiz and is buried in the cathedral's crypt. The admission fee to the cathedral includes entry to the *Museo de la Catedral (Mon–Sat 10am–4pm)*, located in the Casa de Contaduría on the Plaza Fray Fé-lix. You may also enter the ☽ *Torre del Reloj*, a clock tower offering a magnificent view over the city. *Mon–Sat 10am–7pm, Sun 2pm–7pm | admission 5 euros*

### MUSEO DE CADIZ
This museum brings archaeology and

art under one roof. Its treasures include two sarcophaguses from the Phoenician period (5th century BC), a statue of Emperor Trajan found in a Roman settlement and artworks from the 16th–20th centuries. The INSIDERTIP collection of paintings by Zurbarán is also one of a kind. The exceptional talent of this spiritually-minded Baroque artist is particularly apparent in his depiction of saints ('The Ecstasy of St Bruno', 'The Vision of St Francis of Assisi'). *From 10am | free admission for EU-citizens | Plaza de Mina*

## ORATORIO DE SAN FELIPE NERI
A beautiful Baroque church in Andalucía, its elliptical floor is illuminated by the natural light shining through the cupola. This national landmark is where the Cortes (the Spanish parliament) assembled in 1811/ 12 to draw up Spain's first liberal constitution. The monument on the Plaza España depicts a failed democracy *From 10.30am | admission 3 euros | C/ San José 38*

## TORRE TAVIRA ☼
A table-like screen glows in a dark room. You believe it's just an image of the city until you see people moving around in it. Although impressive, the video isn't created using magic or virtual reality. This camera, the camera obscura, was invented in the 10th-century by the Arab astronomer Abu Ali al-Hasan. *Daily 10am–6pm, May–Sept until 8pm | admission 6 euros | C/ Marqués del Real Tesoro 10 | www.torre tavira.com*

## TAPAS
Several tapas restaurants with outdoor terraces are located in the Calle Plocia. Two of many good recommendations are *El Aljibe* and *La Cepa Gallega*.

Spanish or British? For some residents it's an irrelevant question in Gibraltar

## SHOPPING
Next to the Plaza de las Flores with its flower market, you'll find the *Mercado Central*, a neo-Classical market building with a tempting range of culinary delicacies. Caught on the Costa de la Luz, the tuna here is especially good; buy it deep-frozen or pickled at *Gadira (C/ Plocia 8)*.

## BEACHES
West of the Old Town, the *Playa de la Caleta* is just 450 m/1476 ft long. On the south side of the strip is the larger *Playa de la Victoria* (2.5 km/1.5 mi), which connects Cadiz with the rest of Andalucía.

## WHERE TO GO

### SEVILLE ★
Andalucía's hot capital (pop. 694,000) leaves nobody cold. Catch the exuberant zest for life and gaiety of the *sevillanos*,

stroll along the banks of the Guadalquivir River and breathe in the ambience in the squares and the fragrance of the orange trees in the picturesque district of Barrio de Santa Cruz.

Things become quite lively during Holy Week with its famous processions, and during the *Feria de Abril.*

The *Plaza de Toros de la Maestranza* is a sanctuary for bullfight aficionados and the stars among toreros perform here. Designed by the German architect Jürgen Mayer H., the futuristic *Metropol Parasol (setasdesevilla.com)*, located at the Plaza de la Encarnación, is an eye-catcher.

### JEREZ DE LA FRONTERA

A day in the life in Jerez (pop. 215,000) is best seen on the Calle Larga. Some sit on expensively built terraces with a pint of *fino* (beer); others dress in fine attire and walk up and down the long street.

Jerez is famous for its wine (or *Sherry*, as foreigners call it). The horse breeders are exceptionally talented and flamenco music is still a tradition here. PS fans may see Jerez as the 'Motorcycling Capital of the World' and are familiar with the *Circuito de Jerez* racing circuit. Horse lovers, on the other hand, may know of the city's famous horse riding school. Either way, Jerez remains a city full of surprises. Cosy squares, lively bars and tons of contrasts can be found here, a place where the pretty and ugly sides of Andalucía meet. The churches boast exuberant décor and clash with the city's dreary tower blocks. People who feel fortunate to even have a job mingle with those born into rich and influential families.

# PALMA/ MALLORCA

**One of the things that makes Palma so fascinating to both locals and foreigners is that this town is both old and young.** Stroll through one of the largest pre-

## WHITE OR BLUE?

Nearly all the towns and villages in Andalucía are painted white. Considered a job for the housewife, whitewashing first became a thing in the 17th century. But to be a tourist attraction, a *pueblo blanco* has to offer a bit more than simply a town of whitewashed buildings. They also have to provide tourists with narrow alleyways where they can easily get lost! Only then can a town or village be of Moorish origin. And for picture taking, it doesn't hurt to have the village beautifully placed on a hillside or on a rocky cliff somewhere. The most beautiful *pueblos blancos* can be found in Vejer de la Frontera, Arcos de la Frontera, Grazalema, Gaucín, Comares, Casares and Frigiliana. There is one village, however, that stands out from the rest, called Júzcar. Located between Ronda and Estepona, this village has been painted sky-blue. It started as a pomotional gag by Sony Pictures and required 9000 buckets of light-blue paint – the perfect backdrop for the premiere of the 'Smurfs' movie. Although that was some years ago, after thousands of visitors started coming to see the *pueblo azul*, nobody in the village wanted their whitewashed houses back.

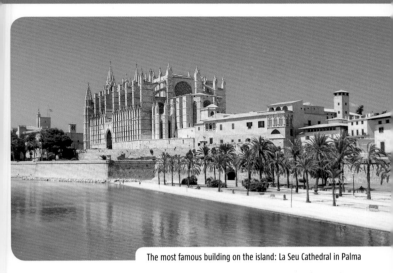

The most famous building on the island: La Seu Cathedral in Palma

served medieval cities of the Mediterranean, once an important hub for the trading and warring powers of the region. Its former – and thanks to tourism, also current – affluence is tangible almost everywhere. And everything is in close proximity: the peaceful inner courtyards of sumptuous noblemen's palaces are next door to busy street cafés surrounded by surging traffic; dark, incense-scented churches can be found next to the bustling activity under the bright lights of the market halls; squares bathed in cheery sunlight are situated next to shady arcades. Palma may not be a Gaudí city like Barcelona, but you will also see architecture in the Spanish Art Nouveau style here. Get a folding map with tour recommendations at *Arca,* the Association for the Revitalisation of Old Centres *(C/ de Can Oliva 10).*

## SIGHTSEEING

### ES BALUARD ★ *(*𝄞 *3/D2)*
This modern building fits in brilliantly with Palma's historic fortifications; great views of port and cathedral can be had from the 🌿 roof terraces. *Plaça Porta de Santa Catalina 10 | www.esbaluard.org | Tue–Sat 10am–8pm, Sun 10am–3pm | admission 6 euros, free on public holidays*

### CASTELL DE BELLVER 🌿 *(*𝄞 *3/A3)*
Sturdy and defensive from the outside, rather elegant in its interior, the royal castle dominates the town. Today, the castle houses the historical museum. *Mon 8:30am–1pm, April–Sept Tue–Sat 8:30am–8pm, Sun 10am–8pm, Oct–March Mon–Sat 8:30am–6pm, Sun 10am–6pm | admission 4 euros, Sun free*

### FUNDACIÓ PILAR I JOAN MIRÓ ★
Part of Miró's bequest can be seen in this beautiful museum building. *C/ Saridakis 29 | Cala Major | miro.palmademallorca.es | Tue–Sat 10am–7pm, in winter 10am–6pm, Sun 10am–3pm | admission 7.50 euros, Sat from 3pm, 1st Sun in the month and on open days free*

## WATERY FUN

### PALMA AQUARIUM

This complex shelters 55 fish tanks with an impressive plant life and 8000 specimens from the world's oceans, a jungle landscape, a Mediterranean garden, restaurant and café. The transparent tunnel lets you get really close to the fish – and the sharks too... *Platja de Palma | motorway exit no. 10 (at Balneario 14, signposted) | www.palma aquarium.com | daily 9:30am–6:30pm | adults 24 euros, children 14 euros*

### ART NOUVEAU BUILDINGS (*3/D2*)

Some beautifully restored facades show the Catalan version of Art Nouveau, modernisme. To name but a few: *Edifici Casayas* on Plaça Mercat and, diagonally opposite, the ★ *Gran Hotel (Mon–Sat 10am–8pm, Sun 11am–2pm | admission 4 euros)*.

### LA SEU CATHEDRAL ★ (*3/D2*)

The main nave boasts 14 slim pillars, the large rose window in the main apse, made up from 1236 pieces of glass and the Gaudí chandelier above the altar. *Plaça Almoina | Mon–Fri June–Sept 10am–6:15pm, April/May and Oct 10am–5:15pm, Nov–March 10am–3:15pm, Sat 10am–2:15pm | admission 7 euros*

### PALAUS (PALACES) (*3/D2*)

Most of the palaces of the local bourgeoisie and nobility, usually erected in the 15th and 16th centuries in the Italian style, can be found in the Old Town and in Sa Portella. Particularly beautiful is the *Can Marquès (C/ Zanglada 2 | Mon–Sat 10am–3pm | admission 6 euros)*. Easy to visit and free: *Casal Solleric (Passeig des Born 27 | casalsolleric.palma.cat | Tue–Sat 11am–2pm and 3:30–8:30pm, Sun 10am–2:30pm)*.

### PORT (*3/C3*)

The fishing port is limited by the long jetty reaching out into the sea below the cathedral. This is also where the ships leave for the one-hour *Cruceros Marco Polo* around the harbour *(www.crucerosmarcopolo.com | March–Oct Mon–Sat hourly 11am–4pm | 12 euros per person)*; a refreshing and relaxing change for visitors whose feet need a break.

## FOOD & DRINK

Starting at 8 pm, the entire district of INSIDER TIP *Santa Catalina* is transformed into an open-air buffet with international offerings. There are many restaurants to choose from in the traffic-calmed *Carrer Fábrica*. In the summer, its sidewalks are packed with tables.

## SHOPPING

Ready for a little shopping spree? First, you must stroll along the stately boulevard *Passeig des Born* and up and down *Jaume III*. If you're up for more, walk up *Carrer Unió* and turn down *Carrer Sant Miguel*, passing Palma's best fashion shops as you go. You will find shops stocked with international designer brands as well as boutiques featuring the creations of Spanish designers.

# EIVISSA/ IBIZA

**Eivissa was once afraid of its Ottoman enemies and barricaded itself behind**

**stout walls. Nowadays peaceful people from all around the world pour into the city (pop. 50,000) – and are welcomed with open arms.**

The situation becomes exceptional in July and August, when a variegated international horde descends on the wider area surrounding the harbour, bent on enjoying themselves in any way possible. The sky is the limit for anything that is fun. In the evenings, streets and squares are transformed into catwalks for show-offs and strollers. Historically, Ibiza has a lot to offer. The Phoenician-Punic necropolises on the "hill of the mills" *Puig des Molins* is a Unesco World Heritage Site alongside the Dalt Vila, whose massive walls date back to the Moorish period, dominate the site.

## SIGHTSEEING

INSIDER TIP CASA BRONER ☼
(🗺 4/C3)

A highlight is the former domicile of the painter and architect Erwin Broner (1898–1971) from Munich, who succeeded in blending traditional Ibizan architecture with modern elements. Enjoy the beautiful view from the roof terrace of the present museum. *From 10am | admission free | Travesía de Sa Penya 15*

### DALT VILA ★ (🗺 4/B3)

Eivissa's historical upper city Dalt Vila gives the impression of being a huge open-air museum: cannon emplacements and squares, tunnels to walk through, promenades with a view and winding alleys, huge towers and city walls dating from a variety of historical periods. There are uneven pavements, whitewashed façades with flowers in bloom and washing hanging on the line, wild tangles of cables, roof gardens and a few derelict houses. This is all part of Dalt Vila, alongside numerous notable buildings including the town hall and the cathedral. The walls circling the hill mainly originate from the second half of the 16th century.

The Upper Town of Eivissa (Ibiza) dates back to the Moorish period

### HARBOUR ★ (🕮 4/C3)

There is plenty to see in Evissa's extended harbour with the constant loading and unloading of container ships and the arrival and departure of cruise ships, ferries, (super) yachts and sailing and fishing boats. In the south, the broadside of the port neighbours the historical districts of fishermen and sailors, *La Marina* and *Sa Penya*. Scores of bars and restaurants with lounge terraces invite you to chill out and smoke shishas. The plump boats from the Spanish mainland arrive at the main ferry station *Estació Marítima*, behind which you can catch sight of the *Monument a los Corsarios*. The monument to the corsairs built in the form of an obelisk at the beginning of the 20th century commemorates the glorious deeds of the local sailors, who took on much bigger ships. A further monument is situated at the crossing of the Avinguda de Santa Eulària d'es Riu honours the more peaceful *Gent de la mar*, the "people of the sea". A great route to walk along leads from the Marina past the Botafoc lighthouse up to the tip of the wharf at the harbour entrance.

### PASSEIG DE VARA DE REY ★ (🕮 4/B3)

The inner-city promenade converted to a traffic-free pedestrian zone is named after one of the most famous islanders: General Joaquín Vara de Rey, who died in 1898 while fighting for the independence of the Spanish colony Cuba. Cafés, restaurants and shops line both sides of the boulevard. The legendary *Grand Hotel Montesol* in neo-Colonial style is an ideal breakfast spot! This location has acquired its special flair through the frequent markets and concerts held here.

### MUSEU D'ART CONTEMPORANI (🕮 4/B3)

The Museum of Contemporary Art is a huge surprise and literally a cool location

# BEACHES FOR SUN LOVERS

### FIGUERETES (🕮 4/A4)

The suburb adjoining Eivissa, with its broad beach of imported sand, is divided into several sections by cliffs. The palm promenade *(Passeig de les Pitiüses)*, which runs down both sides of the Plaça de Julià Verdera (which is closed to traffic), is an attractive location for a walk with its bars, restaurants and great views of Dalt Vila, Eivissa's Puig des Molins and Formentera. *2 km/1.2 mi south-west of Eivissa, accessible on foot via Av. d'Espanya and Carrer País Basc*

### PLATJA D'EN BOSSA

The sandy expanses are enjoyed by all age groups and tastes. Close to the southern end, the Torre d'es Carregador, a watchtower dating from the 16th century, stands sentinel next to the beach and high life.

### PLATJA DE TALAMANCA

The deep, protected bay has calm water for swimming and is therefore particularly popular with families with children. You can continue your walk on a wooden walkway leading along the band of sand at the Platja de Talamanca towards the north-west. Behind the pine groves, the attractive walk ends at the stone slabs near Cap Martinet. *In the summer, a boat will bring you from the harbour in Eivissa to the Platja de Talamanca (otherwise drive via the Av. 8 d'Agost).*

to relax in in the midst of the hectic life in Eivissa! Even the modern architecture of the former barracks, fortified with bomb-proof underground depots in the 18th century, is simply fascinating with its blend of historical walls and modern transparency with plenty of glass and exposed concrete. Archaeological finds were discovered during construction work and are now displayed on the lower floor under glass. On the ground floor, the permanent exhibition is spread between two vaulted halls. The upper floor floor is used for temporary exhibitions. *From 10am | admission free | Ronda Narcís Puget*

### NECRÒPOLIS PÚNICA (Ⅲ 4/A3)

Below the historical hill of the mills *Puig des Molins,* where several windmills continued to grind cereal into flour right into the 20th century, the remains of Eivissa's necropolis can be found, which was used as a cemetery in ancient times, first by the Phoenicians (from the 7th century BC) and subsequently by the Carthaginians (from the 5th century AD). Historians estimate that there could be a total of several thousand graves distributed across the sloping area, of which one is open to the public: the "Mule hypogea", a set of underground vaults, which were discovered when a mule found its way into a broken shaft. Fifteen steep steps lead down into the depths of the vault. Skeletons have been placed inside glass sarcophagi: a journey into the past could hardly be more vivid! The entrance to the historical cemetery leads through the modern museum (*Museu Monogràfic*) with five rooms devoted to themes such as "Death in the time of the Phoenicians" and "Carthaginian burials". Finds displayed include burial objects such as jewellery, amulets and ceramic bowls alongside death masks, bone carvings and a lead sarcophagus. Admission is free on Sundays. *Via Romana 31*

Great beach feeling in Figueretes

## SHOPPING

Shopping fans will be at home in the areas around the P*asseig de Vara de Rey, Plaça del Parc* and *Plaça de la Constitució*. It is also well worth visiting the area near the *Av. d'Isidor Macabich*. In the harbour area, crowds gather near the church *Sant Elm* (or *San Telmo*), in the *Carrer Emili Pou*, *Carrer de Mar* and especially in the *Carrer d'Enmig*.

## LEISURE & SPORTS

A ferry service to Formentera leaves from the harbour every half hour. The crossing lasts 30–45 minutes. It is best to book your tickets online combined with a voucher for a Vespa on Formentera. Return tickets are available from *Cooltra (tel. 9 37 06 69 12 | www.cooltra.com)* for 39 euros including the Vespa.

# TRAVEL TIPS

## ADMISSION

Admission costs to museums and monuments depend on their respective levels of famousness, and range from between 2.50–4 euros in smaller cities up to 5–8 euros in larger cities. However, there are many exceptions! In Barcelona, it is extremely expensive: a basic visit to the Sagrada Família costs 15 euros, and admission to Antoni Gaudí's Casa Batlló is a steep 22.50 euros. A larger budget is also required for family outings to water- and recreational parks, as well as aquariums. Children *(niños)*, students *(estudiantes)* and pensioners *(jubilados)* are usually entitled to discounts. A few museums offer free admission once a week.

## BERTHS

### ▶ BARCELONA
Barcelona has seven cruise-ship terminals. From some terminals, you can walk to the city in 10 to 15 minutes. Use bus services from terminals that are further away.

### ▶ VALENCIA
The modern cruise-ship terminal is approx. 6 km /3.5 mi from the city centre. Public and shuttle-bus services are available.

### ▶ ALICANTE
Shuttle-bus services operate between the cruise-ship terminal and the city centre. A walk to the city centre takes 15 minutes.

### ▶ CARTAGENA
Cartagena has two piers for cruise ships. From the Alfonso XII Pier you can walk to the city centre, but from the Muelle de la Curra you should use the shuttle bus.

### ▶ MÁLAGA
The old town is situated approx. 2 km/1.2 mi from the modern cruise-ship terminal. Smaller ships can be moored directly in the centre.

### ▶ GIBRALTAR
The port of Gibraltar is centrally located, and sightseeing can be done on foot.

### ▶ CADIZ
Cruise ships are moored in central Cadiz; you can easily walk to the city centre.

### ▶ PALMA
The piers for cruise ships in Palma are approx. 5 to 7 km/3 to 4 mi from the centre; bus services are available.

### ▶ EIVISSA
Large ships are moored out of town; the ride with the shuttle-bus transfer to the city centre takes approx. 10 minutes.

## EMERGENCY SERVICES

Countrywide *tel. 112*

## HEALTH

All travellers, regardless of nationality and country of origin, should take out adequate travel medical/health insurance well in advance of the cruise. Citizens of EU member countries may use their European Health Insurance Card (EHIC), but this is not a substitute for travel insurance. In Spain, it does not allow for a free choice of doctors, and the services of the nearest health-care centre *(centro de salud)* will have to be used. At a hospital *(hospital, clínica)*, the emergency section is called *emergencias*.

# Spain

Your holiday from start to finish: the most important addresses and information for your trip

More info and updates for travellers from the UK, USA, Canada and Australia at:
UK: https://www.gov.uk/browse/abroad/travel-abroad and https://www.gov.uk/foreign-travel-advice/spain/health
USA: https://www.state.gov/travel/ and https://travel.state.gov/content/travel/en/international-travel/before-you-go/travelers-with-special-considerations/cruise-ship-passengers.html
CAN: https://travel.gc.ca/travelling/advisories
AUS: https://smartraveller.gov.au/guide/all-travellers/health/Pages/default.aspx

## INTERNET & WIFI

WiFi in Spanish is *wifi*. In some places, there are free WiFi-zones. Barcelona has a good WiFi network and a large number of internet cafes.

## MONEY & CREDIT CARDS

Credit cards are widely used, especially Visa. ATMs *(cajeros automáticos)* are widely available.

## OPENING HOURS

There are no legally enforced business hours. Opening hours for businesses are mainly from Mondays to Fridays, from 9.30am or 10am to 1.30pm or 2pm, and from 4.30pm or 5pm to 8pm; Saturdays sometimes mornings only. Some businesses in tourist places, department stores and large supermarkets are open all day. Museums often change their seasonal opening hours during the year; many close on Sunday afternoons and especially on Mondays.

## PHONE & MOBILE PHONE

For international calls, dial 00, then the country code (Australia 61, Canada 1, UK 44, USA 1), followed by the area code of the city or town (but omit the area code prefix 0) and then the telephone number. For Spain, the country code is 0034, followed by the complete telephone number. You can use your mobile phone without any problems, though it will automatically select a service provider with the strongest frequency. Numbers in Spain that are not free of charge, start with 807, 901 or 902.

## POST

There is no difference in the postage for postcards and international letters of up to 20 g/0.7 oz. At the time of going to press, it was 1.10 euro. Tobacconists *(estancos)* also sell stamps. *www.correos.es*

## TIPPING

In restaurants, five percent is appropriate. Spaniards usually give small tips. In bars, you can leave some change. It is not customary to tip taxi drivers.

## BUDGETING

| | | |
|---|---|---|
| Snack | from £0.85/$1 | *for a small tapa* |
| Espresso | £0.85–£1/$1–$1.60 | *for one café solo* |
| Wine | £0.85/$1 | *for a glass at the counter* |
| Bicycle rental | £10–£17/$14–$23 | *per day* |

# FRANCE

**Do you like contrasts? Fantastic, then the French Mediterranean coast will be the perfect place for you!**

Luxury, a hustle and bustle, palaces and beautiful exotic flower displays await you on your onshore excursions along the Côte d'Azur. Experience glamorous and famous cities like Nice and Cannes, and the noble Principality of Monaco. As a contrast, head inland, where quaint solitary cliff-perched towns and breathtaking landscapes will enchant you. Provence is a feast for the senses: you will delight in the fabulous sights of white cliffs, blue sea, aromatic green pine trees and fragrant purple-blue lavender fields; delicious herbs and wonderful wines will excite your palate. In Marseille, the evocative, bubbly blend of centuries-old Oriental and Western cultures will stir your heart and mind with fervour. As your ship approaches Corsica, look out over the sea and enjoy the scenic beauty of the island's capital Ajaccio.

## MONACO

**The casino and Hôtel de Paris are situated on land that was covered with moss-grown stones, orange trees and pine forests a mere 150 years ago. Such a setting might have been quite idyllic, but it did not offer any economic and social prospects. Casinos were forbidden in France in 1850, but in Monaco, a casino brought about change.** François Blanc, the successful manager of the casino in Bad Homburg in Germany, established

## The Maritime Alps, the sea, glitterati and a sophisticated lifestyle underline the special character of France's Mediterranean coast

the Société des Bains de Mer (SBM) and extended the railway from Cagnes-sur-Mer to Monaco. Within a few years, more than a hundred mansions and twenty hotels sprang up and gave Monaco its unique hallmark: the quintessence of luxury. The Principality comprises four sections: Monaco-Ville (which includes the old town and the Prince's Palace); Monte Carlo, featuring the casino, grand hotels and beaches; La Condamine; and Fontvieille, which is situated on land reclaimed from the sea.

SIGHTSEEING

### CASINO DE MONTE CARLO ★

Charles Garnier, the architect of the Paris opera house, designed the casino in 1878. Built in the style of the Belle Époque, it has been a setting for many films. Access to its lavishly and extravagantly decorated halls is free of charge. The terrace overlooks the sea and offers an exceptionally glorious view from Monaco to the Italian Riviera. *Place du Casino | admission 10 euros | www. casinomontecarlo.com | www.opera.mc*

### CATHÉDRALE DE MONACO
The cathedral, consecrated in 1911, is in the old town. Beneath the choir stalls, members of the Grimaldi family, including Princess Gracia Patricia and Prince Rainier III, are buried. *Daily 8.30am–7pm | 4, Rue Colonel Bellando de Castro | admission free | www.visitmonaco.com*

### COLLECTION DE VOITURES ANCIENNES (OLDTIMER COLLECTION)
About one hundred vehicles of the Prince's collection are on display in a beautiful exhibition hall. The legendary Mediterranean-blue Bugatti 35 B, which won the first Grand Prix of Monte Carlo in 1929, has a place of honour. *Daily 10am–6pm | Les Terrasses de Fontvieille | admission 6.50 euros | www.palais.mc*

### JARDIN EXOTIQUE ★ ☀
Throughout the year, and thanks to a microclimate, this lovely garden presents an amazing display of small and big cacti with colourful flowers, many exotic plants, and African trees. A flowering cactus will delight you year-round in this spellbinding garden. There is also a cavern with stalactites and stalagmites, and a gorgeous sea view. *Daily 9am–6pm | 62, Blvd. du Jardin Exotique | admission 7.20 euros | www.jardin-exotique.mc*

### INSIDER TIP ▶ JARDIN JAPONAIS
A legacy of Princess Gracia Patricia: in accordance with her wishes, the Japanese architect Yasuo Beppu designed and landscaped the Japanese Garden. He based the layout on Shinto principles, thereby creating an oasis of tranquillity. Situated in the modern Larvotto quarter, it covers an area of more than an acre. *From 9am | Av. Princesse Grace | admission free*

### MUSÉE ET INSTITUT OCÉANOGRAPHIQUE DE MONACO (OCEANOGRAPHIC MUSEUM) ★ ☀
Prince Albert I established the museum in 1910 with a view to making marine treasures accessible to everybody and for all times. In the 90 aquariums, 350 fish species and 100 coral species are on display. Visitors can watch films made by the world famous oceanographer, Jacques-Yves Cousteau, who was the museum's director for many years. *2, Av. Saint-Martin | admission varies seasonally, 11–16 euros | Info & opening hours at: www.oceano.mc*

# P AS IN PROMINENCE

Paparazzi, prominent people, pop stars and poodles – a myriad of Ps revel on the coast in summer. The more expensive it gets, the more it teems with celebrities. Those who wish to watch Madonna, Paris Hilton, Adele and Jayzee with their enormous sunglasses and obligatory mini-dogs should head to Cap Ferrat or Saint-Tropez. There celebrities sit in restaurants or hide behind high walls and uniformed guards. They might also profit from Monaco as a tax haven, like motor-racing drivers and tennis pros. It is quite acceptable that stars like Leonardo di Caprio or Bono sail with their yachts to the beach restaurant in Pampelonne, but it is a different scenario for Jean-Pierre Tuveri, the mayor of Saint-Tropez, when 30,000 helicopter shuttles fly over his area every summer. Then glamour imposes a noisy handicap on seemingly idyllic places.

### LE PALAIS PRINCIER ★ ☽

The palace of the Monegasque Princes is a magnificent seat of residence. Visit the interior; admire the beautiful Throne Room, and the lavishly furnished *State Apartments*. The Galerie d'Hercule offers a good view onto the lovely Cour d'Honneur. The private apartments of the Grimaldi family are in the southern wing of the palace. The Changing of the Guards ceremony is performed daily at 11.55am in front of the palace. *April–mid-Oct daily 10am–6pm | admission 8 euros (ticket reservations online available) | www. palais.mc*

### LE ROCHER (THE ROCK)

The old town, Monaco-Ville, also known as "the Rock", is situated on a rocky promontory. Following the steep narrow and winding alleys, you will find the Palace of Justice, the picturesque Place Saint Nicolas, the lovely Jardins Saint Martin (gardens) and the Prince's Palace.

## SHOPPING

All leading haute couture designers and their boutiques have a presence in Monaco. Shops in the streets close to the casino are expensive. The shopping mall of Le Métropole is located opposite the *Jardins du Casino*. In the city quarter of La Condamine, around Rue Grimaldi and Rue Princesse Caroline, about 200 stores offer many opportunities for browsing and shopping sprees. Sales *(soldes)* occur in January and July, and even high-end and luxury boutiques reduce their prices considerably.

# NICE

**You can really let it all hang out in Nice: enjoy a chic cocktail wearing a jogging suit. Enjoy a cool swim on the beach**

The charming old town of Nice with its narrow alleys

**promenade in the morning, and in the afternoon take the bus to the skiing region. Dance the salsa in the moonlight at midnight as you enjoy a violet and chestnut ice cream.**

Above all, Nice is famous for its 7 km/4.4 mi beach promenade, the *Promenade des Anglais*. The new *Promenade du Paillon* starts a few feet farther: the lovely park with play areas, fountains and impressively tall palm trees is so popular with families that children actually queue for the slides. Right next to it are the crooked streets of the old town. Even at the height of summer it's pleasantly cool here, and the air is full of the wonderful smells of hand-made leather bags, soaps and spices.

## SIGHTSEEING

### VIEILLE VILLE (OLD TOWN)

Alleys, squares and houses in deep ochre yellow and rust red: the old town is irresistibly charming. The impressive INSIDER TIP *Palais Lascaris (Wed–Mon 10am–6pm | 15, Rue Droite)* dates back to the 17th century and has a distinctive Genoese style. Three squares give the old town its architectural style; *Place Garibaldi* – with its statue of the freedom fighter – is surrounded by arcades, *Place Saint-François* with the town hall and fish market and *Cours Saleya* in the south with the colourful flower market.

### MUSÉE MATISSE

Henri Matisse (1869–1954) resided in Nice from 1917 until his death, and this 17th century Genoese villa in an olive grove in Cimiez has a large collection of his work and displays his artistic beginnings through to his last work. *Wed–Mon 10am–6pm | 10 euros | 164, Av. des Arènes de Cimiez | bus Arènes/Musée Matisse | www.musee-matisse-nice.org*

### MUSÉE NATIONAL
### MARC CHAGALL ★

Cimiez is home to a purpose-built museum with the most comprehensive collection of Marc Chagall's (1887–1985) works. Its focus is the biblical messages contained in his paintings, sculptures and tapestries, as well as mosaics of the Prophet Elijah on the building's façade. *May–Oct Wed–Mon 10am–6pm, Nov–April 10am–5pm | 8 euros | Av. du Docteur Ménard | bus Musée Chagall | www.musee-chagall.fr*

### INSIDER TIP VILLA ARSON

This beautiful 18th century villa estate with its modern Bauhaus extension is a modern art academy. The academy puts on some of the most exciting exhibitions on the Mediterranean art circuit. *Wed–Mon 2pm–6pm | entrance free | Av. Stephen Liégard | bus Le Ray or Deux Avenues | www.villa-arson.org*

## SHOPPING

For olive oil, head to INSIDER TIP *Nicolas Alziari (14, Rue Saint-François de Paule)*. Candied fruit, bars of chocolate and chocolate are available from *Maison Auer (7, Rue Saint-François de Paule)*. Browse the small antiques market *Les Puces de Nice (Tue–Sat 10am–6pm)* in the harbour. If you're looking for fashion, head for the streets around the Rue de la Liberté. You'll find the major brands in the quarter to the west of Avenue Jean Médecin between Boulevard Victor Hugo and Promenade des Anglais. For 100 boutiques under one roof, go to *Nicetoile (30, Av. Jean Médecin | www. nicetoile.com)*.

## WHERE TO GO

### CAP FERRAT ★

You'll see better in the dark: if you want to understand the unimaginable wealth of the millionaires' peninsula at the old fishing village of *Saint-Jean-Cap-Ferrat* (pop. 2100, 6 km/3.7 mi to the east), you'd best come in the middle of the night, when you'll be able to see the sparkling chandeliers inside the villas and the liveried staff at the tall entrances. By day, it's better to take the *coastal trail (sentier littoral)*, which will take you once around the peninsula in about two hours.

### EZE ★ �≈

This village is said to have been named after the Egyptian goddess Isis. With a population of around 3000, Eze is 10 km/6.2 mi east of Nice and is a typical example of a *village perché*. Eze is known for its *Jardin Exotique (summer 9am–8pm, otherwise 9am–5.30pm | 6 euros)* on top of the hill in the grounds of a ruined 14th century castle. Enjoy spectacular views of the Riviera from its terraces.

# FOOD & DRINK

Fertile soil, culinary innnovations and original flavour experiences – that's what French cuisine is all about

**In France, the art of living, *l'art de vivre*, stands for the art of eating and good food. The French celebrate each and every meal and visiting a restaurant resembles a real event.**
The pioneering French Cuisine has been included in the **Unesco World Heritage** since 2010. Correspondingly high are the standards on chefs and restaurants. There is hardly any other region in France with as many Michelin star chefs as on the French Riviera. But even smaller taverns in remote villages almost always meet the expectations. Suited to different climatic conditions, specific soil and differing traditions, each region developed a typical cuisine and its own *specialities*. Go for local food and dishes and combine these with regional wine. Most restaurants are closed on Sundays because the locals traditionally eat at home with their family. Instead you can visit one of the many daily opened *bistros* that are an important part of French food

culture. Grab a quick petit noir (espresso) or a petit crème (a small cup of coffee with a dash of milk) at the counter or have a snack and aperitif. Opting for the special of the day *(plat du jour)* is usually an excellent choice.

## LOCAL SPECIALITIES

aïoli – a mayonnaise made from garlic, egg yolk and olive oil
bouillabaisse – fish soup made of scorpion fish *(rascasse)*, gurnard *(grondin)* and sea eel *(congre)*. Other ingredients include onions, tomatoes, saffron, garlic, bay leaf, fennel, sage, orange zest and of course olive oil
bourride – similar to a bouillabaisse, but with sea bass *(loup)*, monkfish *(baudroie)* and whiting *(merlan)* and thickened with aioli
ratatouille – a vegetable dish of aubergines, peppers, tomatoes, onions and courgettes, braised in olive oil and garlic, served hot or cold

# CANNES

**Cannes (pop. 74,500) is the famous capital of glamour and films, yachts and stars, yet it encompasses much more.**

Over just a few decades, Cannes remarkably transformed itself from humble beginnings into a stylish city. In the 19th century, it was a poor and isolated agricultural area and fishing village. Today it is fashionable and chic, notably during festivals and trade fairs. In summer, it is a pre-eminent attraction for the rich and famous and their private yachts. In winter, on the other hand, it is peaceful and tranquil, and prosperous elderly people amble on the promenade. What happens off the Croisette? Just a few paces away from this resplendent promenade, everyday life takes place: fishing boats and anglers enter the harbour with their fresh catch; locals carry newspapers and baguettes under their arms and meet in bars; and the markets go about their regular business, humming with merry chatter.

## SIGHTSEEING

### BOULEVARD DE LA CROISETTE ★

The Croisette is the iconic promenade for strolling and people watching! Lined with palm trees and sandy beaches, the boulevard is the perfect setting for palatial hotels like the Carlton, the Majestic and the Martinez. The *Allée des Etoiles* features a walk of fame: concrete slabs with the handprints and signatures of over 200 stars.

### CENTRE D'ART LA MALMAISON

The striking white manor house, with its large forecourt on the Croisette, attracts attention. Today the former games and tearoom of the Grand Hôtel houses a small art museum. *Sept–April Tue–Sun 10am–1pm and 2pm–6pm, July/Aug Tue–Sun 11am–8pm | 47, Blvd. de la Croisette | admission varies, depending on exhibitions.*

Cannes is not only a stronghold of cinema, but also features a picturesque old town

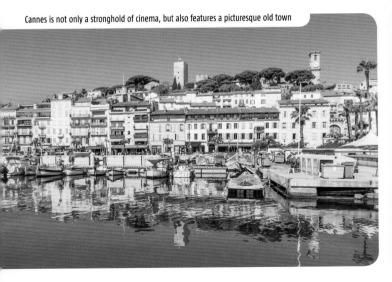

## PALAIS DES FESTIVALS ET DES CONGRÈS ⭐

Here you will see the famous staircase that draws cameras from around the world every year in May! When the red carpet is not in use, the Palais des Festivals et des Congrès serves as venue for fairs and events *(www.en.palaisdesfestivals.com | www.festivalcannes.fr)*. A special homage to cinema: 15 impressive frescoes on facades adorn the city.

## LE SUQUET

Narrow alleyways wind their way up the Mont Chevalier: Le Suquet is the historic centre of Cannes. Lined with many restaurants, the ascent leads on to the Chapelle Sainte-Anne and the medieval castle that houses the historic Musée de la Castre (from 10am | admission 6 euros). The ⚘ INSIDERTIP tower and ⚘ a shaded terrace offer stunning views.

## SHOPPING

From Zara to Dior – Cannes is a shopping paradise that offers every purse something. On the *Boulevard de la Croisette*, high-end designers' outlets display elegant creations. The *Rue d'Antibes* is a shopping and commercial area, abounding with boutiques. Discover some obscure and small authentic shops on the side streets of the Rue d'Antibes.

## BEACHES

Shopping bags in one hand, beach towel in the other: city and beach life literally go hand in hand in Cannes. At the farthest end of the Croisette, close to the Palm Beach Casino, there is an especially lovely beach, the INSIDERTIP *Bijou Plage*. Of note is also the long sandy beach that stretches for over half a mile (a kilometre) from the old harbour Quai Saint-Pierre to Mandelieu-La Napoule.

## WHERE TO GO

### ÎLES DE LÉRINS

Take a 20-minute boat trip to the two islands of *Île Ste-Marguerite* and *Île St-Honorat*, and indulge in a welcome escape from the bustling city. Franciscan monks still inhabit the monastery of St-Honorat. Wander around the island, swim in the sea and visit the church and the monastery shop. On the larger, but uninhabited Île Ste-Marguerite, you can also enjoy lovely strolls and a visit to the *Musée de la Mer* (admission 6 euros).

### GRASSE ⭐

Put your "nose" to the test! Indulge in fragrances and become a perfume devotee. Endless flower fields grow in the vicinity, especially roses, tuberose, May rose, jasmine and lily of the valley. The city has an unpretentious character. The Italian influence is still traceable in the old town with its narrow alleys, arcades and five-storey buildings.

### SAINT-TROPEZ ⭐

Situated on a sheltered bay, Saint-Tropez boasts vineyards on its surrounding hills and charming, first-class sandy beaches. Between the 15th and 17th centuries, the once tiny Saint-Tropez was an autonomous republic. Today, it is a preferred hotspot on the Riviera for chic Parisians and the international jet set. It was made famous by Roger Vadim's film "And God Created Woman" (1956) with Brigitte Bardot, which was shot in the bay of La Ponche. As soon as the holiday season is over, Saint-Tropez re-awakens to its original beauty and locals play *pétanque* on the Place des Lices, peacefully and undisturbed.

# SHOPPING

## Thinking of those who stayed at home: some souvenir ideas besides the usual edible treats

Colours, smells, fragrances, tastes – the French Mediterranean coast offers an abundance of souvenirs that are typical of the region. For instance, consider a bar of fragrant soap from Marseille, hand-made with olive or coconut oil; or one or two lovely colourful fabrics from Provence; or maybe some dried lavender; or maybe... the choice is endless. Immerse yourself in an exhilarating feast of the senses!

### GASTRONOMY AND TABLEWARE

Throughout France, you can find faience earthenware and pottery. Artisanal olive-wood products and accessories make lovely souvenirs from southern France, for instance from INSIDER TIP *Grain d'Olive (www.graindolive.com)* in *Puyloubier* near Aix-en-Provence.

### CULINARY IDEAS

**Olive oil** is always a good idea. It is best to take "extra vergine", the premium quality, which is a classic in southern France. The highest-quality sea salt, "fleur de sel", is harvested in the Camargue and you can buy it directly from farmers. The flavoursome herbs of Provence, including thyme and rosemary, are proverbial. Herbs also make pretty decorations.

### FASHION AND TEXTILES

Exclusive boutiques in larger cities like Cannes offer luxury and upmarket fashion collections. Those who want to spend less may wish to consider the pretty Provençal fabrics with colourful designs and lovely images of indigenous nature.

### MUSIC, BOOKS AND FILMS

Keep the holiday mood acoustically alive! Terrific selections of classic-chanson CDs are available at stores, for instance at retail outlets of the media company FNAC, where one can also find film classics on DVD.

# MARSEILLE

**Marseille is impervious to subtle differentiation: you either love or hate the oldest city of France. Featuring one of the most beautiful bays in the Mediterranean, the city is a melting pot of nations. With over 100 city districts, it can be somewhat chaotic, though full of contradictions and poetry.**

With a history of over 2600 years, Marseille fairly recently started to focus on tourism, taking full advantage of its fine sea-facing setting and lovely sandy beaches. If you want to know why the locals love their city, take a tour eastwards along the seaside on the coastal route, the Corniche, from the Vieux Port (Old Port) to the tiny harbours of Les Goudes or Callelongue. The basilica of Notre-Dame de la Garde offers arresting views over the city, especially at sunset when an exquisite golden crowning of the day is unmissable. As the sun descends behind the hills, a golden-hued light majestically envelops the city, its seafront and the Mediterranean, creating an unforgettable and spellbinding scenery.

## SIGHTSEEING

### CHÂTEAU D'IF AND FRIOUL ARCHIPELAGO

Take a boat from the Old Port to the island of If and view the fortress of *Château d'If* and the ⬛ observation tower. Visit the other islands in the Bay of Marseille: the Frioul Islands of Ratonneau and Pomègues *(Frioul-If-Express | daily, hourly, in summer | combined ticket 16.20 euros)*.

### CHURCHES

The medieval basilica of Major, built in the 12th century, was partially demolished in the 19th century, when the new *Cathédrale de la Major (Place de la Major)*

was built. The Marseille people held this against the architects and took punitive measures by restricting the completion of the cathedral's interior decoration. Yet the forecourt of the new cathedral, superbly overlooking the sea, was entirely rebuilt. The crypt of the fortified-looking Abbey of *Saint-Victor (daily 10am–7pm | 2 euros | Place Saint-Victor)*, dating from the 11th and 13th century, is worth visiting. The question of the architectural aesthetics of ⭐ ⬛ *Notre-Dame de la Garde (daily 7am–6.15pm, summer until 7.15pm | Rue Fort du Sanctuaire | www.notredamedelagarde.com)*, dating from the 19th century, remains controversial. Nevertheless, it affords visitors a magnificent view over the city.

### MUSÉE DES CIVILISATIONS DE L'EUROPE ET DE LA MÉDITERRANÉE (MUCEM) AND FORT SAINT-JEAN

The ⭐ *MuCEM (Wed–Mon 11am–6pm, summer until 8pm | exhibitions 9.50 euros, free admission to the grounds | www.mucem.org)* presents the connecting elements between the various cultures of the

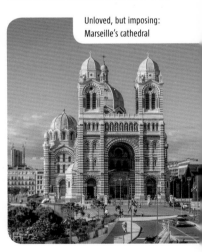

Unloved, but imposing: Marseille's cathedral

Mediterranean world. The INSIDER TIP *tower Roi René* at the *Fort Saint-Jean* is part of the site. It offers extraordinary views of the city and the port. 1, Esplanade du J4

### INSIDER TIP MUSÉE D'HISTOIRE DE MARSEILLE (𝄞 *5/C3*)

When the shopping centre Centre Bourse was built in the 1960s, archaeologists uncovered the ancient port. The museum, in the basement of the shopping centre, presents the 2600-year-old history of the city and houses a Roman ship discovered during the excavations. *Tue–Sun 10am–6pm | 6 euros | 2, Rue Henri Barbusse | musee-histoire-marseille-voie-historique.fr*

### INSIDER TIP MUSÉE REGARDS DE PROVENCE (𝄞 *5/A3*)

The museum exhibits pictures, sculptures and photographic work of artists of the region, and runs special exhibitions depicting the rich artistic tradition of Provence. *Daily 10am–6pm | combined ticket permanent and special exhibitions 8.50 euros | Av. Vaudoyer | www.museeregardsdeprovence.com*

### INSIDER TIP VALLON DES AUFFES AND MALMOUSQUE

Right in the centre of the city a picture-postcard small fishing harbour lies tucked away. The *Vallon des Auffes* is accessible via a staircase opposite the War Memorial of the Far East, *La Porte de l'Orient*. Another surprising secret one would not expect in a large city is the Malmousque cove, featuring a small village and tiny beach.

### VIEUX PORT AND LE PANIER (𝄞 *5/B3–4*)

The Vieux Port, the ★ *Old Port*, has been the heart of Marseille for 2600 years and is still the starting point for exploring the city. Every morning on the Quai des Belges (or on the *Quai de la Fraternité*, its official name since the beginning of the millennium), there is a picturesque fish market. From the Quai du Port, one can easily head to the old town of *Le Panier* and the Place des Moulins, with their prevailing village character.

# FRAGRANT FIELDS

The endless lavender fields flower between June and August. Of the total world production, approx. 70 percent of lavender oil and 90 percent of lavandin oil are from Provence. Lavender and lavandin differ in the sense that the latter is a hybrid, Lavandula x intermedia, a cross between "true" lavender, Lavandula angustifolia, and Lavandula latifolia. The lavandin hybrid, with its more intensive fragrance, is used for pharmaceutical and cosmetic purposes. "True" lavender is oilier and has a more delicate scent.

## SHOPPING

Shoppers in Marseille get value for their money. Shopping excursions promise not to be boring at all, whether the desired objects are shoes at La Canebière, or fragrant Oriental specialities along the alleys surrounding the *Place du Marché-des-Capucins*, or olive-oil chocolate. Cruise-ship tourists, but also people who want to do their shopping directly at the seaside, can browse from boutique to boutique and stroll on the enormous terrace high above the harbour dock at the shopping mall of *Les Terrasses du Port (9, Quai du Lazaret)* with over 150 stores, including high-end outlets, cafes and restaurants.

The world-famous white horses of the Camargue

## BEACHES

Marseille has spruced up its beaches. On the roundabout at the intersection of the coastal road and the *Avenue du Prado* stands a statue of David, a replica of the famous work by Michelangelo: a landmark at the *Plages Gaston-Defferre*. This seaside park covers over 110 acres and has sandy and pebbly beaches, showers, large lawns, cafes and restaurants. The *Base Nautique de Corbières* overlooks the Bay of Marseille and is worth visiting.

## WHERE TO GO

### CASSIS ★
On the hills, winegrowers still produce AOP-certified white wine, although urban sprawl straddles vineyards. The seaside resort has a picturesque port. Delightful pebbly and rocky beaches adorn the stretch of coast, which is renowned for its high sea cliffs. Take in the exquisite scenery between the Plage du Bestouan and

the peninsula, and view the unique steep-sided fjord-like inlets, Les Calanques: Port-Miou, Port-Pin and En-Vau.

### CAMARGUE ★
Rice paddies, as far as the eye can see, salt marshes, flamingos, seemingly endless meadows with black bulls and white Camargue horses – the Camargue, embodying the flat delta plains of the Rhône, is a unique landscape! Excellent information is available at the *Musée de la Camargue (5 euros | D 570 | Mas du Pont de Rousty | www.parc-camargue.fr)*, where you can enjoy a discovery path of 3.5 km/2.2 mi.

### AVIGNON ★
The town's curious landmark is the 12th-century Saint-Bénézet bridge, made famous in a well-known folksong. Rhône-flooding in the 17th century damaged several of its arches. Since then, the bridge ends in the middle of the river. Among other sights, the Pope's Palace and the 4.3 km /2.7 mi ramparts also warrant a visit.

Beautiful colours in Ajaccio

# AJACCIO/ CORSICA

**Ajaccio (pop. 68,600), situated on the northern shore of the Gulf of Ajaccio, is Corsica's largest city. Palm trees, beautiful boulevards, the deep-blue sea, white sandy beaches and terracotta-hued buildings evoke Ajaccio's Mediterranean allure.**

Buzzing with southern European vibrancy, the city is calm at lunchtime though. In the old town, bars and restaurants lining the narrow alleys pulsate well into the wee hours. Wander around the lovely *Rue Fesch* and the *Cours Napoléon*. Ajaccio is the birthplace of Napoleon Bonaparte, the French emperor who had world-power ambitions. His name and image characterize the city, which is often alluded to as the "imperial city" *(Cité Impériale)*. Ajaccio is the seat of the Assemblée Régionale de Corse, the legislative assembly of the Corsican territorial collectivity of France.

## SIGHTSEEING

### MAISON BONAPARTE *( 6/B3)*
This is the house of the Bonaparte family, where Napoleon I was born. *Tue–Sun*

*10.30am–12.30pm and 1.15pm–6pm | 3 rue St-Charles | admission 5–7 euros | www. musee-maisonbonaparte.fr*

### NOTRE-DAME DE LA MISÉRICORDE *( 6/B4)*
This 16th-century cathedral, with a prodigious dome, houses the marble font where Napoleon was baptized in 1771. Shortly prior to his death on St Helena, he expressed the wish to be buried here, should Paris decline his body. *From 8am | Rue Forcioli Contiin in the old town*

### PALAIS FESCH *( 6/C2)*
Napoleon's uncle, Cardinal Fesch, bequeathed his valuable Italian art collection to his home city. The *Chapelle Impériale*, next to the Palais Fesch, is also worth visiting. It contains the tombs of the Napoleon family. *May–Sept | 50 rue Fesch | admission 8 euros | Info & opening hours at: www.musee-fesch.com*

### PLACE D'AUSTERLITZ
A large statue of the Emperor Napoleon, with an inscription of his victories, adorns the square. From the top of the ⚘ steps one can enjoy a splendid view over the city and the bay. Napoleon apparently liked playing in the adjacent cave when he was a child. *At the end of the Cours du Général Leclerc*

### PLACE MARÉCHAL FOCH *( 6/B3)*
The square is the principal core of the historic city. Surrounded by palm trees, this landmark features the lion fountain with its centrepiece, a towering marble statue of Napoleon Bonaparte.

## SHOPPING

### MARKET ★
Corsica's loveliest market brims with colourful, aromatic local produce *(Tue–Sun*

*8am–noon | Place Foch)*. Expand your experience in the area and catch a glimpse of the fish market, the *Halle aux poissons. Daily 7.30am–12.30pm (Oct–April Mon closed) | Quai Napoléon*

### PATISSERIE AU BON PAIN DU CASONE

Though inconspicuous, this bakery and pastry shop sells delicious and typical Corsican breads, cakes and pastries. The *beignets au brocchiu*, small sweet pastry balls with sheep-milk-cheese filling, are especially commendable. *12 cours Général Leclerc*

### SCARBONCHI U POGHJU ❂ ⬝⬝

Marie-Claude beckons with homemade jams and chestnut flour, made with produce that she grows on her farm. View cattle, a tree nursery and an orchard; located at Curintina Suprana in Cuttoli-Corticchiato. *April–Sept daily until noon, Oct–March by appointment | tel. 04 95 25 83 46*

## LEISURE & SPORTS

INSIDER TIP COULEUR CORSE

Among activities arranged by Laetitia and her team, there are mountain-hiking excursions and canyoning day trips in a lovely gorge near the city. *6 boulevard Fred Scaramoni | tel. 04 95 10 52 83 | www. couleur-corse.com*

## WHERE TO GO

### PORTO

Among Corsica's many tourist attractions, Porto, with its red stone buildings, stands out in the ⭐ *Gulf of Porto*, a Unesco world heritage site. Climb to the top of the Genoese watchtower at the end of the headland, or enjoy a sightseeing boat ride in the Gulf, so that you can indulge in the mesmerizing splendour of the beautiful scenery and colourful interplay of water and cliffs.

### CALANCHES DE PIANA ⭐

South of Porto you will find the Calanches, a magnet in the region. Fantastic and bizarre formations of dazzling weathered red granite rocks add splendour to the landscape. Rushing rivers, steep wooded mountainsides, and green meadows enhance the scenic beauty, set between Porto, the main town, and Piana, the second main town in the gulf.

### SCANDOLA ⭐

The Scandola Nature Reserve covers the entire Scandola peninsula northwest of Osani and encompasses large marine areas where depleted fish stocks can regenerate. Ospreys build their nests on the cliffs, and visitors can watch their elegant flight. *www. visite-scandola.com*

# STRENGTH IN PEACE AND CALM

#### TORTOISE ZOO A CUPULATTA

This sanctuary for tortoises from all over the world is situated on the N 193-route from Ajaccio to Bastia. At noon, when it is hot, the tortoises tend to go into hiding. It is best to visit INSIDER TIP as early as possible. Afterwards, there will be time for a picnic at the nearby river. *21 km/13 mi from Ajaccio, in Vignola | admission 12 euros, children (ages 5–11) 9 euros | Info & opening hours at: www. acupulatta.com*

# TRAVEL TIPS

## ADMISSION

In general, state and city museums have considerably cheaper admission fees than private collections and attractions. State and city museums grant free admission to EU citizens below the age of 26 and to everyone on the first Sunday of the month. Children and senior citizens can expect discounts of up to 50 percent and over 75-year-olds often have free admission. Some museums and attractions have seasonally adjusted price grades; July and August are the most expensive months.

## BERTHS

▶ MONACO

The port, with its Pier Quai Rainier III for cruise ships, is centrally located. If piers are fully booked, ships drop anchor offshore and tender boats take passengers ashore.
▶ NICE

The Nice-Villefranche port is the second largest cruise-ship port in France and has more than 500 piers. Larger ships that are more than 200 m/219 yd in length use the piers at the tender of port Villefranche, east of the centre; smaller ones are moored at the Port de Nice. From Villefranche you can reach the centre by bus or taxi; from the

## BUDGETING

| | | |
|---|---|---|
| Coffee | £1.30–£2/$1.70–$2.60 | |
| | *for a petit noir at the counter* | |
| Ice cream | £1.70–£3/$2.30–$4 | |
| | *per scoop* | |
| Wine | from £3.40/$4.50 | |
| | *per glass in bistros* | |

Port de Nice you can walk to the old town.
▶ CANNES

Since Cannes does not have its own port for cruise ships, ships drop anchor offshore; tender boats provide the transfer to one of the three quays ashore. From here, you can get directly to the centre of Cannes.
▶ MARSEILLE

In Marseille, cruise ships dock approx. 8 km/5 mi north of the Vieux Port. There are bus and taxi services to take you to the Vieux Port.
▶ AJACCIO

The port of Ajaccio is very centrally located; you can head to the city centre on foot.

## CLIMATE & WHEN TO GO

The north of France is relatively humid and the south enjoys long sunny periods. The best travelling time in most regions in France is from late spring to autumn. Along the Côte d'Azur, one can already enjoy some sunshine in January.

## CUSTOMS

UK citizens do not have to pay any duty on goods brought from another EU country as long as tax was included in the price and are for private consumption. The limits are: 800 cigarettes, 400 cigarillo, 200 cigars, 1kg smoking tobacco, 10l spirits, 20l liqueurs, 90l wine, 110l beer.
Travellers from the USA, Canada, Australia or other non-EU countries are allowed to enter with the following tax-free amounts: 200 cigarettes or 100 cigarillos or 50 cigars or 250g smoking tobacco. 2l wine and spirits with less than 22 vol % alcohol content, 1l spirits with more than 22 vol % alcohol content.

# France

Travellers to the United States who are returning residents of the country do not have to pay duty on articles purchased overseas up to the value of $800, but there are limits on the amount of alcoholic beverages and tobacco products. For the regulations for international travel for US residents please see http://www.cbp.gov

## EMERGENCY SERVICES

In all EU countries, the emergency-service number is 112. You can reach it by telephone and mobile phone, even without a SIM card or contract.

## HEALTH

All travellers should take out adequate travel medical/health insurance well in advance of the cruise. Citizens of EU member countries may use their European Health Insurance Card (EHIC), but this is not a substitute for travel insurance. More info and updates for travellers from the UK, USA, Canada and Australia at:
UK: https://www.gov.uk/browse/abroad/travel-abroad and https://www.gov.uk/foreign-travel-advice/france/health
USA: https://www.state.gov/travel/ and https://travel.state.gov/content/travel/en/international-travel/before-you-go/travelers-with-special-considerations/cruise-ship-passengers.html
CAN: https://travel.gc.ca/travelling/advisories
AUS:https://smartraveller.gov.au/guide/all-travellers/health/Pages/default.aspx

## INTERNET & WIFI

Good news for frequent internet users and web surfers: all state and city museums, almost all private museums, all libraries, all train stations, fast-food chains and shopping centres offer free, unlimited internet access, which is very fast and without any log-in hurdles.

## MONEY & CREDIT CARDS

ATMs offer the easiest and most convenient way to make cash withdrawals. Plenty of ATMs are available, and they accept credit cards and EC cards. In France, credit cards are accepted almost everywhere, even for smaller amounts.

## PHONE & MOBILE PHONE

For international calls to the UK, dial 0044, for the USA and Canada 001, for Australia 0061, followed by the area code of the city or town (but omit the area code prefix 0) and then the telephone number. For calls to France, dial the country code 0033 and the phone number, but omit the introductory 0. Within France, you have to dial the complete 10-digit number

## POST

Letters up to 20 g/0.7 oz and postcards to countries in the European Union and to Switzerland cost 1 euro postage, at the time of going to press.

## TIPPING

It is customary to give tips. However, when paying in cafes and restaurants, one usually waits for the change and then leaves the tip on the table.

# ITALY

When you arrive in Italy, the first thing you should do is to go to the piazza; it is the sitting room, hub of urban life and stage for the Italians all rolled into one. Sit down in the café with the best view, order a cappuccino, a Campari or even a local aperitif and simply watch the Italians.

# ROME (ROMA)

Rome's appeal is in its unique mix of ancient past, dynamic present and a mild climate that allows much of life to be al fresco.

In the centre of this metropolis awe-inspiring ruins bear testimony to the city's time as the pulsating heart of the Roman Empire, while magnificent churches and palazzi from the medieval, Renaissance and Baroque periods provide equally clear evidence of its role as a centre of Christianity. Enthroned above it all is the monumental Vittoriano "altar of the fatherland", offering a breathtaking panorama from the Terrazza delle Quadrighe. Museums for contemporary art (MACRO and MAXXI), first-class concerts, exhibitions and film festivals are regular features in the lively cultural scene, and besides well-established, traditional trattorias and local bars, there are sophisticated restaurants and trendy lounge bars, and in addition to the classically elegant boutiques, there are also stores of a younger style. Walk through the fashion-

Photo: Seen from afar, Vesuvius dominates the Gulf of Naples

## The Boot of Italy is surrounded by water: the Ligurian, Tyrrhenian, Ionian and Adriatic Seas welcome you

able areas such as the serene Trastevere and vibrant Testaccio or to the elegant Piazza del Popolo.

### SIGHTSEEING

**BOCCA DELLA VERITÀ** (*📖 7/D4*)
The "mouth of truth" is a strange marble face as tall as a man on the left of the atrium of *Santa Maria in Cosmedin*. The left eye seems to be shedding tears, and only the mouth has been worn smooth, as visitors place their hands into the

monster's jaws. By tradition jealous married people send their partners there. If they don't tell the truth, this ancient lie detector is said to bite off the hand. Don't miss the 1000-year-old gold mosaic inside the church. *Daily 9.30am–6pm, in winter 9.30am–5pm | Piazza Bocca della Verità 18 | Santa Maria in Cosmedin*

**CAMPIDOGLIO** ⭐ (*📖 7/D3*)
The Capitol is just a magical place! Where the Temples of Jupiter and Juno once stood, in 1536 Michelangelo laid out the

One of the most impressive relics from Roman times is the Colosseum

trapezium-shaped square of the Capitol, flanked by the *Palazzo dei Senatori*, the *Palazzo dei Conservatori* and the *Palazzo Nuovo*. The pedestal from which the riding Emperor Marcus Aurelius greets passers-by with a raised hand today bears a copy of the original statue dating from the 2nd century, which needed protection from pollution and was moved inside the *Musei Capitolini*. If you take the steps to the left of the Piazza del Campidoglio, you have a wonderful view of the ⌇↯ *Foro Romano*. On the way, pause to look at the small bronze statue of the Roman she-wolf, which Romulus and Remus, the founders of Rome, was said to have raised. *Piazza del Campidoglio*

## COLOSSEO (COLOSSEUM) ★ (*[m 7/E3*)
The gigantic arcades of the Colosseum were Emperor Vespasian's attempt, as

successor to cruel Nero, to enhance his popularity with his citizens and staged "bread and circuses". It was inaugurated by his son and successor, Titus, following an intensive period of building activity lasting just eight years. The arena had seating capacity of 50,000 spectators; the first three rows were reserved for the Roman aristocracy. Women, slaves and plebeians crowded into the top wooden stand below sun canopies. Today, sophisticated underground passages, trap doors, enclosures and the lifts for wild animals are still exposed in the foundations of the building as well as changing rooms and weapons stores for the gladiators. Safety guidelines were also extremely elaborate: in case of emergency, like a fire, the arena could be cleared in five minutes via 80 entrances and exits. Highly recommended are the INSIDER TIP night tours "La Luna sul Colosseo". *Admission daily 8.30am until one hour before dusk | Admission 12 euros (also valid 2 days for Foro Romano and Palatine), Online reservation recommended at www.coopculture.it | Piazza del Colosseo 1 | Metro B Colosseo*

### FORO ROMANO ★ (*♨ 7/E3*)
The Forum Romanum, originally conceived as a sanctuary of Vesta, evolved from a cattle market to a political arena from which not only Rome but the whole Roman Empire was ruled. Today you don't have to wear a toga to stroll between columns and triumphal arches on warm evenings: INSIDER TIP▶ "Roma sotto le stelle" (Rome beneath the stars) is the name for night tours. *In Italian and English | June–mid-Sept | dates from the tourist information pavilions and newspapers, e.g. La Repubblica.*

### CAMPO DE' FIORI ★ (*♨ 7/C3*)
Here is a lively party atmosphere. This is the piazza for meeting in the evening and is especially popular with young people. At the centre of Rome's popular square, surrounded by tall and restored palazzi, stands a memorial to the Dominican monk, Giordano Bruno, who was burned at the stake here by the Inquisition at the start of the Holy Year of 1600. From beneath his hood Bruno looks defiantly towards the Vatican past the lively goings-on of the market in the mornings and the party people and restaurant-goers in the evenings. On Rome's favourite vegetable market fewer stands are to be found nowadays than in the past, as the competition from supermarkets takes its toll, but many Roman women still swear by the Campo, where lots of greens, root vegetables, spices and even clothes are on sale, though not many flowers despite the name of the square, which comes from a flower-covered meadow that was here in the Middle Ages.

### PANTHEON ★ (*♨ 7/D2*)
A cylinder with a dome on top: the Pantheon, built in 27 BC at the behest of Marcus Agrippa, the son-in-law of Augustus, to honour all the gods, is a seemingly simple construcion. From the outside, the 2000-year-old temple looks slightly grey and pockmarked, but when you walk through the high, bronze doors you will be surprised: inside, you marvel at the largest, unsupported dome of ancient Rome with a giant, open skylight. On sunny days, the effects of light are astonishing, and even more so if it rains, when water drains through a recess at the centre of the building. *Mon–Sat 8.30am–*

# FONTANA DI EUROS

It is the dream of every European minister of finance to possess such a source of money, one that even flows in times of crisis: the *Trevi Fountain*. Every year, Caritas helpers fish 35,000 kg/ 77,000 lbs worth of coins (often more than 900,000 euros) out of Rome's most beloved baroque fountain. Chances are high that more millions of euros will be reached, as the city of Rome has made it illegal to fish the fountain dry and declared it a crime. This money can only be used for humanitarian purposes and not to fill holes in the tax budget.

*7.30pm, Sun 9am–6pm | free admission | Piazza della Rotonda*

## PIAZZA NAVONA ⭐ (*𝔐 7/C2*)

The most beautiful and cheerful arena of the Baroque period, elongated but enclosed, lively and colourful but at the same time intimate, is the work of Renaissance and Baroque popes, like so many attractive squares and streets in Rome. To please his beloved sister-in-law Olimpia, Innocent X (1644–55) not only ordered the construction of Palazzo Pamphilj, today the seat of the Brazilian embassy, for her, but also spread this wonderful piazza at her feet. It was laid out on the site of the *circo agonale*, out of which the people of Rome made the word navona. Until the late 18th century princes of the Church and patrician families enjoyed contests and horse races here from the windows of their palaces. To cool the Romans down in the summer, the piazza was flooded in August so that miniature naval battles could be staged. Gianlorenzo Bernini's *Fontana dei Quattro Fiumi* is the centre of attention on the piazza. Four river gods are seated on a rocky grotto crowned by an obelisk. They represent the Danube, Nile, Ganges and Rio de la Plata. The church of Sant'Agnese opposite was built two years after completion of the fountain by Bernini's rival Francesco Borromini.

## SANTA MARIA DELLA PACE (*𝔐 7/C2*)

The cloister, art, coffee and light snacks offer a charming mixture here. They are located in the ⭐ *Caffetteria Chiostro del Bramante (Mon–Fri 10am–8pm, Sat/Sun 10am–9pm)* on the first floor above the Renaissance cloister created by Florentine star artist Donatello Bramante. Before or after you enjoy a cappuccino you can visit one of the numerous touring exhibitions in the cultural centre INSIDER TIP ▶ *Chiostro del Bramante (daily 10am–9pm | Arco della Pace 5)*. Wonderful! *Via della Pace 5*

## FONTANA DI TREVI (TREVI FOUNTAIN) ⭐ (*𝔐 7/D2*)

It was the last great monument of the Baroque popes, whose power was waning by 1750, the year of its construction. The god of the sea, Oceanus, rides through a triumphal arch with two horses. Incidentally, tourists not only arrive because of "La dolce vita". Those who throw a coin into the fountain will return to Rome at some point in the future. Perhaps it will work. *Piazza di Trevi*

## GALLERIA BORGHESE ⭐

Miracles happen, but in the Eternal City they sometimes take an eternity: after a 17-year restoration, the Baroque pleasure palace of Cardinal Scipione Borghese reopened. The prelate was one of the world's great patrons of art. Ever since there has been a rush for admission tickets, advance booking online is essential. On the ground floor you will see Bernini's sculptures "Daphne and Apollo", "David", "The Rape of Proserpina" and the semi-nude "Paolina Borghese", Napoleon's sister, by Antonio Canova. On the first floor, however, you are on the safe side. Here, mainly clothed figures are displayed by the artists Lucas Cranach, Titian, Paul Veronese, Raphael, Peter Paul Rubens and Caravaggio. *Tue–Sun 8.30am–7.30pm | admission 15 plus 2 euros | registration only (Italian/English) tel. 0 63 28 10 or www.ticketeria.it | Piazza Scipione Borghese 5*

## SCALINATA DI TRINITÀ DEI MONTI (SPANISH STEPS) ⭐ (*𝔐 7/D1*)

The Spanish Steps always were the favourite place for visitors to Rome. In the

Probably the most famous steps in Rome: Scalinata Trinità dei Monti (Spanish Steps)

late 18th century, English poets like John Keats and Percy Bysshe Shelley sat quietly writing their poetry on the curved balustrades that were built by Alessandro Specchi and Francesco di Sanctis in 1723. Today, the wide steps are filled with young Romans and tourists. The jeweller Bulgari recently paid 1.5 million euros for the restoration of the elegant steps. Bulgari also restored the tinkling *Fontana della Barcaccia*, the fountain in the shape of an old boat, and designed in 1629 by Pietro Bernini, the father of the even more famous sculptor Gianlorenzo Bernini, and now flowing crystal clear at the foot of the Spanish Steps. But on Rome's favourite square litter is still quietly left behind.

## SAN PIETRO (ST PETER) ★ (𝄞 7/A1–2)
St Peter's Basilica can only be described with superlatives. In size it far exceeds any other European church, measuring 211 m/692 ft in length, 186 m/610 ft at its widest point and 132 m/433 ft in height. In 1506 Pope Julius II gave Donato Bramante the task of building a new church to replace the ancient basilica that Emperor Constantine erected over the tomb of St Peter. In the 120-year period of construction, the best architects in Italy came up with many mutually contradictory models. Inside, you can admire Michelangelo's "Pietà" and the cathedra altar with the papal throne. To get up to the roof, where you'll find INSIDER TIP a nice café and souvenir shop, you take a lift to the right of the church. After that 320 steep steps lead up to the 🔆 *dome,* from where the view of Rome is superb. Be sure to wear decent clothing, i.e. long trousers, no uncovered shoulders! *Church daily 7am–7pm, sacristy 9am–6pm | admission 5 euros; roof and dome 8am–6pm | admission 5 euros, with lift 7 euros, security checks beneath the right-hand colonnade*

# ROME (ROMA)

**VATICAN MUSEUMS** ⭐ *(ᗩ 7/A1)*
With 14 museums, the Vatican City has one of the largest museum complexes in the world; an immeasurable abundance of masterpieces from antiquity and leading artists such as Giotto, da Vinci, Caravaggio, Raphael and many others. The highlight has to be the ⭐ *Sistine Chapel (Cappella Sistina)* with Michelangelo's paintings based on the Book of Genesis (1508–1512) on the ceiling of the large chapel, still used by Catholic popes today. It is generally worth reserving a ticket *(biglietteria-musei.vatican.va)* in order to avoid having to queue. *Mon–Sat 9am–6pm, last Sun of the month (no admission fee) 9am–2pm | main entrance Viale Vaticano | mv.vatican.va*

### CAFÉS & ICE CREAM PARLOURS

**INSIDERTIP GINGER** ⊙
In this organic bistro and café situated on the exclusive Via Borgognona, health-conscious Romans sip their smoothies, organic fruit juices, herbal teas and even a good old cappuccino from time to time. *Daily 10am–midnight | Via Borgognona 43–44 | bus 62, 63 | Metro A Spagna*

**INSIDERTIP GROM** ⊙
Two young Turinese had the perfect slow-food ice idea, grew their own organic fruit on their plantations in Piedmont – and voila: a new super-gelato was born. Insider tip: cantaloupe melon! Also situated near the Pantheon *(Via della Maddalena 30). Sun–Thu 11–1am, Fri/ Sat 11–1.30am | Piazza Navona 1 | bus 40, 64, 70, 81, 492*

### SHOPPING

The best fashion designers have their fine shops on and around *Via Condotti*; the *Via del Corso* offers more variety. On Sundays, there is a flea market At *Porta Portese* in Trastevere.

# VATICAN CURIOSITIES

**Miniature state.** Rome's church state is 44 ha/109 acres – it previously extended across the whole of Central Italy. The 572 residents of the Vatican state have everything, and they don't even pay taxes. The population growth is, of course, zero.
**What is an ipsophonum?** Catholics live around the world – how can Babylonian confusion be prevented? It's easy: Latin is the official Vatican language. The problem is that a lot of contemporary vocabulary is missing in Latin. Since 1976 there is a New Latin dictionary in which an answering machine is called an *ipsophonum*, a mobile phone *telephonum manuale* and

a cash machine an *automata monetalia*.
**Railway without trains.** The Vatican rail service is the smallest in the world: 400 m/1312 ft tracks, one platform, a single set of points, yet no trains. The Italian railway service provides trains and personnel just in case.
**Popemobile.** Pope John Paul II tested the popemobile on an "official visit" in 1979 in his home country of Poland. Afterwards, he introduced it on all of his 104 visits to be as close as possible to the faithful. Most of these 60 papal vehicles remained in the host countries and are re-used for each visit.

# FOOD & DRINK

## Pasta is the basis of Italian food – and each region produces the right wine to accompany it

The *salumerie*, the cheese shop, and the food markets will have your mouth watering within seconds. However, it is the simple, but ingenious, durum wheat flour pasta that is the traditional mainstay of Italian cuisine.

The imagination and creativity of the Italians have produced around *250 different types of pasta*, first and foremost spaghetti. In southern Italy, *maccheroni* holds sway, also *tubetti*, *rigatoni* or *penne*. Then, there are the more typically central or northern Italian pasta, and finally the *filled pasta* made of egg and flour dough in many forms and with different fillings. Many pasta dishes are traditionally topped with grated cheese. A meal begins with *antipasti*, which include starters such as salami, ham, pickled onions, aubergines, artichokes or seafood; this is followed by the *primo* (first course), a pasta dish, soup or *risotto*; the *secondo* (main course) is braised or grilled meat, or fish, also often simply grilled, and a choice of vegetables (*contorno*). *Vegetables* provide the cue for the south, which is where the tomatoes taste particularly good, as do the aubergines, artichokes, fresh *fave* (green, sweet broad beans), hearty leaf vegetables, such as *cicorie, cime di rape, friarielli* and *broccoli*. The meal culminates with *creamy desserts* such as *tiramisu* as well as biscuits which you dunk into sweet fortified wine.

## LOCAL SPECIALITIES

(insalata) caprese – the classic summer snack: tomatoes, mozzarella (preferably made of buffalo milk), basil

gnocchi – tiny potato flour dumplings served, like pasta, as a primo with a sugo

zabaione – light and fluffy custard cream with wine, originally from Piedmont

insalata di frutti di mare – a seafood salad with a lemon, olive oil, garlic and parsley dressing comprising of chopped squid, octopus and mussels

ossobuco – braised veal or beef shanks in a tomato sauce, typical for Lombardy

spaghetti alle vongole/allo scoglio – spaghetti with clams or seafood

# LIVORNO

The people of Livorno are merry folk; their local dialect has a distinctive twang, reminiscent of American English. It is the language of seafarers, the result of the meeting of many cultures and traditions. Livorno truly is a well-kept secret. The lively yet humble seaport does not boast the pomp of the Renaissance, nor will you find winding medieval alleyways here. Instead, the streets and piazzas are broad and sunlit. Livorno came into its own in the 16th century, when the powerful Medici clan needed access to the sea. And in order to attract wealthy Jewish merchants to the city, the freedom of speech and religion was established early on.

## SIGHTSEEING

### FORTEZZA VECCHIA AND FORTEZZA NUOVA

Back in the 16th century, the two brick fortresses served as outposts to secure the seaport of the rich and powerful Medici clan. Nowadays, the *Fortezza Vecchia* is a busy venue with events almost every summer evening. Every year during the *Effetto Venezia (www.livornoeffettovenezia.it)*, a major music festival taking place in July, the entire city district of *Venezia Nuova* will be heaving with visitors. The *Fortezza Nuova* is now a major park where the locals come for their lunch break or take a leisurely evening stroll to enjoy the lovely view over the battlements.

### LUNGOMARE

As soon as the sun appears, this 4 km/2.5 mi long seaside promenade – between the bathing beach Scoglia della Regina and the circular pine grove Rotonda Ardenza – fills up with pedestrians, cyclists and joggers. Along the way are the ⚡ *Mascagni*

*panorama terrace,* art nouveau villas, bars and cafés. In the evening the promenade is full of people strolling leisurely along.

### INSIDER TIP MUSEO CIVICO GIOVANNI FATTORI

During the 19th century the local painter Giovanni Fattori was a leading member of the "Macchiaioli", a Tuscan group of artists that, like the French Impressionists, resisted the dominant academic style. Artworks by Fattori and other group member are on display in the art nouveau Villa Mimbelli. *Tue–Sun 10am–1pm and 4pm–7pm | 6 euros | Via San Jacopo in Acquaviva*

### VENEZIA NUOVA

The old district of merchants and fishermen is the heart of the town. Here, the gozzi, the traditional rowing boats emerge from the network of ancient canals to commence their daily training in the harbour basin. From the harbour, another network of tunnels reaches the buildings' foundations. In the past, the riches of the city were stored here, but today the tunnels are occupied by studios and bars, such as INSIDER TIP *La Bodeguita (Mon closed | Scali Finocchietti 28)*. You can explore the teeming life on top of Venezia Nuova's wooden foundations by boat: *Giro in Battello (10 euros | tickets in the Punto Informazioni | Via Pieroni 18)*

## SHOPPING

### BOTTEGA CAMPAGNA AMICA 🌐

A local cooperative specializing in the direct selling of regionally sourced food. *Piazza dei Legnami 22*

### MARKETS

Do try to prise your eyes away from the mouth-watering local delicacies of the 180-odd market stalls for long enough to admire the imposing art nouveau cast-iron and stone construction of the *Mercato Centrale (Mon–Sat 7.30am–1.30pm | Via del Cardinale/Via Buontalenti)*. The INSIDER TIP *Mercatino Americano (Mon–Sat 10am–7pm | Via della Cinta Esterna/Piazzale del Portuale)* still feels like a temporary post-war structure. But the countless stalls of local handicraft and foreign imports are a veritable treasure trove for collectors and bargain hunters.

## WHERE TO GO

### LUCCA ⭐
Its 16th century fortified walls encircle the old town, which is brimming with treasures such as the *San Martino cathedral* (6th/13th century) or the oval *Piazza del Mercato* with the medieval houses lining a Roman amphitheatre. Standing in the shade of the trees on ⬙ *Torre Guinigi,* you can look across to Garfagnana, a beautiful place for day trips and walks in the north of Lucca. One highlight: th INSIDER TIP camellia blossoms in spring in the gardens of the old villas.

### FLORENCE (FIRENZE)
It is Europe's richest art centre, full of incomparably exquisite architecture, monuments, sculptures and paintings. From the 14th century, the powerful Medici family steered the city's political and cultural destiny, which reached its zenith during the Renaissance. It was here in 1256 that Dante was born, the writer whose poetical language was to provide the basis for the Italian language. From the raised square, ⬙ *Piazzale Michelangelo* on the left bank of the Arno, there is a fantastic view of the whole town, including the river banks, the palaces, the towering ⭐ cathedral dome.

### PISA
Hardly any other monument in Pisa is as famous as the *Leaning Tower (current ope-*

Is the tower going to topple over or not?

*ning times and tickets via www.opapisa.it | no children under 8)*. Its tilt started quite soon after its construction in 1173 on the shifting sands of a former estuary. It stands on the ⭐ ⬙ *Campo dei Miracoli* (Field of Miracles), as do the magnificent Romanesque cathedral, the baptistry and the *Camposanto*, a cemetery full of precious sculptures and frescoes from the town's golden age.

# LA SPEZIA

**Surrounded by hills, La Spezia nestles securely in the furthest land-reaching arc of the lovely Gulf of La Spezia.**
In 1808, Napoleon started expanding La Spezia's significance as a naval base. In recent times, the Italian government strengthened the city's naval status. Although modern post-war reconstruction and industrial developments were not conducive to reviving La Spezia's former radiance, it today embodies culture and

The Duomo San Gennaro in Naples

charming urban appeal. Visit the interesting archaeological and art museums, and stroll around the lively city-centre district of Prione. Closer to the sea, there are lovely places: Portovenere and the island of Palmaria to the west, and Lerici to the south-east. On ⚓ approaching the *Cinque Terre*, you will be afforded the most glorious view over the gulf.

## SIGHTSEEING

### CAMEC
The name Centro d'Arte Moderna e Contemporanea says it all: now La Spezia also has a place for modern and contemporary art. *Tue–Sun 11am–6pm | Piazza Cesare Battisti | camec.spezianet.it*

### CASTELLO SAN GIORGIO/MUSEO ARCHEOLOGICO U. FORMENTINI ⚓
From the hilltop fortress, once a stronghold of Genoa against the seaport Republic of Pisa, you have a magnificent view over the gulf. It houses the Archaeological Museum, which exhibits prehistoric finds from the vicinity and valuable objects from the old Roman port city of Luni. The main attractions are the famous and secretive stone figures of men and women, the ⭐ stelae statues from Lunigiana, the area bordering Tuscany. *From 10.30am |Via 27 Marzo*

### MUSEO DEL SIGILLO
View an impressive collection of seals from all over the world and of all times. *Tue 4pm–7pm, Wed–Sun 10–noon and 4pm–7pm | Via del Prione 236*

### CINQUE TERRE ⭐
Situated in the lovely Cinque Terre National Park, the five idyllic fishing villages Monterosso, Vernazza, Corniglia, Manarola and Riomaggiore are among the most attractive coastal spots in Italy. Strict nature-conservation measures are enforced in the park, including the protection of the endangered mountainous landscape.

## SHOPPING

La Spezia also offers a pleasant shopping experience, notably in the pedestrianized old town. Stroll around the orange-tree-lined boulevards, the Piazza Verdi and the Piazza Europa, and browse in shops galore. Visit a delightful market in the morning: the Piazza Cavour or the Piazza Mercato. Outside the city, in Santo Stefano di Magra, at the A 12/A 15-highway-junction, there is a large, modern shopping centre, *La Fabbrica*.

# NAPLES (NAPOLI)

**Seen from the sea, in the distance, Naples appears wonderfully promising. Dominating the south is the broad cone of Mount Vesuvius.**

In the city's interwoven fabric, you will find legacies of the French, Spanish, Habsburg and Bourbon royal families – elegant public squares, palazzi and gardens – right next to labyrinthine districts of chaotic proportions. Yet the city also boasts a lot of contemporary culture. Contemporary art centres such as *PAN (Palazzo delle Arti di Napoli)* and *MADRE (Museo d'Arte Contemporanea Donna Regina)* contribute to the cultural variety.

## SIGHTSEEING

### CAPPELLA SANSEVERO (*9/D1*)
The small rococo church contains some exceptional sculptures, especially the "Veiled Christ" with its intricate drapery – a masterpiece by Giuseppe Sammartino (1753). *Wed–Mon 9.30am–6.30pm | Via de Sanctis 19–21 / www.museosansevero.it*

### CASTEL DELL'OVO (*9/C–D4*)
This Norman castle stand on a small rocky outcrop. The castle overlooks the busy fishing harbour of *Porto Santa Lucia* and the *Borgo Marinaro*, popular with night owls, with its trattorias and cafés.

### CATACOMBE DI SAN GENNARO
The most impressive subterranean cemetery in southern Italy with early Christian graffiti (2nd century). *Mon–Sat 10am–5pm, Sun 10am–1pm | Tondo di Capodimonte 13 | entrance near the Basilica della Madre del Buon Consiglio www.catacombedinapoli.it*

### DUOMO SAN GENNARO (*9/E1*)
In the repeatedly redesigned French Gothic cathedral of the patron saint of Naples is the San Gennaro chapel with reliquaries, also a vial of what is thought to be his blood. Enjoy the panoramic view while INSIDER TIP taking a stroll on the cathedral's roof. *Via Duomo*

### MUSEO ARCHEOLOGICO NAZIONALE ★
The museum contains one of the largest and most famous archaeological collections in the world, with murals from Pompeii and Herculaneum. Don't forget to go and see the collection of artistic and unambiguous erotica from ancient pleasure houses, exhibited in the Gabinetto Segreto. *Wed–Mon 9am–7.30pm | Piazza Museo.*

# MAFIA

In Italy alone, the Mafia makes around 100 billion euros a year. Yet there are constantly successful results in the quest to catch the "untouchable" mob bosses, and the civilian population is contributing increasingly to the efforts. Throughout Italy, the Italian association Libera promotes a law-abiding culture against organised crime on a communal and regional level. Organic oil, wine and pasta, produced on land confiscated from the mafia are now being sold under the label ⊕ "Libera Terra" (*www.liberaterra.it*). The Addiopizzo movement ("goodbye to protection money") is drawing attention to hotels, restaurants and shops in Sicily where the owners are bravely resisting the extortion rackets. In Calabria, the Ammazzateci tutti ("kill us all") movement stages campaigns to raise public awareness of legality.

### MUSEO E GALLERIE NAZIONALI DI CAPODIMONTE ⭐

The magnificent royal palace of Capodimonte, set in a beautiful 🌿 park high above the city, houses the art collections handed down over the years by the different rulers of Naples and includes works by Caravaggio, Titian and Breughel. The residential chambers include a salon made entirely of porcelain, a work by the famous porcelain manufactory of Capodimonte. *Thu–Tue 8.30am–7.30 pm | Via di Capodimonte | www.museocapodimonte.beniculturali.it*

### INSIDER TIP NAPOLI SOTTERRANEA (NAPLES UNDERGROUND) (🛍 9/D–E1)

The town is built on tuff, into which caves, cisterns and catacombs have been dug. On the *Piazzetta San Gaetano 68* in the old town you can walk down into Naples's underworld, a labyrinth cut into the volcanic rock by the Greeks and Romans. *Guided tours (also in English) daily 10am–6pm | www.napolisotterranea.org*

### SAN LORENZO MAGGIORE (🛍 9/E1)

One of the most stunning medieval churches in Naples. Remains of the ancient Roman market have been found under the Franciscan monastery. *Daily 9.30am–5.30pm | Piazza San Gaetano*

### SANTA CHIARA (🛍 9/D1)

The *Convento dei Minori* belongs to the French-Gothic church, famous for its *Chiostro delle Clarisse*, a cloister with majolica tiled porticos. *Mon–Sat 9.30am–5.30pm, Sun 10am–2.30pm | Via Benedetto Croce | www.monasterodisantachiara.com*

## SHOPPING

The streets *Via Chiaia, Via dei Mille, Via Roma* are full of exclusive boutiques. The *Spaccanapoli* and their side streets are full of small shops and tradesmen. In the INSIDER TIP *Via San Gregorio Armeno* ("Christmas Alley") you can watch the artisans at work all year.

## WHERE TO GO

### POMPEII (POMPEI) ⭐

What makes this town excavated from the hard lava stone *(daily 9am–5pm, April–Oct until 7.30pm | www.pompeiisites.org)* so unique is the insight it provides into everyday Roman life. Shops, bars, cobbled streets worn with deep grooves from the wagons and famous frescoes of the ancients Romans.

### VESUVIUS (VESUVIO) 🌿

An absolute must when visiting Naples is a trip to the impressive, still active volcano,

# PIZZA NAPOLETANA

It appeared for the first time in the 18th century as a fast and cheap snack on the streets of Naples: a simple, malleable dough made of flour, yeast, water and salt, seasoned with olive oil, oregano and garlic. Tomatoes, mozzarella and basil came later. At the beginning of the 19th century, Naples was already full of pizzerias, but nobody had heard about them in the rest of Italy. They only caught up in the 20th century and then via America. The taste of a real pizza napoletana (with tomatoes, mozzarella and basil, also known as Pizza Margherita) in Naples remains a special experience.

Stunning Venice: the Canal Grande

Mount Vesuvius (1281 m/4200 ft) in the south-east of the city. You can walk across the lava fields to the rim of the crater (20 min), where you can get a glimpse of the abyss. *From 9am | www.epnv.it/grancono*

# VENICE (VENEZIA)

**"Serenissima", her serene highness: this is how Venetians called their once powerful, rich seaport republic, built on 118 islands.**

With every visit, one stands in awe and marvels how this seemingly unreal, magnificent and beautiful city (pop. 60,000, with suburbs pop. 270,000) could have been built on water. Year after year, the splendour attracts millions of visitors. Yet even this city of museums offers something new: the elegant pedestrian bridge, designed by the Catalonian architect Santiago Calatrava, at the Piazzale Roma, and the

INSIDER TIP collection of contemporary art in the *Punta della Dogana*.

## SIGHTSEEING

### CANAL GRANDE ⭐
Along the main canal, there are wonderful palace facades, featuring Gothic, Renaissance and Baroque architecture. Directly after the first canal loop, one finds the *Rialto bridge* of 1592. The Palazzo *Ducale (daily 8.30am–5.30pm, April–Oct until 7pm)* houses resplendent works of art and is located at the Piazzetta *San Marco*.

### BASILICA DI SAN MARCO ⭐
A pinnacle of magnificence: five domes, perfectly adorned arches and windows, mosaics, icons, a high altar with the sarcophagus of St Mark, countless bronze figures – the cathedral is a feast of art! Those who want to save time (but not money) can book a one-hour tour online offered by *Skip-the-Line-Tour (21.50 euros | www.venetoinside.com)* to see the cathedral

and all its treasures. Note: no luggage is allowed into the church.

### CAMPANILE DI SAN MARCO ★ ☆

A lift takes you conveniently up to the top of the famous tower, where a gorgeous view over Venice's rooftops awaits you. The panorama provides an initial, yet helpful overall orientation and a sense of the unique location and structure of the city and the lagoon. Originally erected in the 10th century and then made considerably taller in the 12th century, the 100 m/300 ft-high landmark collapsed in 1902. The original material was saved and it was rebuilt immediately afterwards. While waiting in the line for tickets, you can delight in the sight of the *Loggetta*, built around 1540 by Jacopo Sansovino. *From 9am | Pier: San Marco*

### PALAZZO DUCALE ★ ☆

The palace of palaces: the stunning, colossal marble-lined facade deserves the greatest admiration, especially the countless exquisite columns and arches in the edifice's ground and first levels. The interior is overwhelming: it is adorned with magnificent paintings of the most significant artists of the 16th century, notably Tintoretto, Titian and Paolo Veronese. *Daily 8.30am–6pm, April–Oct until 7pm | combined ticket with Biblioteca Marciana, Museo Correr and Museo Archeologico | palazzoducale.visitmuve. it | Pier: San Zaccari*

### PIAZZA SAN MARCO ★

Napoleon spoke of "the most beautiful drawing room in Europe": two centuries later, his comment is still valid. St Mark's Square, 175 m/574 ft in length and somewhat trapezium-formed, is truly unique. Here one can experience a wide range of moods and atmospheric nuances, as they unfold within the scope of a day and over seasonal changes. It was the scene of countless processions and very worldly festivities. Like all other travellers, relish the allure of this extraordinary place! *Pier: San Marco*

### MADONNA DELL'ORTO

Due attention to this wonderful celebration of art has been scant. Situated in Cannaregio, the northernmost part of Venice, it is a superb Gothic church. Let your eyes feast on the brick facade, the statues of the Apostles and the fine tracery of the windows. The interior is decorated with some INSIDER TIP top-class paintings –

# TIME TO CHILL

If you need a break from the noisy confinements of the old town, visit the *Lido*. At the end of the 19th century, this narrow 12 km/7.5 mi sandy island, which shelters Venice and the lagoon from the open sea, blossomed into a fashionable beach resort, as cinema buffs would recall from Luchino Visconti's film "Death in Venice", based on the novella by Thomas Mann. Meanwhile, life on the Lido has become relaxed, tranquil and somewhat bucolic, with the exception of the annual film festival, when movie stars from all over the world assemble in the *Palazzo del Cinema*. Yet it has not lost its quality as a preserve for friends of *dolce far niente* (sweet idleness), thanks to a seemingly endless stretch of beach on the Adriatic Sea, beckoning all and sundry to come and swim or take a stroll. In addition, there are many pizzerias and ice-cream parlours.

among them "John the Baptist" by Cima da Conegliano and many by Tintoretto, who is buried in the apse of the church. *Mon–Sat 10am–5pm, Sun noon–5pm | Pier: Madonna dell'Orto*

### PONTE DI RIALTO ⭐

In Venice, more than 400 bridges span approx. 150 canals and serve as fixed structures connecting more than 100 islands. Throughout the centuries, financial, trade and business activities in Venice, once an important metropolitan and commercial centre, took place around the famous *Rialto bridge*. Built with Istrian stone, the bridge was completed towards the end of the 16th century. It replaced an old, dilapidated wooden bridge. Until the mid-19th century, it was the only pedestrian crossing over the Grand Canal. *Pier: Rialto*

Best views over Venice:
the Campanile di San Marco

### GALLERIA DELL'ACCADEMIA ⭐

Bellini, Carpaccio, Giorgione, Tintoretto, Titian and Veronese, Canaletto, Guardi, Longhi, Mantegna, Lotto, Piazzetta and Tiepolo... all the rooms of this famous museum on the south bank of the Canal Grande showcase works of almost all prominent artists representing the 500-year-long history of Venetian painting. The gallery is rightly revered as one of the most significant art treasures in the world. A ticket reservation to secure your visiting date *(Tel. 04 15 20 03 45)* costs an additional 1.50 euros, but saves time in the long lines. *Tue–Sun 8.15am–7.15pm, Mon 8.15am–2pm | www.gallerieaccademia.it | Pier: Accademia*

### FINDING A BAR (BACARO) & AN EATERY (OSTERIA)

#### INSIDER TIP DA ALBERTO

Savour local Venice! Alberto serves typical dishes like *sarde in soar*, marinated fried

sardines, and *baccalà mantecato*, creamy mashed codfish, exactly as Venetians themselves prepare these classic dishes at home. *Daily | Calle Giacinto Gallina 5401 | tel. 04 15 23 81 53 | www.osteriadaalberto.it | Pier: Ospedale*

#### INSIDER TIP OSTERIA BANCOGIRO

This hotspot at the fish market near the Rialto bridge draws crowds of Venetians, flocking at the entrance, enjoying aperitifs and the ultimate midnight cocktails. The cuisine is also great. *Mon closed | Campo San Giacometto 122 | tel. 04 15 23 20 61 | www.osteriabancogiro.it | Pier: Rialto*

### SHOPPING

Two kinds of classic souvenirs from Venice are produced on islands in the lagoon: glass from Murano and lace from Burano. You can sample these in many stores in the city or on the islands, for example, vases

# SHOPPING

## Cuisine, clothing and crafts: there is something for everyone in the markets and shopping centres

The Italians display their exquisite taste in fine food and wine, sophisticated fashion and accessories as well as traditional craftsmanship in the country's many ateliers, markets and elegant shops.

### DELICATESSEN & WINE

Culinary specialities make ideal souvenirs, e.g. extra virgin olive oil *(olio d'oliva extra-vergine)*, or wine bought directly from the wine dealer *(enoteca)*, vineyard or local supermarket. A nice accompaniment is air-dried salami, a thick slab of Parmigiano-Reggiano, dried porcini, top-quality charcuterie like the *culatello*, balsamic vinegar and grappa.

### FASHION & SHOES

Top of the list are the big fashion names such as Armani, Dolce & Gabbana, Prada, Versace, followed by the more casual brands such as Benetton, Stefanel and Diesel. Look out for the sales *(saldi)* if you want to avoid high prices; they usually start in January and July.

### HANDICRAFTS

Tourism can be thanked for its role in helping to preserve local craft traditions. Even young people are now learning the old crafts and combining them with attractive new design ideas.

### MARKETS

Practically every town has a market. There you will find the *moka* for making espresso, the milk frother for the cappuccino, the cheese grater, the truffle slicer, the mortar in marble or olive wood, the vinegar and oil set – all things that have been available at home for a long time, but which acquire an additional local flair when you buy them in Italy. Buy regional fruit and vegetables at the farmer's markets bearing the motto ⊕ *chilometro zero*. And at the weekly markets, every kind of clothing is for sale, including surprisingly high-quality items at reasonable prices.

and glass-bead jewellery at *Ferrevetro (Campo Santo Stefano 7)* in Murano, and genuine lace in the workroom of *La Merlettaia (Calle San Mauro 298)* in Burano.

# RAVENNA

**Continuous silting placed this once seaside city (pop. 165,000) farther inland, and today a canal of 10 km/6 mi constitutes its connection to the Adriatic Sea.**
Splendid vestiges of early Christian culture characterize the city. In the 5th century, after the decline of the Roman Empire, Ravenna became a centre of power and maintained that status for 300 years.

## SIGHTSEEING

All sights are open *daily 9am–5.30pm, in summer until 7pm.* Request price-reduced group tickets!

### MAUSOLEO DI TEODORICO
The tomb of the Ostrogoth King Theodoric (he died in 526) in the north-east of Ravenna was constructed out of huge stone blocks assembled without mortar.

### MOSAICS ⭐
Brilliant early Christian mosaics characterize Ravenna's main sights: blue-golden sparkles in the *Mausoleo di Galla Placidia*; lustre in Bishop Neon's baptistry *(Battistero Neoniano)*; exquisite adornments in the glorious basilica of *Sant'Appolinare Nuovo* (6th century), the octagonal basilica of San Vitale (consecrated in 547) and the *basilica of Sant'Appolinare*, 5 km/3 mi southwards.

## WHERE TO GO

### BOLOGNA
In the extensive and well-preserved old town of Bologna (pop. 373,000), tourists are outnumbered by young people who study at the oldest university in Europe (founded in 1088). Accordingly, the city boasts many interesting bookstores. Check out the bustling hall of the city library, the Biblioteca *Salaborsa*, built in art deco style, on the Piazza Maggiore. Sheltered by endless yet elegant porticoes and arcades covering a distance of 37 km/23 mi, one can enjoy ambling and shopping around the city centre in all weather conditions.

### MODENA
The iconic Maseratis and Ferraris are produced here. View historic models at the INSIDER TIP *Panini Motor Museum (only by appointment | Via Corletto Sud 320 | www.paninimotormuseum.it)* and the Ferrari Museum *(daily 9.30am–6pm, April–Oct until 7pm | Via Dino Ferrari 43 | museomaranello.ferrari.com)* in nearby Maranello. Art lovers will delight in the ⭐ *cathedral* of Modena, a masterpiece

Most beautiful mosaics in Ravenna

of Romanesque architecture and sculptural art, and the impressive cemetery of the architect Aldo Rossi in the town's district of Madonnina, a rare INSIDER TIP example of contemporary cemetery architecture.

# BARI

**Apulia's capital (pop. 327,000) is also called the "Milan of the South": for centuries it has been a trade window to the Orient, and each year in September, it hosts the largest trade fair in the Mediterranean, the Fiera del Levante.**

Bari's white old town with the beautiful old church exudes the air of a kasbah. Until a few years ago, it was still a bit grim and by no means completely safe, but in recent years a lot has been restored, and the two attractive squares *Piazza Ferrarese* and *Piazza Mercantile* have become a centre of the *baresi* nightlife thanks to the new cafés, bars and nice restaurants. The elegant hotels as well as vibrant shopping avenues full of people browsing are in the chessboard-styled new town of Bari, which is on the other side of the massive road *Corso Vittorio Emanuele*. You should however, avoid the proliferating, neglected outskirts at all costs.

## SIGHTSEEING

### BASILICA SAN NICOLA

This stately Apulian Romanesque church (11th/12th century) in the old town is very impressive. Inside, look out for the ancient episcopal throne, made of marble and borne by tiny, groaning figures. Below the silver altar is a crypt supported by 26 columns holding the reliquary of St Nicholas, Bishop of Myra, patron saint of Bari and highly respected in the Orthodox Church –

which is why there are a lot of Russian pilgrims. *Piazza Elia*

### CATTEDRALE SAN SABINO

Bari's cathedral, like the Basilica San Nicola, is one of the best examples of Romanesque architecture in Apulia. In the church's archive, there is a precious Exsultet Roll (scroll bearing the Catholic Easter liturgy) from the 11th century. *Piazza Odegitria*

### HOHENSTAUFEN CASTLE

This massive castle overlooking the sea was reconstructed by Emperor Frederick II of Hohenstaufen on an earlier Byzantine Norman bastion. Inside, a collection of plaster casts show how artistic the decoration on Apulian church façades can be. *Thu–Tue 8.30am–7.30pm*

## WHERE TO GO

### ALBEROBELLO

Home of a unique vernacular architecture: the *trulli*, little circular white dry-stone houses with dark conical roofs. You can see them dotted around in the triangle between Bari, Taranto and Brindisi, scattered among the olive groves, almond orchards, vegetable fields and grapevines of the garden-like Valle d'Itria. In Alberobello (pop. 10,000), they form a town, even the Sant'Antonio church is built in *trulli* style, which has turned Alberobello into a tourist hotspot. Inhabited until into the late 20th century, some of the buildings have now been transformed into hotels, holiday homes, souvenir shops and pizzerias.

### CASTEL DEL MONTE AND CANOSA DI PUGLIA

From afar, one sees the "crown of Apulia" on the hill, the octagonal ★ ⁎⁎ *Castel del Monte (www.casteldelmonte.beniculturali.it),* built in 1240–50, with eight towers, eight interior rooms and an octagonal courtyard. It was one of the architectural projects of Emperor Frederick II of Hohenstaufen, and displays an almost esoteric touch. Once this austere castle was richly adorned with marble and Byzantine mosaics. Plan a culinary treat in the nearby village of *Montegrosso d'Andria* and enjoy the meticulous Apulian Slow Food cuisine in *Trattoria Antichi Sapori (closed Sat evening and Sun | Piazza Sant'Isidoro 10 | tel. 08 83 56 95 29 | antichisapori.pietrozito. it | Budget–Moderate)*.

You can drive to the castle inland via *Canosa di Puglia*, a fine example of Apulia's cultural diversity: the Romanesque *cathedral ruins*, the Byzantine *Basilica San Leucio* and in the Via Cadorna the Roman *Ipogei Lagrasta*, burial caves dug into the tuff and dating back to the 4th century BC.

### MATERA

Matera (pop. 52,000), chosen as Europe's Capital of Culture for 2019, boasts a Romanesque Norman cathedral (13th century), a *feudal fortress* from 1515 and naturally the main sight, the ⭐ *sassi:* a subterranean cave town with enchanting cave churches cut into the rock beneath the new Matera. Over 20,000 people lived here well into the 1950s, but their living conditions in the dark, unhealthy cave homes were regarded as a national disgrace. New buildings and resettlements were the results; there is now a resurgence of interest (using public funds) because, ironically, the *sassi* are now on Unesco's World Heritage List.

# CAGLIARI/ SARDINIA

**Old Cagliari occupies a commanding position on a rocky plateau above the Campidano plain, which at this point spreads out to the sweeping Gulf of**

As strange as their name: trulli, the round structures in and around Alberobello

Colourful houses define Cagliari's face

**Cagliari, and is bounded by lagoon lakes and salt flats.**

When the Punics from North Africa landed in Sardinia some 2700 years ago, 'Karalis' with its natural port was one of the first settlements they founded. Each historical period left its mark on Cagliari's cityscape; the legacy of Punic culture was subsumed into the subsequent Roman culture. Apart from the medieval Castello with the cathedral, the palaces of the archbishop, viceroy and aristocratic families, today's old town is dominated by baroque façades and domes – three quarters of which are around the castle mount.

## SIGHTSEEING

### CASTELLO (𝄐 10/B2)

The old town on the hill is fortified like a castle and still has only two entrances. Just like 100 years ago, one may enter the dark and narrow alleys through either of the two city gates. The two tall towers, the *Torre San Pancrazio* and the *Torre dell'Elefante* with its stone elephants, were constructed by Pisan architects from the High Middle Ages. Today's access from Via Manno via the ☀ *Bastione di San Remy*, a meeting point for Cagliari's youngsters, was only created in the 19th century, when the viewing terraces were laid out. The dark streets, lined by the tall palaces of the *Casteddu* (as the Sardinians call the castle quarter), is gradually taking on a new life, now attracting young artisans, goldsmiths and restorers to move into the houses and narrow courtyards that were previously inhabited mainly by the old and poor. Climbing up to the castle is a steep and sweaty affair. But those who know the location of INSIDER TIP the three slightly hidden lifts up to the Castello may visit the quarter even in the heat of summer without getting out of breath. The lifts can be found above the Piazza Yenne next to the Santa Chiara church, as well as at the Viale Regina Elena, one near the Bastione San Remy, the other below the Piazza Palazzo.

### CATHEDRAL SANTA MARIA (𝄐 10/C2)

Amidst this maze of streets a square with several mansions opens up. A brilliant white marble façade in between looks like from the Middle Ages, but actually dates back to 1933. The interior presents a heavy and extremely ornamental baroque. The numerous Spanish inscriptions are testimony to the fact that Sardinia once belonged to the Spanish Empire. The crypt, with its glorious baroque vault and 300 burial chambers, is particularly worth seeing. At the entrance to the cathedral is the marble Guglielmo pulpit featuring reliefs from the life of Jesus, which were created between 1159–62 for Pisa's cathedral. Once the Pisan pulpit by Giovanni Pisano was completed in 1311, the older piece was moved to Cagliari. *Mon–Sat 8am–1pm and 4pm–8pm, Sun 8am–1pm and 4.30pm–8.30pm | www.duomodicagliari.it*

### MUSEO ARCHEOLOGICO NAZIONALE (NATIONAL ARCHAEOLOGICAL MUSEUM) ⭐ *(ᗕ 10/B1–2)*

The richest and most comprehensive collection of prehistoric and ancient finds in Sardinia is housed in the new *Cittadella dei Musei* (which includes an art museum with 16th/17th century Sardinian paintings and three other museums) at the highest point of the city. Most of the space is taken up by the Nuragic culture; the collection of small bronze statuettes placed as votive offerings in the well sanctuaries is impressive. Even more stunning is the exhibition of the the *Giganti di Mont'e Prama* – a sensational find for the Mediterranean. Out of 15 000 individual fragments the archaeologists recreated 38 almost 300-year-old vast stone sculptures. *Piazza Arsenale | Tue– Sun 9am–8pm | museoarcheocagliari.beniculturali.it*

### ORTO BOTANICO *(ᗕ 10/B1)*

Situated in the university quarter west of the city centre and below the amphitheatre, the Botanical Garden offers a good overview of Sardinian and Mediterranean flora.

*Via Fra Ignazio da Laconi | Apr–Oct Tue–Sun 9am–6pm, Nov–Mar Tue–Sun 9am–2pm*

## FOOD & DRINK

Going out for a meal in Cagliari is always a special experience. All nuances of Sardinian cuisine are on offer: the traditional and the experimental, ingredients from the sea and the mountains. Those who want to just head off and go exploring should choose the *Marina quarter* with the Via Sardegna.

## SHOPPING

Luckily, the main shopping streets, Largo Carlo Felice and Via G. Manno, are still free of the international chains – instead there are numerous smaller fashion boutiques, shoe, lingerie, hat and tie shops. The four floors of the traditional department store *La Rinascente (Mon–Fri 9am–8.30pm, Sat 9am–9pm, Sun 10am– 9pm)* on the Via Roma offer the usual department store merchandise as well as numerous Italian designer and fashion labels, shoes and perfumes. Its best feature, however, is the ☕ *café* on the top floor, where you can enjoy fabulous views of the harbour while sipping a cappuccino. Delicacies from all over Sardinia can be purchased in sinfully expensive delis and in the slightly less expensive market halls. What is worthwhile are the gold and silversmiths in the Marina quarter *(Via Sardegna, Via Manno)* and the Castello quarter.

## BEACHES

Beyond the Capo Sant'Elia Peninsula in the south-east begins a 10 km/6.2 mi long sandy beach, *Poetto* (with municipal bus connection) with a typical Italian beach atmosphere: lidos with changing huts, bars and restaurants.

## WHERE TO GO

### MONTE ARCOSU

Stretching west of the capital is the near-inaccessible and unpopulated Sulcis Mountain, an area of unspoilt nature that is a protected reserve. This is home to the *Monte Arcosu WWF reserve (Sat/Sun 9am–6pm, in summertime 8am–7pm, 15 July–15 Sept access only with guide | Registration required, tel. 32 98 31 57 54)*, which is only open at weekends and offers a refuge to the *cervo sardo*, a small Sardinian deer threatened with extinction.

### BARUMINI

In 1949, following days of rain, a hillside started sliding, revealing ancient walls and foundations. The ⭐ *Su Nuraxi nuraghe fortification (daily 9am–one hour before sunset)* was once a castle and the seat of a mighty tribal fiefdom and was listed as a Unesco World Heritage Site in 1997. The citadel, with four corner towers and a central tower, was surrounded by a thick turreted wall; some of the 150

round huts of the village outside – still clearly visible today – served as workshops.

### COSTA VERDE ⭐

The 'Green Coast' is one of Italy's most valuable nature reserves. Most of the endless sandy and dune beaches south of Marina di Arbus (75 km/46.6 mi north of Iglesias) are only accessible on foot. The nature reserve starts some distance south of the (not very appealing) Marina di Arbus holiday village with a beach that runs on for miles, with sand dunes up to 300 m/984 ft high.

# PALERMO/ SICILY

**The location of Palermo (pop. 669,000) in the Conca d'Oro – "the Golden Shell", framed by the mountains behind Monreale and Monte Pellegrino, is magnificent. In the 18th century the setting was even**

# ISLAND OF TOWERS

Some 60 towers are evenly spaced along the West Coast of Sardinia: the Saracen towers were built between the 15th and 18th century by order of the Spanish viceroys in order to repel attacks by pirates (Saracens), who plundered villages, even those far from the coast, abducting their inhabitants as slaves. Even more stunning are the nuraghi. These mighty, megalithic, cone-shaped towers lent their name to the nuraghi civilisation, one of the most interesting cultures of the Bronze Age. There are over 7000 of

these stone towers in the deserted countryside. Many have only the foundation walls left while others are three storeys tall, with heights of over 12 m/39.4 ft. The nuraghi formed defensive lines, as is easily visible at Macomer and around the Giara di Gesturi. Other eye-catchers are the more than 100 tombs (the so-called giants' graves), various small temples related to the water cult (sacred wells) and thousands of bronze figures representing warriors, pilgrims, priests, animals and nuraghi.

described as "the most beautiful in the world".

Even today, the most evocative way to approach Palermo is by ship. First you catch a glimpse of the theatrical mountains on the north coast before entering the bay, where the towers and domes become increasingly clear. As everywhere in Sicily, the dominant architectural style is Baroque. The magnificence of the Norman buildings and mosaics stopped later generations from demolishing, remodelling or covering them up.

## SIGHTSEEING

### CATTEDRALE (CATHEDRAL) (*8/B3*)

Only the dimensions of the cathedral and the Norman style of the unaltered choir are remnants of when the building was erected (1185). The impressive Late Gothic side façade with the main portico is of Catalan influence; the dome and the interior are from the late 18th century – very austere. Inside, the polished porphyry sarcophagi of Frederick II (1194–1250) and other members of the royal and imperial families can be seen. *Admission 1.50 euros*

### GALLERIA D'ARTE MODERNA (GAM) (*8/C3*)

Art from between 1800 and 1900. An excellent collection of works, also by Sicilian artists, is displayed in the beautifully restored former monastery of *Santa Anna alla Kalsa. Tue–Sun 9.30am–6.30pm | Via Sant'Anna 21 | admission 7 euros*

### GALLERIA REGIONALE DELLA SICILIA (*8/D3*)

Housed in the Gothic Catalan Palazzo Abatellis, the museum showcases Sicily's artistic past including the bust of Eleonora d'Aragon by Francesco Laurana, the head of a boy by Antonello Gagini, and paintings on panel such as INSIDER TIP Anto-

Palermo Cathedral, a magnificent building

nello da Messina's "Annunciation". *Tue–Fri 9am–6pm, Sat/Sun 9am– 1pm | Via Alloro 4 | admission 8 euros*

### LA KALSA (*8/D3*)

Al-Halisah, "the Chosen One", is the name the Arabs gave this district on the shore and around the harbour. There is a wonderful view of the coastline and the Old Town from the *Passeggiata delle Cattive*. A visit to *Palazzo Mirto (Tue–Sat 9am–6pm, Sun 9am–1pm | Via Merlo 2 | admission 6 euros)* provides a glimpse of upper-class life in the 18th-century. *La Magione (daily 9am–7pm, in winter Sun 9am–1pm only | admission 2 euros),* is a plain Norman church with an enchanting cloister.

### INSIDER TIP ORTO BOTANICO (*8/D4*)

Laid out as a pleasure garden in 1792 for the upper classes, the garden today is a shady paradise with huge trees from both the Mediterranean and the Tropics. It provides an extensive overview of the regional flora and those plants from all over the world that have become established here. *From 9am | Via Lincoln 2 | admission 5 euros | www.ortobotanico.unipa.it*

## PALAZZO DEI NORMANNI AND CAPPELLA PALATINA ★ *(📖 8/A4)*

The origins of the former *royal palace* date back to the 9th century. The interior of the capella is completely covered with gold mosaics and marble intarsia. The chancel contains King Roger II's (Ruggero's) coronation throne, with rich intarsia work, and the high altar. The wooden "stalactite" ceiling looks as if it has come out of an Oriental fairytale. *Mon–Sat 8.15am–5.40pm, Sun 8.15am–1pm (not during mass 9.45am–11.15am), last admission 5pm/12.15pm | Piazza Indipendenza | admission Tue–Thu 7, Fri–Mon 8.50 euros | tel. for reservations 09 16 26 28 33 | www.ars.sicilia.it | www.federicosecondo.org*

### INSIDER TIP ▶ LA ZISA

In the 12th century, Arabian builders erected this royal summer residence. The tall cube is elegantly subdivided by decorative arches, windows and portals. The fountain niche, with its delicate pendant arches, from which the water flows outside, can be seen in the imposing hall decorated with mosaic friezes and marble tiles. Concealed flues, clay pipes and running water create a form of air

conditioning that still works 800 years on. *Mon– Sat 9am–7pm, Sun 9am–1.30pm | admission 6 euros | Piazza Zisa*

## SHOPPING

### LA COPPOLA STORTA

This is where you can buy a genuine Sicilian coppola from San Giuseppe Jato, in any number of colours, for men, women and children, made of coarse or soft material, and for every conceivable occasion. And just to rid any doubt as to who wears this cap today: the shop is on the "Addio pizzo" list. *Via Bara all'Olivella 74*

### STREET MARKETS ★

There are several famous food markets in the Old Town. The largest, in the *Capo district* is held around Sant'Agostino church and stretches down several roads as far as the Teatro Massimo; the Ballaró market caters for the area around Porta Sant'Antonio, the Chiesa del Carmine and Chiesa del Gesù.

## WHERE TO GO

### MONREALE

The ★ *Cathedral of Monreale (from 8am | admission 4 euros)* 8 km/5 miles west of Palermo was founded as a Benedictine monastery in 1174 under the Normans. It is the largest and most compact ecclesiastical building of that era. Well worth seeing is the cloister *(Mon–Sat 9am–6.30pm, Sun 9am–1pm | admission 6 euros)*.

### CEFALÙ

The massive ★ *Norman cathedral of Cefalù (pop. 14,500)* looks like a toy set against the huge rocky Rocca mountain. The roofs of the houses are clustered around the landmark of this town, which was a burial place in the early Norman period and had a brief heyday as an im-

# PUPPET SHOWS

## MARIONETTE THEATRES IN PALERMO

See wild fights and loud kisses in the marionette theatres, the *Opera dei Pupi*, in Palermo, where knights of old fight the Saracens or come to the rescue of damsels in distress.

portant harbour before falling into a deep sleep until the 20th century. This left the medieval town virtually unaltered. The *Corso Ruggero*, the main street lined with austere palaces with pointed arched windows, opens onto the cathedral square. The Old Town is protected from the sea by a huge wall.

# MESSINA/ SICILY

**For tourists coming by car or train from Calabria, Messina (pop. 237,000) is the gateway to the island. The city is modern, with broad and straight roads.**

And it's brimming with life – especially in the principal shopping areas *Via San Martino*, the tree-*lined Piazza Cairoli* and *Via Garibaldi*. The heart of Messina can be found a little behind these around the *Piazza Duomo* with its magnificent cathedral. But even here as elsewhere in Messina, there are few stones that have been standing longer than 1908 when a terrible earthquake destroyed towns both sides of the straits, the *Stretto di Messina*.

Cefalù will take you into the middle ages

by the Sicilian Antonello Da Messina and two paintings by Caravaggio, who lived on Sicily in 1608/09. *Tue–Sat 9am–7pm, Sun 9am–1pm | on the Punta del Faro road | admission 8 euros*

## SIGHTSEEING

### CATHEDRAL

Originally built in 1197 in the Norman style and rebuilt after the earthquake in 1908 and again after bombing during the war in 1943. The belfry contains an astronomical clock from Strasbourg (1933) that includes a parade of figures with the city heroines Dina and Clarenza at noon.

### MUSEO REGIONALE

The museum contains a picture gallery as well as displays of archeological finds, small artefacts and majolica. The most valuable exponents include an altarpiece

## WHERE TO GO

### REGGIO DI CALABRIA

Ferries *(www.carontetourist.it)* leave every 40 minutes for the mainland at *Reggio di Calabria,* where the *Museo Archeologico Nazionale (Tue–Sun 9am–8pm | Piazza Giuseppe De Nava 26 | admission 8 euros, Wed 6 euros)* exhibits the well preserved Greek bronzes of naked warriors, the Bronzi di Riace (cast in the 5th century BC).

# CATANIA/ SICILY

**Chaotic, volcanic, seductive – due to Mount Etna, Sicily's second biggest city is also known as La Nera, "the black city".**

Mount Etna towers majestically near to Catania

The architectonic ensemble of lava and basalt palazzi not only appeals to Baroque lovers – the city was completely redesigned by architects after the eruption of Etna in 1669 and the earthquake of 1693. A more frenzied location is the city's morning market, just a few steps away from the Cathedral with its variety of colours, fruits, fish, noise and bustle, the close proximity of waste and picturesque market stalls, smells and aromas from its century-old multicultural cuisine. This is the pulsating heart of Sicily!

## SIGHTSEEING

### CASTELLO URSINO

The castle, constructed of black blocks of lava and with four massive corner towers, is Catania's most distinctive medieval building. In 1669, it became surrounded by streams of lava. It now houses the *Museo Civico* with a picture gallery, collections of antiques, weapons and ceramics,

as well as views of Mount Etna and ambitious special exhibitions. *Daily 9am– 7pm | Piazza Federico II di Svevia | admission 6 euros*

### CATANIA LIVING LAB

The ancient monuments of Catania reanimated in 3D. An experience not just for kids and computer fans. *Mon, Wed, Fri 9am–12.30pm | free admission | Via Manzoni 91 | www.catanialivinglab.it*

### PIAZZA DUOMO

Cathedral Square with the black lava elephant is the central hub of the city, with the main shopping streets branching off it. The fish market on Porta Uzeda is just a short walk and the square is surrounded by the huge Baroque town palaces of the nobility and church leaders. The *Cattedrale di Sant'Agata* is dedicated to St Agatha, the patron saint of Catania, whose reliquary is housed here. A fresco in the sacristy depicts the eruption of Etna in 1669.

## VILLA BELLINI ⚘

The park in this district of 19th-century houses is named after the opera composer Vincenzo Bellini ("Norma"), who came from Catania. It contains busts of major Sicilian figures as well as an Art Nouveau music pavilion and good views.

## SHOPPING

You should definitely find time for a stroll through Catania's ⭐ *fish market at the Porta Uzeda* in the pescheria district. It is Sicily's liveliest and most beautiful market, and it doesn't just sell fish, but all foods you can think of and all the fruit of Mount Etna. Don't forget, while you're being distracted by all the colours, smells and sounds, pickpockets like being in the thick of things too.

## WHERE TO GO

### MOUNT ETNA ⭐

Europe's tallest active volcano is 33 km (20½ miles) from Catania. *Piano Provenzana* and *Rifugio Sapienza* are the principal starting points for tours up to the top of the volcano. Information from the Mountain Guides' Office in Nicolosi *(tel. 09 57 97 14 55 | www.etnaguide.eu)* or in Linguaglossa *(tel. 09 57 77 45 02 | www.guidetnanord.com)*.

### ALCANTARA GORGE ⭐

18 km (11 miles) west of Taormina the River Alcantara and its waterfalls have cut a narrow gorge through the basalt up to 50 m (165 ft) deep. Can be accessed down steps from the road to Francavilla as well as by a lift *(7–13 euros, depending on the season)*.

### SYRACUSE

With a reputed population of half a million, this ancient city with its gigantic quarries was far bigger than its size today. However, today the provincial capital of Siracusa (pop. 122,000) with its fascinating monuments is fully on a par with its ancient rival. Its historical centre with medieval lanes is situated on the "quail island" of ⭐ *Ortygia*; a romantic district which has seen a recent revamp. Amphitheatre-style entertainment can still be found at the *Opera dei pupi* when the marionettes are dancing or at the *Teatro Greco* for performances of Ancient Greek tragedies.

# VOLCANOES & EARTHQUAKES

Geologically speaking, most of Sicily was part of Africa. Only the north is part of the Eurasian Plate and is being pushed by the African Plate, which resulted in the formation of the mountain ranges in northern Sicily. Earthquakes are caused by tension and the sudden release of energy in the earth's crust. Volcanoes often appear along the seams where cracks and faults cause chambers of magma – which rises from the molten centre of the earth – to form. Etna and Stromboli are the two most visibly active volcanoes on Sicily. For volcanologists, the islands of Lipari, Vulcano, Panarea and Pantelleria are still active, although their last eruptions were more than 100 years ago. Deep under the Tyrrhenian Sea, north of the Aeolian Islands, lies Europe's largest active volcano, Marsili, which covers an area of more than 770 sq miles and rises to a height of some 3000 m (9850 ft).

# TRAVEL TIPS

## BERTHS

▶ **ROME/CIVITAVECCHIA**
The port of Civitavecchia is approx. 70 km/43 mi away from Rome. Use the shuttle-bus service to depart from the harbour. Rome is accessible by taxi, bus or train.

▶ **LIVORNO**
Cruise ships drop anchor at the container port and the city centre is accessible by shuttle bus.

▶ **LA SPEZIA**
Cruise ships dock centrally in the city at the Molo Garibaldi. Since walking in the harbour area is not allowed, a shuttle-bus service is readily available.

▶ **NAPLES**
The city centre is just a stone's throw away from the Stazione Marittima, where cruise ships dock.

▶ **VENICE**
Venice has three berths for cruise ships. The elevated shuttle train People Mover takes you to the Piazzale Roma. From there, you can explore the city on foot or use the waterbus services.

▶ **RAVENNA**
In Ravenna, cruise ships dock at the cruise-ship terminal Porto Corsini. From here, the old city is approx. 15 km/9 mi away and it is accessible by shuttle bus, taxi or the public transport service.

▶ **BARI**
Cruise ships dock at the terminal Crociere in the new port. You can walk to the old town.

▶ **CAGLIARI**
In Cagliari, cruise ships berth close to the city centre. A 15-minute walk takes you to the old town. Alternatively, a shuttle-bus service is available.

▶ **PALERMO**
Since the port is in the centre, the latter is readily accessible on foot.

▶ **MESSINA**
Cruise ships berth close to the centre and you can easily walk there.

▶ **CATANIA**
In Catania, ships dock not far away from the centre, to which you can readily walk.

## CUSTOMS

UK citizens do not have to pay any duty on goods brought from another EU country as long as they are for private consumption. The limits are: 800 cigarettes, 400 cigarillo, 200 cigars, 1 kg smoking tobacco, 10 L spirits, 20 L liqueurs, 90 L wine, 110 L beer. Travellers from the USA, Canada, Australia or other non-EU countries are allowed to enter with the following tax-free amounts: 200 cigarettes or 100 cigarillos or 50 cigars or 250g smoking tobacco. 2L wine and spirits with less than 22% vol. alcohol, 1L spirits with more than 22% vol. alcohol content. Travellers to the United States do not have to pay duty on articles purchased overseas up to the value of $800, but there are limits on the amount of alcoholic beverages and tobacco products. For the regulations for international travel for U.p. residents please see www.cbp.gov.

# Italy

Your holiday from start to finish: the most important addresses and information for your trip

## EMERGENCY SERVICES

Emergency call *(pronto soccorso)* free from every public telephone:
- Police *tel. 113*
- Fire brigade *(Vigili del Fuoco) tel. 115*
- Ambulance *tel. 118*
- Breakdown service *tel. 80 31 16,* with international mobile phone operators *800 11 68 00*
- European emergency number *tel. 112*

## HEALTH

At hospitals or the local health authority ASL *(Agenzia Sanitaria Locale)*, European residents should present their European Health Insurance Card (EHIC). Additional travel insurance is advisable and for non-EU residents essential. Remember to ask for receipts for any treatment that you have to pay for, so that you can apply for a refund from your own health authority upon your return home. The ambulance emergency services *(pronto soccorso)* are generally swift, good and uncomplicated.

## INTERNET & WIFI

There are internet cafés everywhere (2–6 euros/hr); in the larger towns, you will also find cafés with WiFi access. Community websites provide information about free WiFi for both locals and tourists.

## MUSEUMS & SIGHTS

The admission price ranges from 4–10 euros, occasionally with an additional charge for reservations. The state museums *(musei nazionali)* are also free of charge for EU citizens under 18; young adults aged between 18 and 25 only have to pay half price. Admission to all state-owned museums is free on every first Sunday of the month. You can buy online tickets for all the major museums and most popular sights. Take advantage of this service to avoid hours standing in queues.

## MONEY & CREDIT CARDS

Banks have ATM cash dispensers *(bancomat)*. Almost all hotels, petrol stations and supermarkets and most restaurants and shops accept major credit cards.

## PRICES

At the bar, an espresso will cost you about 1 euro, but if you sit down at a table or on the terrace to drink it, it may well cost you twice as much or even three times as much.

## TIPPING

Don't be too stingy: waiters, chambermaids, porters etc. get a five to ten per cent tip – if you were satisfied with their services.

## BUDGETING

| | | |
|---|---|---|
| Coffee | £1–£1.30/$1.35–$1.68 | *for a cappuccino at the bar* |
| Ice cream | £1.75/$2.25 | *for one large scoop* |
| Wine | from £2.65/$3.35 | *for a glass at the bar* |
| Museums | £3.50–£8.80/$4.50–$11 | *for admission* |
| Beach | from £12.30/$15.70 | *Daily rental for sunshade and lounger* |

# MALTA

Malta is not a small idyllic island, but almost as densely populated as highly industrialized areas elsewhere in the world. Despite the inexorable urbanization, places are not without charm, thanks to countless historic architectural monuments and the typical Maltese architecture.

When you leave the cities, you can discover green oases on Malta, for example by opting for simple hikes. North of Malta lies the small island of Gozo, which is mainly rural and rather thinly populated, compared with its large sister island. Green, low table mountains characterize the landscape of Gozo. Here you will perhaps find the kind of romanticism that would be up to your expectations of a Mediterranean island.

## VALLETTA

What a transformation! What was once a lifeless administrative city with churches and museums aplenty has now been revitalised into a vibrant capital of culture with many trendy bars, theatres and street cafés.

Malta's capital (pop. 7100) used to go to sleep at the close of business. Nowadays the city is still buzzing well after midnight. New people and businesses have breathed new life into Valletta; a whole row of small boutique hotels has even opened in the city's old fortification walls. The facelift is mainly attributed to the city's new status as the European Capital of Culture 2018.

In tune with life: culture in the mornings, parties in the evenings and throughout the days, many restaurants and shops

## SIGHTSEEING

### BALLUTA BAY ☀

One of the most photogenic spots on the entire island: in summer hundreds of brightly coloured boats squeeze into this narrow harbour while Malta's night life pulsates all around the bay. "Love" is the title of the modern sculpture by Richard England, an internationally acclaimed Maltese architect, poet and artist. Why are the letters deliberately turned upside down? So they can be read when they reflect in the water. *Promenade between Sliema and St Julian's*

### INSIDER TIP CASA ROCCA PICCOLA (𝄞 11/C2)

Although you wouldn't necessarily choose to live here, visits to this 16th century palazzo allow a unique insight into the privileged lifestyle of the aristocracy, in this case the 9th Marquis de Piro and his family. Those interested in delving into the palace's history should go down into the WWII air-raid shelters where the Piro family sought ref-

Comino is a little paradise

uge from German and Italian bombs. *Mon–Sat 10am–3pm hourly | admission 9 euros | 74 Republic Street | Valletta | www.casa roccapiccola.com*

### GRAND MASTER'S PALACE ★ (📖 11/C2)

The palace is situated in the heart of Valetta and was originally built as the palace of the Grand Master when the Order of St John established the new city of Valletta. The austere two-storey façade is typical of the style of the 16th century. The wooden corner bays are more recent, and the Baroque gateways were not added until the 18th century. Inside, thanks to numerous frescoes and ceiling paintings, you will learn a lot about the history of the Order of St John. Armoury and State Rooms: *Daily 9am–5pm | joint ticket 10 euros*

### ST JOHN'S CO-CATHEDRAL ★ (📖 11/C3)

No other church is like this one! The most unusual feature is the floor of the church. It is completely covered with 375 tombstones, inlay work in different colours of marble, beneath which Knights of St John are buried. The walls and the ceiling are almost as impressive. Adjoining St John's Co-Cathedral is a museum. *Co-Cathedral and Museum Mon–Fri 9:30am–4:30pm, Sat 9:30am–12:30pm | admission 10 euros | www.stjohnscocathedral.com*

## WHERE TO GO

### GOZO AND COMINO

Gozo — Malta's little sister island — still reminds much of the traditional Maltese culture. Most of Gozo consists of a plateau crossed by low, long flat-topped hills. The INSIDER TIP temple of *Ggantija* should definitely be visited. Between Gozo and Malta lies the little island of Comino, which consists of thyme-covered scree fields and scores with the Blue Lagoon, which lives up to its name.

### MARSAXLOKK

Marsaxlokk is the only location on the island where you can still see colourful fishing boats bobbing on the waters and moored along the harbours with families of fishermen mending their nets. The promenade is lined with low-rising houses towered over by the village church's dome and towers.

# DEVIL'S TIME

A word of caution before looking at the time on Maltese church tower clocks: almost every second clock stands still or indicates the wrong time. This is no coincidence. It is done in the hope to confuse Satan from disturbing the mass. Some of the clocks are painted on for decoration, others tell completely the wrong time. If a church has two towers with two clocks, only one will show the correct time.

# FOOD & DRINK

## Culinary variety: Maltese dishes and international delicacies are served on the archipelago

Although under British rule for almost 150 years, there is hardly a trace of Englishness in the island's cuisine – except for the full English breakfast. The restaurant scene is dominated by Italian and especially Sicilian cuisine. *Authenticity is guaranteed*. Pizza and homemade pasta are served everywhere as well as other specialities from all parts of Italy. After long years of neglect, the availability of *Maltese specialities* has greatly improved. These include a great variety of soups and casseroles, rabbit recipes and vegetable dishes. The national dish on Malta is *fenek*, rabbit, usually served in a garlic and red wine sauce. Good restaurants are also cooking with genuine Maltese olive oil once again, as the cultivation of olives on the island has taken an upward turn. The Maltese are also keen on cakes and biscuits, which are sold in any number of *confectionery shops,* the place to buy typical Maltese *pastizzi*. These are rolls or pouches with extremely diverse kinds of filling, from pureed peas to cream cheese. One of the pleasures of a holiday here is to try out all the different varieties. A *pastizzerija* will have a particularly good selection and usually also sell little pizzas and small portions of *timpana*, a pasta casserole.

### LOCAL SPECIALITIES

**Aljotta** – fish soup with lots of garlic, herbs and rice

**Bragioli** – roulade of beef, stuffed with egg, mincemeat and peas

**Gbejniet friski** – cream cheese from goat's and sheep's milk, usually from a dairy on Gozo

**Kannoli** – a pipe-shaped pastry filled with cream cheese, chocolate, candied cherries and roast almonds

**Pastizzi** – rolls of puff pastry, stuffed e.g. with cheese, meat or fish – and eaten for breakfast

**Qara'bagli** – creamy vegetable soup made from small pumpkins

**Ravjul** – ravioli filled with Maltese ricotta cheese

**Ross fil-Forn** – cheese-topped rice casserole with mincemeat, eggs and tomatoes

# SHOPPING

## Culinary specialities and crafts made on Malta

If you're looking for authentic, original Maltese products to take back home as souvenirs, prepare to be disappointed about the choice available. However, if you are still in a shopping mood, you can find a large selection of well-known international jewellery, watch and fashion labels on sale. They are no cheaper here than elsewhere, though.

### CULINARY CHOICES

Maltese liqueurs bearing the name *Zeppi's* are colourful gifts to take home – and they taste good, too. They are made in all sorts of exotic flavours, including prickly pear, almond, honey, pomegranate, fennel, carob and fig. Other treats for the palate such as wine, honey, halva and the rare pure Maltese olive oil are also worth taking back.

### MALTA STONE

Maltese limestone is not only used to build almost all the buildings on the island, but it is also suitable for making items of everyday use such as ashtrays, paperweights and modern sculptures.

### SHOPPING CENTRES

*The Point* in Sliema is Malta's newest shopping mall. Fifty stores on three floors sell everything that an international clientele longs for. The island's two craft centres, Ta'Qali near Mdina on Malta and Ta'Dbiegi near San Lawrenz on Gozo, are centres of production as well as sales.

### TRADITIONAL CRAFTS

For centuries, Maltese and today Gozitan women in particular have been making Maltese lace to adorn tablecloths and handkerchiefs, napkins, scarves and stoles. These enormously industrious women also knit pullovers, cardigans and caps or weave colourful woollen carpets by hand. The wood of a species of heather that grows on the island is carved into tobacco pipes with a characteristic shape that is easy to hold.

# TRAVEL TIPS

## Useful addresses and information for your trip to Malta

### BERTH

▶ **VALLETTA**

Cruise ships are moored at the Valletta Cruise Terminal at the Grand Harbour, which is located quite close to the city centre. The old town, perched above the port, is accessible on foot. Alternatively, take the lift directly to the Upper Barrakka Gardens.

### CUSTOMS

EU citizens can import and export goods for their own personal use without paying duty (800 cigarettes, 10 litres of spirits or 90 litres of wine per adult person). Citizens of other countries, e.g. the USA and Canada, can import the following without paying duty: 200 cigarettes , 100 cigarillos, 50 cigars, 250 g of tobacco; 1 l of spirits, 2 l of wine, 16 l of beer; 50 g of perfume or 250 ml of eau de toilette; and other goods up to a value of 175 euros.

### PHONE & MOBILE PHONE

Country code for Malta and Gozo: 00356. Code when calling from Malta to the UK: 0044; to the USA and Canada: 001; to Ireland: 00353, then the local code without 0. If you plan to use your mobile phone on Malta frequently, it pays to invest in a Maltese SIM card.

### TIPPING

In some restaurants no service charge is included in the bill; in this case give the waiter about 10 per cent, and otherwise round up the amount.

### WHEN TO GO

Thanks to its many historic sights, Malta is a year-round travel destination. Hotels, restaurants, language schools and souvenir shops are open all year. Spring is the most colourful time in the countryside. Advent on Malta is also a festive time of year. Many of the main roads are decorated with lights and Christmas carols play on loudspeakers all around.

### WIFI

Free WiFi hotspots exist on many public squares, and more and more cafés and bars provide Internet access free of charge. A smartphone app provides information about WiFi access.

## BUDGETING

| | |
|---|---|
| Espresso | £ 0.90/$ 1.20 |
| | *for a cup of espresso* |
| Wine | from £ 9/$ 12 |
| | *for a bottle of wine in a restaurant* |
| Cake | £ 2.70/$ 3.60 |
| | *for a slice of cake in a café* |
| Taxi | £ 1.40/$ 1.80 |
| | *per kilometre* |

# CROATIA

Imagine the following: 1,777 km (1,100 miles) of coastline, off which there are a total of 1,184 islands. Most of the islands lie directly off the Dalmatian coast in the Adriatic. There are large ones such as Brač and tiny ones such as Lokrum, inhabited islands and inhospitable rocky reefs, lavishly green ones and ones only suitable for sheep grazing. Some are given a jagged appearance by their countless bays, while others are lined by beaches. An absolute dream destination! It is not surprising that this coastline is one of Europe's most beautiful sailing spots and a holiday landscape whose diverse appeals, changing moods, ruggedness and charm will create lasting memories.

## ZADAR

**Dalmatia's second-largest port preserves three millennia of art and architecture, but there are also traces left by the city's more recent history – and here we don't just mean the enchanting art installation of the Sea Organ and the Greeting to the Sun, where the city's inhabitants gather to watch the sunset.**

The city was expanded under Venetian rule into a naval fortress from 1409 onwards, complete with walls and towers. Zadar was the capital of Dalmatia until 1918 and its culture was strongly influenced by a large Italian community until 1947, when they left the city after it became part of Yugoslavia. This Italian flair

## Metropolitan flair meets unique landscapes: turquoise water, secluded coves and bustling harbour towns

can still be felt today in the city centre, with its many cafés.

### SIGHTSEEING

#### SEA ORGAN (MORSKE ORGULJE) ⭐

Under the steps are a number of plastic tubes of varying length, each with a pipe attached to the end. These pipes produce noises that are sometimes eerie, sometimes contemplative, depending on the rhythm of the waves – and occasionally recalling the song of a whale. Only when

the mighty Bora threatens, the holes are closed. The installation is rounded off by the 🌐 *Greeting to the Sun* (Pozdrav suncu). This is a disc made up of 300 glass plates that store energy in their solar cells during the day, before releasing it at night in the form of colourful light signals that are triggered by people's footsteps on the disc.

#### SV. DONAT AND SV. STOŠIJA ⭐

The idiosyncratic rotunda of the *Sv. Donat church (daily from 9am | 20 kuna)* was built in the 9th century. This pre-Romanesque building is unusually tall, at 26 m/85 ft, and offers superb acoustics. Inside, the remains of Roman columns and capitals are preserved alongside old Croatian reliefs. Zadar's *Sv. Stošija cathedral (summer Mon–Fri 8am–2pm, 5–7pm, Sat/Sun 8am–noon)* next door constitutes a 12th/13th-century expansion of the city's sacred centre. Its Romanesque-Gothic architecture and elegant rose windows are reminiscent of Tuscan churches. The 56 m/184 ft-high ☼ bell tower *(Mon–Sat, June–Sept 9am–10pm, April, May, Oct 10am–5pm | 15 kuna)* offers superb views over the old town.

## ARCHAEOLOGICAL MUSEUM (ARHEOLOŠKI MUZEJ)

Starting on the top floor, travel chronologically through Zadar's history – from the Illyrians to the Romans, Slavs and the early Croatian middle ages – as documented in this museum by means of some sacrophagi, baptismal fonts and shrines dating from the 9th to the 11th centuries. A special section tells of the time when the Romans ruled Dalmatia. The museum shop sells INSIDER TIP handmade jewellery. *Further information & opening times at: www.amzd.hr | Trg opatice Čike 1 | www.amzd.hr*

## GLASS MUSEUM (MUZEJ ANTIČKOG STAKLA)

Playing with fire is fun to watch in this museum, where you can see how glass jewellery is moulded from a liquid mass. The well-made replicas of the Roman exhibits such as cups, bowls, perfume bottles and lamps can be purchased in the museum shop. *Mon–Sat 9am–9pm | 30 kuna | Poljana Zemaljskog odbora 1 | www.mas-zadar.hr*

## TRG PET BUNARA (SQUARE OF THE FIVE FOUNTAINS)

In earlier times the only way to reach the peninsula was to cross a drawbridge and pass through the Land Gate. Behind the gate lies the enchanting *Trg pet bunara* with its five Renaissance wells, beneath which Zadar's largest cistern used to collect rainwater. You can still see parts of the crenellated medieval City Wall here, along with a watchtower and two beautiful palaces from the 14th/15th centuries. In the Baroque *Sv. Šimun* church, two angels support the imposing gold and silver sarcophagus of the city's patron St Simeon (14th century). To the northwest of the square lies the lively district of INSIDER TIP Varoš with numerous small shops and bars.

## WHERE TO GO

## MURTER AND THE KORNATI ARCHIPELAGO

The 148 islands and rocky outcrops that make up the ★ *Kornati archipelago* are sprinkled along the coast between Biograd na Moru and the island of Murter. The true beauty of the island can only be seen from the sea, travelling by boat around the islands, spotting rare water birds, dolphins and maybe even sea turtles. Moor and enjoy a hearty meal in one of the traditional konobas that open their doors in summer.

## PAKLENICA NATIONAL PARK ★

The two canyons, Mala (little) and Velika (big) Paklenica, which were carved into the karst by the wild streams of the Velebit mountains, are the heart of this park. The main attraction in both canyons is the free climbers who hang like colourful spiders on the rocky walls. At a height of 400 m (1,312 ft), the wall Anića kuk is considered to be quite the challenge. The routes vary in difficulty from 3 to 8b+. Beginners and

A unique spectacle of nature: the Plitvice Lakes

parents with small children will find easier climbing routes in the INSIDER TIP *klanci section* – but please make sure that kids wear a helmet! *Tel. 023 36 91 55 | www. paklenica.hr*

### PLITVICE LAKES NATIONAL PARK ★
The thickly forested mountains are dotted with valley basins in which waterfalls and streams cascade over the sides, connecting 16 lakes with each other. Paths wind through the magical landscape to highlights such as a 76 m (250 ft) high waterfall. *Tel. 053 75 10 15 | www.np-plitvicka-jezera.hr*

### ISLAND OF PAG
The island stretches long and narrow in front of the steep slopes of the Velebit Mountains. Pag stands for the aromatic sheep's chees *paški*, for filigree doilies and salt. Alongside this, you can also enjoy a number of attractive shingle beaches. The best international DJs play one after another at Zrće, Croatia's most famous party beach, near the city of Novalja.

## SHOPPING

### MARKET (TRŽNICA)
Zadar's lively market sees fruit and vegetable stands arranged between the city wall and Narodni trg, while the nearby *indoor fish market* on the edge of the harbour is where you can inspect the catch of the day. Haggling is not forbidden! *Daily 6am–3pm*

### SUPERNOVA CENTAR
This shopping centre will set fashionable pulses racing with its selection of international chains from Calzedonia to Zara, alongside a few native Croatian brands. *Daily 9am–9pm | Akcije Maslenica 1*

# FOOD & DRINK

## Slow food is no trend here – Dalmatian cuisine has always been prepared with time and care

**With the sea on their doorstep, kitchen gardens full of herbs and vegetables, and a down-to-earth Slavic tradition and temperament, Dalmatia couldn't ask for any better ingredients for its cuisine – which is as delicious as it is unpretentious.**

The Dalmatians, like most southern Europeans, aren't big on breakfast. They are happy with a cup of coffee. It is not until the *marenda*, the second breakfast, served in late morning, an early lunch break, when many cafés sell cheap *hearty small plates* such as rižot, njoki, girice or pašticada. On Sundays and public holidays the marenda is extended into a lavish feast with multiple courses. A lighter meal is then served in the evening, such as a cold plate of starters, salad or a soup. The most commonly available dishes are *pasta and risotto* together with the most popular (and on hot days the most digestible) starter of pršut, cheese and olives. The majority of main courses involve grilled meat or fish, deliciously seasoned with fresh herbs such as rosemary or thyme, garlic and *naturally pure olive oil*. Vegetarians and vegans will gener-ally struggle to find suitable fare. But the trend is moving, albeit slowly, to plant-based cooking: especially in larger towns and cities there are now restaurants that cook without meat. Whether you eat in a konoba (a folkloric extension of a rustic wine cellar), in one of the many mid-price restaurants that can be found on the shoreline promenades, or in a fine dining venue, you will almost invariably be served with *authentic Dalmatian cuisine*. Most restaurants in tourist hotspots open continuously from lunchtime until late in the evening, and in the high season they are generally open seven days a week.

## LOCAL SPECIALITIES

**ajvar** – spicy paste made of red peppers, served with grilled meatt
**arancini** – candied bitter orange peel, a speciality of Dubrovnik
**čevapčići** – grilled minced meat rolls made from pork and beef, or lamb
**fritule** – deep-fried yeast dough, dusted with icing sugar
**girice** – deep-fried fish, to be eaten whole

# SPLIT

**In the foreground, there's the bustling harbour. Residents and tourists stroll along the Riva in front of the walls of Diocletian's palace, admiring its floral decorations. Dalmatia's biggest city and most important ferry port offers visitors an attractive vista.**

The centre of Split (180,000 inhabitants) is shut off from all traffic, noise and crowds: behind the mighty walls of the Roman imperial palace you will hear nothing but the cooing of pigeons and the church bells. The huge palace district (215 x 180 m/705 x 590 ft) was built around 240–312 for the Emperor Diocletian, a persecutor of Christians, and formed the basis for the city of Split: today, it harbours sections of the old town. Inhabitants of the Roman city of Salona sought refuge behind the palace walls in the face of Slavic incursions during the 7th century, and the Roman buildings have withstood 1,500 years of habitation almost miraculously well. In 1979 the palace was designated a Unesco World Heritage Site.

History lives on in Split

## SIGHTSEEING

### DIOCLETIAN'S PALACE ⭐ (*m 12/C3*)
From the Riva, visitors enter this ancient complex through its basement, the *Podrumi (June–Sept daily 8.30am–9pm | 42 kuna)*. The high ceiling is supported on brick arches and walls. From here, a staircase takes you up to the open air, where you will find a peristyle surrounded by arcades with Corinthian columns. A further staircase leads to the vestibule, the only room still preserved today, which offers a good overview of the rest of the ancient structure. On the right, the emperor's mausoleum was converted into *Sv. Duje* Cathedral, which rises from the peristyle, while diagonally opposite stands the baptistery, a former Temple of Jupiter.

### SV. DUJE CATHEDRAL ⭐ (*m 12/C3*)
At the heart of the cathedral is the octagonal mausoleum of the Roman emperor Diocletian, whose ornamented Corinthian columns now frame one of Dalmatia's most beautiful altars: Juraj Dalmatinac created the touching relief of the Flagellation of Christ in 1422. Also worthy of note are the richly decorated Roman portal and the treasury containing the relics of St Domnius *(15 kuna)*. Travellers with a head for heights should climb the 60 m/197 ft ᴧ⅄ᴧ *bell tower* to enjoy the glorious views. *Mon–Sat 8.30am–7pm, Sun 12.30–6.30pm*

### MARJAN HILL (*m 12/A2–3*)
Split's green lung starts to the west of the harbour: the 3.5 km² peninsula of Marjan is covered in thick and shady greenery. Nestled among the trees you will find chapels and churches dating from the 16th and 17th centuries, while

The historic scenery of Trogir invites for a stroll

a 378-step staircase built in 1924 takes you to the highest point (178 m/584 ft). Ivan Meštrović (1883–1962) is Croatia's most renowned sculptor and is mainly known for his monumental sculptures. His summer residence, the Galerija Meštrović, shows the diversity and intricacy of his works. *Further information & opening times at: www.mestrovic.hr | Šetalište Ivana Meštrovića 46*

## BEACHES

Split's city beach *Bačvice* (shingle/concrete) lies to the south-east of the old town. Residents come here not just to bathe, but also to play the popular sport of INSIDER TIP *picigin*, a kind of volleyball played in shallow water. Additional beaches can be found on the Marjan peninsula and in the coves to the south, such as the popular *Obojena svjetlost* in *Kaštelet*.

## SHOPPING

### STARI PAZAR MARKET
A fruit and vegetable market next to Diocletian's Palace. Also sells souvenirs. Daily

### FASHION
Creations from Croatian fashion designers hang from the racks at the *Think Pink (Zadarska 8 and Marulićeva 1)* boutique. The store *Krug (Nepotova 1)* in the old town specialises in natural chic clothing made from sustainable and fair-trade materials. The *ID Concept Store (Bana Jelačića 3)* offers an eclectic mix of romantic clothing from Croatian and international designers.

### PODRUMI
Parts of the subterranean vaults of Diocletian's Palace are devoted to market stands selling souvenirs, books, handmade jewellery and replicas of Roman mosaic motifs.

## WHERE TO GO

### KRKA NATIONAL PARK ★
The water of the Krka is high in calcium carbonate and it made the typical karst formations. The lower course of the river here tumbles over cascades into the valley. From the park entrance, take a boat to the 46 m (150 ft) high waterfall *Skradinski buk*, which is considered to be the highest tuff barrier in Europe. Put on your swimsuit and take a shower under the foaming water. *Skradin entrance | tel. 022 20 17 77 | www.npkrka.hr*

### TROGIR ★
No city in Dalmatia boasts such well-preserved Romanesque and Gothic architecture as Trogir (pop. 13,000). The elongated island, running between the mainland and the much larger island of Čiovo, has a dense covering of churches, palaces and town houses lining narrow streets, and the city's facades and courtyards boast 13th-15th century architectural details such as mullioned windows, arcades and fountains. The old town is connected to the modern quarters in the north and south by two bridges.

### BIŠEVO (BLUE GROTTO)
If you want to take a trip to this neighbouring island to see its famous ★ *Blue Grotto (Modra špilja)* you should enlist the help of an agency to take you from Komiža to the cave at the right time of day. Sunlight causes the water in the cave to glow with a radiant turquoise colour, but only for a short time around midday *(numerous agencies in Komiža, admission 70 kuna)*.

### BRAČ
La dolce vita on idyllic beaches meets traditional agriculture in the hinterland: the island of Brač shows visitors two very different sides. Brač's most famous beach

★ *Zlatni rat*, or the "Golden Cape" is a strip of fine shingle that sometimes points to the east, sometimes to the west, depending on the currents of the sea. Bare, macchia-covered surfaces are as much a part of the landscape here as the irrigated and cultivated valley slopes planted with olive and fig trees or vines.

# DUBROVNIK

**Visitors first have to make their way past crooked city gates and massive bastions before they can fall under the spell of this bright and elegantly beautiful city.**

Nonetheless, this fully preserved city wall forms a large part of Dubrovnik's charm, and visitors feel themselves transported back through the centuries to a time when Ragusa defied both the city republic of Venice and the Ottoman Empire, and was conquered by neither. Ragusa's strength was its tightly interlinked and far-reaching network of diplomatic and trade relations, and its military endeavours were restricted to an attempt to make the city unconquerable.

## SIGHTSEEING

### SPONZA PALACE (PALAČA SPONZA) ★
The 1667 earthquake damaged the Sponza Palace, which was used as a customs house at the time; however, the damage was repaired, allowing this wonderful example of Ragusan architecture to survive to the present day. Nowadays it contains the city archives, as well as a memorial to the victims of the Siege of Dubrovnik by Yugoslavian troops in 1991/1992. Just a few streets further is the *War Photo Limited Gallery (daily 10am–10pm | 50 kuna | Antuninska 6)*, which exhibits moving war photos.

# SHOPPING

## Fleur de sel, award-winning olive oil, fancy schnapps – culinary souvenirs are very popular

Unusual souvenirs are unfortunately uncommon in Dalmatia. The souvenirs available here are still typical of tourist destinations. That is why your best bet is "back to nature", because the regional products are unrivalled!

### HONEY

Dalmatian herbs and scented maquis produce the perfect conditions for lots of differently flavoured honeys. The island of Hvar has lavender-flavoured honey. Honey, like oil, is sold at markets and at the side of the road by the producers. At the market you can also find Dubrovnik's speciality *arancini*: bitter orange peels that are preserved by being candied.

### LAVENDER

When the lavender fields are in bloom on Hvar, the entire island is immersed in the scent of this aromatic, moth-repellent herb. Lavender can be bought in a small pouch or in bulk, as an oil or as a soap or bath product.

### OLIVE OIL

Producers often sell their cold-pressed oil by the side of the road or at the market. Sometimes they refine it with herbs such as rosemary or with garlic. Tourist information centres will be able to tell you where you can get truly pure oil. It is also available in supermarkets. The brand Zvijezda has a particularly good reputation!

### SALT

Sea salt has been obtained in Dalmatia through the process of evaporation since time immemorial. Coarse and fine sea salt as well as "fleur de sel", "flower of salt", is available in supermarkets.

### WINE & SCHNAPPS

Along Pelješac's wine route there are several establishments offering tastings. The grappa-like *lozovaca*, the aromatic *travarica* (herbal schnapps) or the rare *rogač*, obtained from the fruits of the carob tree, should be bought from specialist suppliers.

Opposite the Sponza Palace stands the Orlando Column, which was erected in 1418. At the western end of the Palace is the 31 m/102 ft *Clock Tower* (1444), whose two bronze figures strike the bell every hour.

## FORTIFICATIONS (GRADSKE ZIDINE) ⭐

The 1,940 m/6,365 ft City Wall was expanded enormously by the city fathers during the 15th/16th centuries. The best architects of the age einforced the monumental structure with five forts, 16 towers, 120 cannons and two main gates: the *Pile Gate* in the west and the *Ploče Gate* in the east. The main entrance can be found next to the *Pile Gate*, two other access points are by Sv. Luka church and Sv. Ivan Fortress. In the latter you can inspect the fortifications from the inside, as the basement contains an attractive *aquarium (daily from 9am / 60 kuna)*, displaying Mediterranean flora and fauna in 20 tanks. The rooms above contain a *Maritime Museum (Tue–Sun from 9am)* explaining Ragusa's naval history.

## DOMINICAN MONASTERY (DOMINIKANSKI SAMOSTAN)

This monastery situated on the approach to the Ploče Gate was founded in 1225, and in the 16th century an enchanting cloister was added to it. Palms and orange trees grow in the courtyard, which is a peaceful and idyllic place. The monastery's *Gallery* is also worth a look – in particular its triptych painted by Nikola Božidarević in the early 16th century, showing St Blaise holding a model of Ragusa in his hands. *daily 9am–6pm / 30 kuna / Svetog Dominika 4*

## GREAT ONOFRIO FOUNTAIN (VELIKA ONOFRIJEVA FONTANA)

This polygonal fountain built by the Pile Gate in 1438 has sustained a great deal of damage over the years, and aside from its 16 cisterns (or *maškeron*) is almost devoid of ornament. It formed the end point of an eleven-kilometre-long water pipe leading from a karst spring into the city – a technological masterpiece created by the architect Onofrio della Cava. Another smaller fountain also used to supply the Luža market square.

## RECTOR'S PALACE (KNEŽEV DVOR)

Although the city governor's palace harks back to the 15th century with its typically Ragusan blend of Gothic and Renaissance styles, its current form actually dates from the 17th/18th centuries. The ground floor contains guardrooms and a dungeon, while the Rector's apartments can be seen upstairs. Each Rector was only elected for a one-month term, and during that period was not permitted to leave his quarters in order to prevent anybody from influencing his judgment. *Daily from 9am / 80 kuna / Pred dvorom 1*

## SHOPPING

The main shopping streets are the *Placa* and the *Pred Dvorom* that branches off to the south; here you can find plenty of souvenir and fashion shops.

## BEACHES

Close to the old town lie the coves of the island *Lokrum* (shingle and rock), as well as the sand/shingle beach *Banje* near the Lazareti (Ploče Gate). Here you can also find the *East-West-Beachclub (ew-dubrovnik.com)* with its luxurious loungers (approx. 100 kuna per lounger) and DJ sets. Other beaches are available in the hotel quarters in *Lapad* and *Babin Kuk*, they may be subject to an admission fee.

## WHERE TO GO

### ARBORETUM TRSTENO ★

A magical park created in the 15th century at the behest of a Ragusan noble family at their similarly well-preserved *Summer Palace* around 18 km/11 miles to the north. Palm, eucalyptus, laurel, bougainvillea, oak and Aleppo pine surround statues, fountains and a villa. Its port used to be a docking point for ships from Ragusa and other cities. Today, it's pleasure boats. If you brought your bathing costume, then take a INSIDER TIP dip in front of this opulent backdrop! A number of scenes for "Game of Thrones" were filmed on this location, which served as the palace garden of House Baratheon. *May–Oct daily 7am–7pm, Nov–April 8am–4pm | 50 kuna | Potok 20*

### NERETVA-DELTA

The coastal mountain range opens up between *Neum* and *Ploče* to make room for the 280 km/174 mile Neretva River. At the mouth to the Adriatic Sea, this river flows into another delta, known as the Neretva Delta. In "California in Croatia" mandarins grow on trees like in the Garden of Eden. You can even roll up your sleeves and join in the INSIDER TIP *mandarin harvest*. Day pickers come from Dubrovnik and Makarska to lend a hand with the picking. The frogs and eels from this former swamp region were once seen as poor man's food and are today sold as a delicacy. Try a Neretva stew *(brudet)* in the restaurant *Đuda i Mate (Vid | tel. 020 68 75 00 | djudjaimate.hr | Moderate)*.

### SRĐ ⚓

This 412 m/1,352 ft hill is both Dubrovnik's most beautiful viewpoint and a memorial to the Yugoslavian War in 1991/1992. The 60-man unit stationed in *Fort Imperial* on its summit put up a spirited resistance to the much larger attacking forces during the Siege of Dubrovnik, and a *museum (winter daily 8am–4pm, summer 8am–6pm | 30 kuna)* inside the fort tells the story. Both the summit and the museum can be reached by car, on foot, or by means of a modern *cable car (daily from 9am | return trip 140 kuna | Petra Krešimira 4 | www.dubrovnikcablecar.com)*. The city administration has given their approval for the development of hotels, villas and a golf course on the top of the hill, despite bitter resistance from environmental campaigners.

# BACKSTAGE

Film tourism is a growing phenomenon, once fuelled by the western films set in the country's national parks, today sparked by the fantasy series "Game of Thrones". Fans from around the world flock to Dalmatia and especially Dubrovnik, a main filming location. With its historic fortifications and authentic medieval flair, it's no surprise that the city was chosen for the fantasy capital of the Seven Kingdoms. Take the opportunity, for one glorious moment, to sit on the Iron Throne on the island of *Lokrum*. Then you can stroll around the Royal Gardens Arboretum Trsteno pretending to be one of the lords or ladies plotting intrigues. Dalmatia is now geared to accommodate fans: many operators offer tours to the film sets.

# TRAVEL TIPS

## Croatia: the most important information for your trip

### BERTHS

▶ **ZADAR**

Zadar has two berths. One is close two the old town, the city centre can easily be reached on foot. The ferry terminal Gaženica Luka is situated 5 km / 3 miles away from the historical centre and can be reached by shuttle buses.

▶ **SPLIT**

Smaller boats moor in the port while larger vessels anchor outside. Tender boats take the passangers of cruise ships to the shore.

▶ **DUBROVNIK**

Cruise ships moor in the port of Gruž. The old town is about 3 km / 2 miles away and can be easily reached by foot, taxi, public transport or with shuttle buses.

### PHONE & MOBILE PHONE

The international dialling code for Croatia is 00385; Britain: 0044; North America: 001. If you plan on using your mobile phone often when on holiday, it is advisable to purchase a Croatian pre-paid card.

### WIFI

WiFi access is available in the public spaces of most larger towns, often at the main square, sometimes in the entire old town. In addition most of the ACI (www.aci-club.hr) marinas, almost all hotels, hostels and guesthouses have WiFi access.

### WHEN TO GO

The summers tend to be sunny and warm during the day, while the nights are refreshingly cooler. From time to time black clouds build up that turn into thundershowers in the afternoon. The best time to go is mid-May to the end of June, when the gorse is flowering, and September, when the summer heat is not so intense anymore but the Adriatic is still pleasantly warm. During the late summer and autumn months, the cold katabatic bora wind can bring changes in the weather and choppy seas.

### TIPPING

Good service in a restaurant should be rewarded with around 10 to 15 percent of the bill. The time-tested rule for hotels is to sweeten the employees' job a little with an appropriate tip shortly after you arrive as you will benefit by receiving their attention during your stay.

## BUDGETING

| | |
|---|---|
| Coffee | £1.30/$1.75– £1.75/$2.30 |
| | *in a café for one espresso* |
| Ice cream | £1.75/$2.30 |
| | *for two scoops* |
| Snacks | £1.30/$1.75 |
| | *for a piece of burek (dumpling with a filling)* |
| Pizza | £5.25/$7– £8/$10.50 |
| | *in a restaurant* |

# GREECE

**Relish perfect beaches and over 2000-year-old temples, medieval castles and archaic monasteries, besides sheep-milk cheese, sirtaki sounds and sunshine.**

Moreover, you will experience unexpected beauty, fanciful vagaries and unforeseen human encounters. When it comes to planning a visit to Greece, few people realize that the beauty of nature should enjoy preference. The amazingly lovely landscape features dense woods, deep gorges, fairy-tale caves, rushing mountain rivers, lakes abounding with fish, steep coastlines, cotton plantations and sunflower fields, orange and olive groves, pelicans, flamingos, vultures and perhaps even brown bears.

## ATHENS

**Half of Greece's total population of 11 million lives in Athens and its many suburbs. Holidaymakers usually focus on the city-centre area, where one can conveniently walk to all destinations, by day or by night.**

The pearl of ancient times is more modern than ever before. It is a city eminently filled with antiquity and museums, tavernas and trendy spots. Here one can observe how the past, spanning 2500 years, and the present have become intertwined. Furthermore, views from hilltops, like the Acropolis, reveal the close proximity between the mountains and the sea in Greece. Even islands are in clear sight.



Photo: Mykonos – fabulous in white and blue with red dots

Should one regard everything Greek as being antique? Not at all! Dive into unusual sounds, the world of marvels and tales about gods in love.

### ACROPOLIS ★

An absolute must-see sight! The Acropolis, on a 156 m/112 ft-high rocky outcrop, is the city centre's eye-catcher. More than 2500 years ago, people lived around this landmark and built sanctuaries for gods on its hilltop. During 480/79 BC, the Persian invasion posed a threat to Athenian democracy and Europe. The Athenians courageously defeated the Persians, but the Acropolis was destroyed. Thereafter,

Athenian democracy flourished under Pericles and the Assembly of the People (deme). Pericles' aim was the beautification of the Acropolis. Although the deme held divergent views, the period became known as the Golden Age of Athens.

The success of the project depended on political compromise and the expertise of architects, sculptors and artists. Major edifices were: firstly, the small *Ionian Temple* of Athena Nike, dedicated to the goddess of victory; secondly, the *Erechtheion*, dedicated to gods previously venerated on the Acropolis and featuring the famous Caryatids' porch; and thirdly, the *Parthenon*, the temple dedicated to the goddess Athena, the tutelary deity of Athens, and a monument to democracy and personal freedom. The Parthenon architects were geniuses. To counter distortions of perspective, they devised optical illusions: seeming level horizontal structures are actually curved; apparent symmetrical vertical structures have different shapes. No column is like the other, although they all look the same. These "optical refinements" were regarded as a victory of mind over nature.

A monumental gateway, the *Propylaea*, was built at the end of a wide flight of steps, serving as the entrance to the sanctuary. Like the ancient temples, it was also colourfully decorated. In later years, Christians used the Parthenon as a church, in Ottoman times people lived in its ruins and chickens and sheep inhabited the rock. Today the Acropolis, as a sacrosanct national heritage, is the pride of all Greeks. Note: sandwich eating is not allowed! Non-slip shoes and a sun hat are essential. *Entrance on the west side, April–Oct daily 8am–8pm | admission 20 euros*

### ACROPOLIS MUSEUM ★

What a thrilling museum! Designed by Swiss architect Bernhard Tschumi and inaugurated in 2009, this remarkable building stands on reinforced concrete columns above an archaeological site of the ancient city. A glass-panelled walkway and glass platforms reveal the excavations below. The top floor presents a magnificent view of the ancient relics. The sloping floor from the entrance emulates an ascendance up to the Acropolis. For this reason, the sides of the ascending section exhibit artefacts only from the Acropolis slopes. All artworks in the museum are exclusively from the Acropolis; most exhibits are freestanding. Archaeologists are available to answer questions, free of charge. The ☼ top floor affords a splendid view of the Parthenon. It houses reliefs and parts of the Parthenon frieze, depicting mythical battles and the Panathenaic Procession, the Athenians' festive parade to the Acropolis. Take in the view of the Acropolis from the terrace of the stylish ☼ *Museum Cafeteria* (€), which serves many specialities. *April–Oct Mon 8am–6pm, Tue–Thu, Fri 8am–10pm, Sat/Sun 8am–8pm | Odos Dionisiou Areopagitou 15 | admission 5 euros, e-tickets available on website | www.theacropolismuseum.gr*

### ARCHAIA AGORA (ANCIENT MARKET) ★

Visit the ancient marketplace where the famous philosopher Socrates had his shoemaker's workshop. The wholly reconstructed covered market, the *Stoa of Attalos*, was once a commercial hub. Now a museum, it traces life in ancient Athenian

In perfect sight: Likavittos (Mount Lycabettus) dominates Athens

democracy. Exhibits include sculptures, artefacts and artwork depicting private and public life in antiquity, even a baby highchair with potty, standard weights and a kleroterion, a randomization device used to select and allot citizens to state offices or court juries. Adjacent to the grounds, view the well-preserved Temple of Hephaestos/Theseion, dedicated to the god of fire, metalworking and artisanship. *April–Oct daily 8am–8pm (Museum Mon from 11am) | Odos Adrianou 24 | admission 8 euros*

### NATIONAL ARCHAEOLOGICAL MUSEUM ★

This may not seem an atmospheric spot, but take note: the unbeatable museum contains one of the world's most significant collections from prehistoric times to late antiquity, constituting the most precious collection of ancient Greek art. Dive into the creative spirit of four millenniums. View modern-looking Cycladic marble figurines dating from the

3rd millennium BC, and a handsome gold treasure dating from the Mycenaean period (approx. 1500–1200 BC). Track the liberalization of humankind: in archaic times, statues followed a rigid and schematized pattern, but suddenly they appeared with smiles. In Classical times (5th/4th century BC), each figure depicted an individual, but was still not a true portrayal. See the beginnings of idealism and individualism paving the way for something new: Roman emperors wanted to be recognized, and gods played pranks. *April–Oct daily 8am–8pm | Odos 28is Oktovríou 44 | admission summer 10 euros, winter 5 euros | www.namuseum.gr*

### LIKAVITTOS (MOUNT LYCABETTUS) ★ ⚘

Overlooking Athens, this limestone hill of 277 m/908 ft features a green band around a bare rock. Pleasant pathways and a funicular railway take you to the summit, where the dazzling white Chapel of St George and splendid views await you.

Colourful, winding alleys in Plaka: an invitation to linger

*Funicular railway | daily 9am–2am (Thu from 10.30am) | lower station at upper end of Odos Plutarchou | ticket 7 euros | bus 60 from Kolonaki Square and Platia Kaningos*

## COVERED MARKETS ★

Let's go to today's vibrant market! The covered marketplace is over a hundred years old. It offers fresh fish and other fruits of the sea from the Mediterranean, as well as generous fresh cuts of meat at an array of stands. Modest tavernas serve a choice of hearty dishes and soups, including tripe stew, patsá. All around the place, vendors offer a variety of produce: herbs, nuts, stockfish, fruit and vegetables, and even Polish sausages. *Mon–Sat approx. 6am–3pm | Odos Athinas*

## INSIDER TIP NUMISMATIC MUSEUM IN SCHLIEMANN'S HOUSE

Already in his lifetime, the famous German archaeologist Heinrich Schliemann was a celebrity. In the 19th century, he made a fortune in Russia and excavated ancient cities around the Aegean Sea: Troy and Mycenae were undoubtedly his showpieces. He kept a part of the gold that he found in his own possession. He built a stately and beautifully adorned mansion for his young Greek wife. Today the renovated and refurbished edifice is a museum, housing Greek coins from three millenniums. Chill out at the *cafe* in the garden, a haven of tranquillity. *Mon 1pm–8pm, Tue–Sun 9am–4pm | Odos El. Venizelou 12 | admission 6 euros*

## PLAKA ★

Situated on the Acropolis slopes, Athens' old town is ebullient with gregarious tourists until early evening. Pedestrianized alleys throb with cafes, bars and tavernas. Among the buzz, ATMs and endless little shops answer to material needs. Quiet corners, like the *Anafiotika* neighbourhood with its narrow stone-step pathways, are devoid of any commercial activity. In the evenings, the wide steps leading to *Odos Mnisikleous* are astir with people heading to tavernas to enjoy dancing to Greek music. Orientation tip: the old town's principal business streets are Odos Adrianou (many shops) and Odos Kidathineon (many tavernas).

## TAVERNAS

### DIPORTO

Wine is served from barrels mounted on walls and meals are freshly made. Situated in the market neighbourhood, this cellar taverna proudly serves five or six dishes daily, prepared with fresh market produce. There is no menu, and English is not spoken. There are only eight tables welcoming guests of all stripes. A distinctly plain style and communication: that is all that matters here. *Mon–Sat 8am–7pm | Odos Sokratous 9/Odos Theatrou | Agora*

### INSIDER TIP O PLATANOS

This taverna is over 70 years old and located at a tiny concealed place in the middle of the old town. It serves a large selection of cooked traditional Greek dishes. In summer, tables and chairs enjoy the shade of a large plane tree. *April–Oct daily noon–4.30pm, Mo–Sat also from 7.30pm | Odos Diogenous 4 | Plaka*

### O THANASIS ★

On the fringes of the lively Monastiraki square, you will find three similar tavernas. For many decades, they have been serving souvlaki and minced-meat kebab dishes as their specialities. Especially at lunchtimes, tables are not always freely available, since these eateries are also popular with Athenians. Of great significance is the atmosphere of these tavernas as they spill out onto the square: itinerant vendors offer their goods at tables and itinerant musicians entertain guests with music. *Daily from 10am | Odos Mitropoleos 69/Monastiraki Square*

## SHOPPING

You will find affordabe fashion and accessories in *Odos Ermou*, the street between the Sindagma square and the Kapnikarea church. Upmarket stores are in the *Kolonaki neighbourhood* between the Sindagma square and Likavittos (Mount Lycabettus). In the covered market in *Odos Athinas*, there is a kaleidoscope of activity. Every Sunday morning there is a large flea market around the metro station *Monastiraki*; maybe this is just the place for treasure hunting!

# BUILDING INSTEAD OF SAVING

Are Greeks living well? Some people would respond in the affirmative, considering the many lovely houses and expensive cars. Yet appearances are deceiving. Almost all luxury goods were bought prior to the crisis – but not paid for upfront. Banks made regular personal calls to people and offered personal credit lines or loans. Those who wanted 25,000 euros got 60,000 euros. "Think big" – that was the motto of financial markets. Now many Greek people have debts. Moreover, the supposed securities on which the financial institutions based their calculations do not exist any longer. Impounding properties or sending bailiffs on to debtors were no options, since the deluge of impoundable houses, olive groves and agricultural fields deflated the actual value of these assets; and not many people have enough money to buy them from the banks.

# OLYMPIA

**No sports event is older than the Olympic Games. It is an awesome feeling to be at the exact spot where everything started: in ★ Olympia.**

For nearly 1200 years, athletes gathered here every four years for their contests. The history of the Olympic Games can be traced back to the year 776 BC. The games were held in honour of Zeus, the supreme god, and the sacred place was principally dedicated to him. When all pagan cult practices were banned in AD 395, it spelt the end of the original Olympic Games for a long time. They were revived in 1896, when the first modern-day Olympic Games were held in Athens.

## SIGHTSEEING

### ARCHAEOLOGICAL MUSEUM

A visit to this museum provides absorbing insights and puts the sanctuary of Olympia into context: it embodied much more than just a sports event. The core of the museum is the large main hall with marble sculptures from the pediments of the Temple of Zeus and the twelve relief-friezes (metopes) from the front sides of the temple. Among the museum highlights are the marble statue of Hermes; the sculpture of Nike, the goddess of victory; the Roman bull; diverse bronze horses of various sizes and the famous cup of the sculptor Phidias, whose statue of Zeus is one of the Seven Wonders of the Ancient World. *April–Oct daily 8am–8pm | admission: ticket includes visit to excavation sites*

### EXCAVATIONS

The religious centre of the sanctuary, the *Temple of Zeus*, was the focus of excavations. Its former prodigious stature is evidenced by its multilevel platform and many scattered column drums. It housed one of the Seven Wonders of the Ancient World: the chryselephantine (gold/ivory) 14 m/46 ft-tall statue of Zeus, adorned with gold, ivory, silver and gems. Other art treasures are the *Leonidaion*, a lodging place for guests of honour, from the 4th century BC; the large *Palaestra*, from the 3rd century BC; the platform of the Temple of Hera; and the partially reconstructed vaulted stadium-passageway. The stadium seated 40,000 male spectators on embankments. *April–Oct daily 8am–8pm | admission April–Oct 12 euros*

### ARCHIMEDES' MUSEUM: MUSEUM OF ANCIENT GREEK TECHNOLOGY

The modern-day museum exhibits models of ancient operating instruments and gadgets, and traces the foundations of modern technology back to inventions and discoveries of the ancient Greeks – it is definitely an exciting place to visit. *Daily 10am–6pm | Main street in direction of excavations | admission free*

### MUSEUM OF THE HISTORY OF THE OLYMPIC GAMES

On the issue of gender equality, this museum shows, although only in passing, that a kind of Olympic Games for women also existed. Many exhibits of ancient sports apparatus and even winners' lists are on display. *Opening hours as at Archaeological Museum | above the street from the excavations to the town | no extra admission fee*

## SHOPPING

Jewellery and a variety of replicas of museum exhibits are on offer. Check out *Orpheus* in the main street for modern Greek art, superior Greek wine, a comprehensive selection of books on Greece (in many languages), as well as Greek music.

The Old Fort – today, it is the symbol of Kérkyra

# CORFU

**The heart of Corfu has remained Greek despite the influx of foreign visitors.**

The elegant arcades are bursting with rows of shops which line the wide lanes with their marble paving. All over the town small squares appear dotted with cafés. Imposing Italian-style red-dome clock towers soar above five and six-storey century-old houses where washing lines stretch from balcony to balcony, especially in the Old Town district *Cambiéllo*.

## SIGHTSEEING

### OLD FORT ☆

Start your tour of the city at the *Old Venetian Fort* which offers a great view of the city. After that, you'll know your way around! You are treated to splendid views over the whole town if you wander up the first of the two hills on the rocky headland. Although resembling an ancient Greek masterpiece, the temple in front of you was in fact built by the British: the former Anglican *St. George's Church* is modelled on a Doric temple. *May–Oct daily 8am–8pm | admission 4 euros, combined ticket 8 euros*

### OLD PALACE

Just beyond the northern end of the Esplanade, the Old Palace was built from 1819–23 by Maltese workers. The construction was commissioned by the British to house their Lord High Commissioner, and the three large function rooms facing the Esplanade once hosted parties for the island's British elite and later Greece's Royal Family. Asian art is on display in most of the other rooms. Hidden away in one corner of the museum are erotic reliefs portraying "acrobatic" Kama Sutra scenes, taken from the famous temple at the Khajuraho Group of Monuments in India. *April–Oct Tue–Sun 8am–7:30pm | admission 6 euros, combined ticket 8 euros | Esplanade*

### ARCHEOLOGICAL MUSEUM ★

The sight of the horrifying visage of the gorgon Medusa is enough to give anyone a fright. This ancient Greek creature has snakes growing out of her hair

Dramatic as Greek tragedy: Achilles

and shoulders and hanging around her waist. Her googly eyes appear to be popping out of her head, her tongue is hanging out of her wide mouth. No wonder that the Ancient Greeks believed the sight of her turned the enemy to stone and had this gorgon erected on the gable of their most important temple to ward off thieves and fire. The museum also exhibits more attractive artefacts: Dionysus, the God of wine and theatre, is engraved into a second smaller gable as well as several majestic lions. *Odós Wraíla 1.*

### INSIDER TIP ▸ BRITISH CEMETERY

The cemetery with its colonial tombstones seems like an enchanted park and it is not only a romantic place but also a great attraction for flower-lovers in spring and autumn with its many wild orchids. *Daily, from sunrise to sunset | Odós Kolokotróni 25*

### BYZANTINE MUSEUM ⭐

More than 100 valuable icons from the 15th–18th centuries from Corfiot houses of worship have found a dignified new home in the *Panagía Antivuniótissa Church* in the Old Town. Soft Byzantine music can be heard in the background while you make your visit. The fourth icon on the left after the cash desk, a traditional Byzantine icon from around 1490, shows St George on a horse with a young boy holding a teapot and cup sitting behind him (no. 186). *Tue–Sun 9am–4pm | admission 3.50 euros, combined ticket 8 euros | steps lead up from Odós Arseníu*

### CAMBIÉLLO

Put away your Marco Polo guide now and enjoy an aimless stroll between the sea promenade, Odós Filéllinon, Odós Ágios Spirídonos and the Old Palace through the old town's most beguiling district. Pass by the local stray cats and dogs, walk under the washing lines stretched from window to window and meet the locals who live here. There is no store or *kafenío* around here to distract you. It is purely a residential area. The district is proof that beauty can emerge from poverty. The ★ *Esplanade* is a hive of activity. The broad expanse of the Esplanade is the centre of all social life. There is a fountain in the shady park. One of the monuments erected here commemorates the unification of the Ionian Islands with free Greece in 1864. It shows seven bronze reliefs with symbols of the seven main islands.

### ÁGIOS SPIRÍDONAS CHURCH

Its most precious relics are the bones of St Spiridon, a Cypriot martyr from around 300 AD. A noble Corfiot family purchased his remains from a travelling salesman in 1456. Over the centuries the relics have not only blessed the common folk; they have saved entire cities, islands and countries from war and helped to contain the spread of the pest and cholera. Saint Spyridon also exceeded all expectations when he was attributed to saving Corfu from the hands of the Turks in 1716.

### MON REPOS ★

A little-known fact is that Prince Phillip of Greece, who was to marry Queen Elizabeth II, was once pushed around the enchanting grounds of Mon Repos in his pushchair. Born in this small castle on 10 June 1921, there is nothing here to remind you that his family once resided here; the Palazzo now houses a colour collection of memorabilia connected to the island's history and flora. The visit is not mandatory, but you probably won't get another chance to take such a leisurely half-hour INSIDER TIP park stroll anywhere else in Greece. Covered in ivy, most of these tropical trees are almost 200 years old. The remains of two Ancient Greek temples are also dotted around the gardens, the Doric Temple is ideal for a few peaceful moments sitting in the grass or picnicking between the 2500-year old pillars. *Park daily 8am–7pm | admission free*

## SHOPPING

The main shopping streets for the locals are Odós Vularéos in the Old Town and its continuation, Odós G. Theotóki, in the new section with its beautiful arcades. Modern shops, especially those selling electrical items and multimedia, can be found on the wide Odós Aléxandras that runs from Platía G. Theotóki (Sarocco Square) to the sea. Arts and crafts and souvenirs are mainly offered on Odós N. Theotóki, Odós Filarmonikís and Odós Filéllinon in the Old Town. There alre also many small shops in Odós Ag. Sofías in the old Jewish quarter.

## WHERE TO GO

### ACHÍLLION ★

The Kaiser hero-worshipped the figure of the "victorious Achilles" and had a monument built in his memory with his helmet, shield and lance. The statue stands in the splendid gardens which the Kaiser bought along with the castle in 1907. The building of the castle was in fact commissioned by the Empress Elisabeth of Austria (1837–98). In keeping with her melancholic nature, she chose to portray the "dying Achilles" in her garden statue. *May–Oct daily 8:30am–7pm | admission 7 euros | There are four to six buses daily to Achíllion – from San Rocco Square (line 10); tickets are not available on the bus*

# FOOD & DRINK

Food the Greek way: good dining in Greece means fresh ingredients and easy-going conviviality around a large table

**You can eat gyros and moussaka at home, here you should try real Greek cuisine – it has a lot more to offer.**
Most restaurants and taverns in Greece provide multilingual menu cards. However, you should do as the locals do and ask the waiter for the special of the day. Greeks eat mezedákia, a wide variety of specialities on as many plates as possible. There is not a set sequence of menu courses as we know it; waiters serve dishes to the table as soon as they are ready in the kitchen. Locals would prefer to stay at home rather than eat alone or as a couple. A meal can only be fully enjoyed with the right *paréa*, one single Greek word to mean a group of family or friends gathering together to enjoy each other's company. The waiter places all the dishes in the middle of the table and everybody takes what and as much as they want. Fish and meat are usually served on *large platters* and everyone helps themselves. The waiters don't

take any away so that the paréa can see how well they dined. As a tourist dining out alone or with a partner, you can of course order in the normal fashion – although the Cretan way is much more fun. By the way: it is the Greeke custom that one person usually pays for everyone, if this does not suit you then let the waiter know when you place your order.

## LOCAL SPECIALITIES

**briám, briamé** – a kind of ratatouille
**fáva** – pureed yellow peas which the guests prepare themselves at the table with onions and olive oil
**jouvétsi** – noodle gratin with beef (occasionally, with lamb)
**márides** – crisp, fried anchovies eaten head and all
**spanakópitta** – puff pastry filled with spinach
**stifádo** – beef or rabbit stew in a tomato-cinnamon sauce

# MYKONOS TOWN

**Mykonos Town is mostly closed to traffic. Only small motor-tricycles can ride through the narrow alleys.**

Pedlars still come with their donkeys to sell fruit and vegetables. Take a glimpse (and pictures) of the delightful neighbourhood of *Little Venice* with its seafront houses right on the edge of the sea, and the church of *Paraportianí* or "Our Lady of the Side Gate". The church stands on a promontory close to the sea, in the neighbourhood of *Kástro*, a name dating back to the Middle Ages during Frankish rule. A backdrop of windmills on the elevated margins of the town, the old fishing port with its cafes, the chapel of *Ágios Nikólaos* and the island's landmark town hall round off the charming setting.

## WHERE TO GO

### ANO MERA

Apart from the main town, the only other traditional village lies in the interior of the island. Adjoining the large platía (town square) with its many tavernas, stands the monastery of *Panagia Tourliani*, founded in 1542. Its edifices date back to the 18th century; particularly lovely are the iconostases, the marble fountain and the bell tower adorned with traditional reliefs. A brisk 15-minute walk from the platía will take you to the somewhat impoverished *Paleokastro Monastery* (17th century), a convent that lies just off the asphalt street to Mykonos Town. *9 km/5 mi from Mykonos Town*

### ARCHAEOLOGICAL MUSEUM

Among the many interesting finds from the Delian necropolis on the island of Rheneia is a pithos, a large archaic earthenware storage jar, dating from the time around 670 BC, which is adorned with a INSIDER TIP relief depiction of the legendary Trojan horse with soldiers and terrible war scenes. *Above the street to the ferry pier.*

### MARITIME MUSEUM

The *Aegean Maritime Museum* houses historical models of ships, nautical instruments and maritime paintings. In addition, a historic *kaíki*, a wooden cargo sailing vessel, is on display. *Daily 8.30am–1pm and 6pm–9pm | close to the Tria Pigadia in the centre of town*

### FOLKLORE MUSEUM

Furniture, photos and countless other memorabilia depict life on the island during the past 200 years. *April–Oct daily 5.30pm–8.30pm | on the square facing the church of Paraportiani*

# BEACH LIFE ON MYKONOS

The loveliest sandy beaches of the island are located on the southern coast. If you want to go to the beach of *Platis Jalos*, simply hop in a bus – there is a local bus service from town. From this beach, around-the-day boats provide transport to *Paradise Beach*, popular with nudists, and to *Super Paradise Beach*, preferred by gay people. If you fancy Elia Beach, you can take a bus or boat; or take a bus to the equally popular beaches of *Kalafatís*, *Agios Stefanos* and *Ornos*, or the narrow, somewhat more tranquil beach of *Agios Ioannis*.

Cable car from the port to Fira

# FIRA/
# SANTORINI

**The island's capital, perched on the cliffs of the caldera rim, stretches over a long distance and spreads into the bordering towns of *Firostefani* and *Imerovigli*.**
As far as practically possible, houses have been built on to the edge of the caldera (crater). All the interesting sights and spots are located in this vicinity. Here you will find the oldest hotel of the island, the *Atlantis*, and next to it, the *Orthodox cathedral*, beautifully renovated after the earthquake of 1956, and adorned with contemporary frescoes in the traditional Byzantine style.

## SIGHTSEEING

### SKALA (OLD PORT)
A wide cobblestone path and more than 587 steps provide the steep pedestrian connection between the town of Fira, perched on the caldera rim, and the town's old port, which locals call *Skala* (as many ship moorings in Greece are called). In earlier times, fishing boats and freight-carrying sailing ships were moored here. The port, lying at the base of the steep caldera cliff, today welcomes modern cruise-ship travellers wishing to explore the gorgeous Santorini sights. Dozens of mule drivers wait here to take tourists on a 15-minute ride to the top. The mules have made their mark on the way between Fira and Skala. You should therefore take care when walking up or down the steep path, and look out for mule dung. The descent is nevertheless worth the effort. Alternatively, use the cable car.

### CABLE CAR ★ ⚘
From the early 1980s, two lanes of six concatenated cabins connect Fira with the old port. Within two minutes, the cabins surmount an altitude difference of 225 m/738 ft. The shipping-company owner Evangelos Nomikos donated the Austrian-made cableway to his home island. Today it belongs to the town of Fira. *Hilltop station at crater-rim next to Archaeological Museum (many signposts) | daily 6.30am–9pm, longer hours in the summer season, depending on demand | one-way trip 5 euros*

### ARCHAEOLOGICAL MUSEUM ★
In the cashier area, visitors can admire finds from prehistoric times, which were discovered on the island even before the Akrotiri excavations began. Three small ceramic ewers (jugs) are especially pretty; they stand on the top shelf of a display-case on the way to the large hall. These

ewers are decorated with breast nipples and are called *Cycladic Nippled Ewers*.

In the large museum hall, walk clockwise. To the left of the entrance, there is a hanging display case containing an exhibit, one of the most valuable treasures of the museum: a painted, very well-preserved female *terracotta figurine*, which is about 30 cm/12 in tall, dating from the second half of the 7th century BC. The woman tears her hair: an expression of mourning and grief. Such lamentation of women is also shown in the famous Greek film "Zorba the Greek" (1964). This is still a custom in Greece. *On the northern end of the caldera-rim road, close to the cable-car station | Tue–Sun 8am–3pm | admission 2 euros*

## CATHOLIC QUARTER
### (TA FRANGIKA) ⭐

The neighbourhood of Ta Frangika, known as "The Frankish", lies directly east of the hilltop cable-car station. From the early 18th century, and after the end of the Italian rule, the majority of the Roman-Catholic people on Santorini stayed here. In the vernacular, they are called "the Franks". On the way between the cable-car station and the cultural centre of Megaron Ghizi, you will find the two most significant edifices of the quarter: the *Dominican Convent* and the island's *Roman-Catholic Cathedral*.

On entering the small church of the Catholic convent, one senses the difference to the Orthodox Church. Here one finds a stoup, a confessional and sculptures of saints. The convent's Dominican nuns, originating from different countries, warmly welcome visitors to church services *(daily 6.15am, 7.45am, 12.15pm, 4.10pm, 6pm, 7.30pm, 9pm and 1am)*. The church is always open. Diagonally opposite from the convent, there is the small Roman-Catholic Cathedral dating from 1823. It is dedicated to John the Baptist. *Church services Sat 7pm, Sun 10am and 7pm | church freely accessible during day-time*

## ORTHODOX CATHEDRAL ⭐

The dazzling white dome on the caldera edge of Fira dominates the town's skyline.

# THE DONKEYS OF SANTORINI

For cruise-ship tourists, a mule or donkey ride from the old port of Fira to the town is an adventurous introduction to their tour of the island. Almost 400 mules and donkeys are available in the summer season, and 40 drivers earn their money with them. Every morning they lead the animals from their stables outside the town down to the port and in the evenings back home again. For them the business is equally strenuous as for the mules and donkeys. Drivers improve their income by holding shares in the competing cableway; and get 20 percent of the profits. Animal campaigners are concerned about the hard fate of the mules and donkeys. However, the drivers are emphatic that they look after them very well *(www.santorini-donkey.gr)*. Artists from around the world supported the "Donkey Republic" project and created colourful fibreglass sculptures of mules and donkeys. These are exhibited in public, and miniatures are sold as souvenirs. A part of the revenue goes to SAWA (Santorini Animal Welfare Association) and its shelter for mules, donkeys and other animals at Karterados.

Fira's cathedral radiating virtuously

This landmark was built in 1956/57, shortly after the earthquake had destroyed the old Orthodox Cathedral, which dated from 1827. The revered edifice has an imposing interior: its splendour, its precious crystal chandeliers and an artistically appealing iconostasis are breathtaking. Most beautiful are the extensive murals and frescoes adorning the interior walls and ceilings. Santorini's Orthodox believers financed the murals. The artist Christophoros Assimis painted the murals. He was born in Exo Gonia on Santorini in 1945, and still lives on the island. Explore the glorious images in this Cathedral Church of Candlemas of the Lord, especially if you are interested in learning more about the Orthodox faith and art in the Orthodox Church.

### PREHISTORIC MUSEUM ★

The museum essentially houses finds from Akrotiri, where excavations started in 1976. Tour the museum in an anticlockwise manner.

In room B, there are information boards with very good and extensive explanations (in English and Greek) about the geology and history of the origins of Santorini. A display case on the right-hand side contains *fossil casts of plants and animals*, which were found in ancient lava layers, as well as fossil casts of olive-tree leaves dating back 60,000 years. *Opposite the central bus-stop | Wed–Mon 8am–3pm | admission 3 euros*

### SANTOZEUM ★

Opened in 2011, the museum houses a modern exhibition of 3-D-reproductions of virtually all of Akrotiri's ancient murals and frescoes. Most of the original artworks are older than 3500 years. Meticulous work, combined with strict scientific standards and artistic imagination, led to these first-class reproductions. Compared with the few originals exhibited in the Archaeological Museum in Athens and in the Prehistoric Museum in Fira, one can distinguish quite clearly between the original parts that archaeologists discovered in the excavated houses and those parts that were so exceptionally well reconstructed. The reconstructions outweigh the originals by far in surface area. Close to the cable-car station, good signposts | May–Oct daily 10am–6pm | admission 5 euros | www.santozeum.com

## TAVERNAS

### SIMOS

Though not overlooking the caldera, this classic taverna serves excellent cuisine. Instead of opting for a main course in the evening, you can order typical Greek meze, which is a combination of a variety of smaller dishes. The owner will bring a tray with a selection to your table, and you can order whatever you prefer. *Firostefani, to the left of the main street in Fira to Imerovigli | daily |* Budget

### INSIDER TIP ▶ NAOUSSA ⋏⋏

In 2013, this renowned taverna moved to the caldera rim. Nevertheless, prices were not increased. It is probably the most reasonably priced good taverna offering such a stunning view. Expect waiting times for tables, but the wait is well worth every minute. On the one hand, you get a superb view and affordable prices, and on the other, the owners, who hail from Macedonia, serve Greek taverna cuisine at its very best, often delectably spiced in true Macedonian fashion. *Odos Georgiou D. Nomikou | www.naoussa.restaurant. com | daily from 12pm |*

## WHERE TO GO

### AKROTIRI ★

The excavations at Akrotiri are the Greek Pompeii, although no dead persons or metal objects were found. Given these facts, one can assume that earthquakes or smaller volcanic eruptions acted as advance warnings to the town's inhabitants. Thus they presumably had a chance to flee before the huge volcanic eruption occurred and could take valuable belongings with them, the most important of which have been metal objects.

Compared with most other archaeological sites where remains of foundation walls were found, these excavations reveal much more. Here facades of houses, some up to four storeys high, were preserved, as well as amphorae, still standing in the same position as at the volcano eruption. One can recognize entire streets. In many houses, archaeologists found countless pieces of broken frescoes and laboriously put them together again. These are today housed in the National Archaeological Museum in Athens and in the Prehistoric Museum in Fira. Postcards (available at the excavation site's cashier), and of course the reconstructions exhibited in the Santozeum in Fira, offer a good impression of their gracefulness and beauty. *April–Oct Tue–Sun 8am–8pm | bus to Fira (15 km/9 mi)*

## WHITE-BLUE

There is no absolute certainty as to why so many buildings on Santorini and other Greek islands are painted white and blue. Romanticists refer to the basic colours of the sky and water. Analysts recall the Greek flag and explain: by painting their buildings and houses white and blue, the inhabitants of Santorini and the other Cycladic islands proudly demonstrated their allegiance to the liberated, independent Greek state in the 19th century.

### KAMENI ISLANDS ⭐

The two lava islands in the caldera are worth visiting by boat from Oia or Fira. On the larger one, *Nea Kameni,* some of the craters came into existence in the 20th century. Visitors can feel the heat of the soil and watch rising sulphur vapours. In a small cove of *Palea Kameni,* a thermal source of 45°C/113°F heats up the seawater.

### OIA

Oia lies in the outer northwest and is similar to Fira, but much more tranquil. Many houses here are built into natural caves in the caldera cliffs and some are available as holiday accommodation. In contrast, there are a few classicism-styled villas along the caldera-rim street. These bear testimony to the fact that the inhabitants of Oia, unlike those of Fira, went out to sea frequently and became captains or even ship owners. A small museum presents recollections of this time. *11 km/6 mi from Fira*

### WINERIES

You can visit quite a few wineries in Santorini. The most modern one is *Boutari (Visitors' Centre daily approx. 10am–6pm | follow signposts from the main street | Megalochori)*, offering guided tours of the winery (in several languages) and wine tastings. Alternatively, visit the INSIDER TIP *Art Space Winery (daily approx. 11am until sunset | www.artspace-santorini.com)*, just outside the town of Exo Gonia. The owner, Antonios Argyros, guides visitors in English through his winery, which is carved out of thick pumice rock. There is also a distillery and a well-known art gallery.

Rugged cliffs and water in Oia symbolize Greece's national colours

# SHOPPING

## Arts and crafts, culinary items and music are extremely popular souvenirs

No matter where you go, there will be trash and famous brands, but you will definitely find lovely and useful Greek-made products: handicraft products, arts and crafts, jewellery and culinary delights. Business hours differ from region to region. Souvenir shops are generally open from 9am–10pm, supermarkets Mon–Sat 8am–8pm. Other stores are open Mon–Sat 9am–2pm and Tue, Thu, Fri also approx. 5pm–8pm.

### CERAMICS

Greek ceramics workshops offer an array of products, ranging from plain household articles to artistic sculptures. A particularly large range is offered in the Plaka neighbourhood in Athens.

### GAMES

Consider adding a new board game to your collection: like backgammon, one can easily learn *tavli*; or maybe Greek monopoly could be fun. Streets and stations have Greek names, but the rules are the same.

### MUSEUM SHOPS

Apart from copies of museum exhibits, many museum shops offer objects with a modern design, inspired by antiquity. Check out the shops in the Acropolis and the Benaki Museums in Athens, and the Greek cultural heritage museums of PIOP *(Piraeus Bank Group Cultural Foundation | www.piop.gr)*, highlighting artisanal and industrial technology.

### SHOES

Even in rural areas, it is astonishing to see women's adventurous footwear. Prices are cheap, and there are innumerable shoe stores.

### YOUNG FASHION

Some Greek labels come at affordable prices, for example Anna Riska *(anna-riska.gr)* and Haris Cotton *(hariscotton. gr)*. The less expensive brand Paranoia *(www.paranoia-eshop.gr)* is widely available in rural areas.

# IRÁKLIO/CRETE

**Have no fear! From a distance, Iráklio (pop. almost 200,000) may look like a Moloch, but at the centre the city is pretty, clearly laid out and, above all, bursting with urbane life. By day and night.**

Road traffic has been brought well under control in recent years; traffic lights have been removed and many passenger precincts created. Which means there is now even more room for tavernas and street cafés. As a shopping metropolis, Iráklio is unbeaten on the island – and its museums are among the most important in Greece.

## SIGHTSEEING

### ÁGIOS MÁRKOS CHURCH (📖 15/C2)
The oldest Venetian church, built in 1239 (close to the Morosini Fountain), today hosts concerts and exhibitions. The monolithic pillars of the basilica date back to ancient times. *Opening times differ | admission free | Odós 25 Avgústu*

### ÁGIOS MINÁS CHURCH (📖 15/B3)
The cathedral of Iráklio, about 150 years old, is like a picture book. Cupolas, arches and walls are covered in paintings of biblical stories. *Usually open during the day | admission free | Platía Agía Ekaterínis*

### ARCHAEOLOGICAL MUSEUM ★ (📖 15/D2)
If not here, then where? The two-storey museum contains more finds from Minoan times than all of the other museums in the world combined. And as well as noble art, it also contains numerous items that speak to us of everyday life here – about 3500 years ago. One of the most valuable pieces is a vessel in the shape of a bull's head carved from soapstone with rock crystal eyes and a mother of pearl mouth. The wall murals in the Palace of Knossós and the Minoan villas are staggeringly beautiful. *April–Oct daily 8am–8pm | admission 10 euros | Platía Eleftherías/Odós Xanthudínu*

### EARTHQUAKE SIMULATOR (📖 15/A1)
What does it feel like when the earth quakes? That is something that no one would really want to experience, but in the simulator of the *Museum of Natural History* it's both interesting and perfectly safe. In a replica of an old classroom, earthquakes of various forces give you a good shaking every half-hour. *Admission 9 euros | Leof. Sof. Venizélou | www.nhmc.uoc.gr*

### HISTORICAL MUSEUM (📖 15/B1)
What did Iráklio look like 400 years ago? A large wooden model shows it clearly at a scale of 1:500. Also interesting: medieval hand grenades made of glass and ceramic, Cretan folk costumes and art, an office of the Sorbás author Níkos Kazantzákis. And for art-lovers, two small paintings by El Greco. *Mon–Sat 9am–5pm, winter until 3.30pm | admission 5 euros | Odós Lysimachou Kalokerinou 7 | www.historical-museum.gr*

### KÚLES FORTRESS ☼ (📖 15/D1)
This will get your blood flowing. First you climb under the dark arches of the Venetian harbour fort and up onto the roof to look over the old town to the Cretan mountains. Then you can join the joggers running a circuit along the approx. 1 km/0.6 mi pier. *Tue–Sun 8am–3pm | admission 3 euros | the pier of the fishing harbour*

### MOROSÍNI FOUNTAIN (📖 15/C2)
Arranging to meet somewhere? The Venetian "lion" fountain is the general

Iráklio's citadel offers magnificent views

meeting place of the city. It's where all the main day- and night-time streets come together: the wide pedestrian street is 25is Avgústou, the main shopping streets Dédalu, 1866 and Kalokerinú, and the nightlife areas Handakós and Platía Korái. *Platía Venizélou*

### ODÓS 1866 (*15/C3*)

Although the 200-m/660-ft street is no longer a traditional market for locals, there's still plenty going on. It's an excellent place to shop for culinary souvenirs, to pop into rather old-fashioned tavernas and cafenía or modern bistros and coffee shops. The best place to sit is on the eastern end of the street beside the Venetian Bembo fountain.

WHERE TO GO

### KNOSSÓS

The no. 1 of the island's top sights. 3500 years ago, the so-called "palace" of ⭐ Knossós was already a major town with a population of perhaps 80,000. Here, some people even lived in four-storey houses with sewage systems, paved roads and squares. Pretty frescoes adorned the walls, and works of art of a unique elegance were created in workshops, while the people kept stores of provisions in enormous jugs in storage rooms. And although the people of Knossós used a form of writing, they passed nothing of themselves and their history on to us.

The Englishman Sir Arthur Evans only unearthed the settlement in the first quarter of the last century – and then rebuilt it in sections. *Apr–Oct daily 8am–8pm | admission 15 euros, combi-ticket with Archaeological Museum Iráklio 16 euros*

# RHODES TOWN

**It's all a question of taste, but Rhodes is arguably one of the prettiest cities in the world. There's no doubt, though, that its Old Town is the best preserved city of its size.**

The capital city of Rhodes has been a site of uninterrupted settlement for 2400 years which makes history come alive in this unique and vibrant place. The 2000-year old remains of ancient walls are testimony to the monumental architectural achievement. 500-year-old houses are now used as small boutique hotels and guesthouses, cocktail bars and tavernas. The main streets through the Old Town resemble a bustling bazaar, while the winding side lanes are populated by more cats than people. The Avenue of the Knights is one of the world's best preserved medieval streets – and the Archaeological Museum was once the most modern hospitals of its time.

## SIGHTSEEING

### OLD TOWN ★ (𝄞 14/B–C 3–4)

Recently voted the number one world heritage site by Unesco, the Old Town of Rhodes is fully enclosed by its 4 km/ 2.5 miles long *city wall*. You can either walk on top of the wall or in its 2.5 km/ 1.5 mile long *moat* skirting inland. The best way to find your bearings around the Old Town is by following the main streets and then explore the quieter corners walking in a zig-zag direction. Buildings erected by the Byzantines, Crusaders, Israelites, Ottoman Turks and Greeks are embedded in the ancient fortifications. There is no new building to spoil the view.

### MUSEUM OF ARCHAEOLOGY ★ (𝄞 14/C3)

The island's most significant museum lures even the most reluctant visitor to spend more than an hour inside, because it is far more than just an exhibition space. Surrounded by beautiful gardens, the two-storey building itself is a perfect photo opportunity, overlooking a large courtyard with a pile of cannonballs and an ancient marble lion. Its finest treasure is a small marble Aphrodite statue depicting two women with beautifully sculpted figures. *Approx. Easter–Oct daily 8am–8pm | admission Easter–Oct 8 euros | Odós Apéllou | Old Town*

### MANDRÁKI HARBOUR ★ (𝄞 14/C2)

The question on everyone's lips is "where did the famous Colossus of Rhodes once stand?" Nobody knows for sure. Legend would have you believe it stood astride the entrance to Mandráki Harbour precisely where two pillars are now erected carrying the island's heraldic animals, the stag and the doe. It's well worth a stroll around this picturesque harbour: the jetty with its three windmills and the harbour fortress *Ágios Nikólaos* all date from the 15th century.

### NÉA AGORÁ ★ (𝄞 14/B3)

You cannot overlook this building: it has seven corners, but is only one-and-a-half

## ANIMAL WELFARE

Oh, how cute they are! And how amicable! Stray dogs and homeless cats are not a rare sight on Rhodes. The animals are harmless, but they have a hard life and go hungry, particularly in winter. Animal welfare societies on the island organise animal transports and adoptions overseas, for example *rhodesgreeceguide.com/ animalwelfare.htm*

storeys high. Under the arcades facing the harbour, there are a number of cafés. Inside the Néa Agorá stands the former fish market hall, recognisable only by the fine fish reliefs on the capitals of its columns. *Platía Eleftherías Mandráki*

### ODÓS SOKRATOÚS (SOCRATES STREET) ★
*(📖 14/B–C3)*

Shopping is on the agenda when you arrive at Socrates Street, the main street running through the Old Town. The street climbs gently uphill from the Platía Ippokrátous at the bottom to the Mosque of Suleyman at the top end. The street is lined on both sides with shops selling all the usual souvenirs and more besides: jewellery and freshly roasted coffee, leather and furs, natural cosmetics and Greek culinary specialities, kitsch, t-shirts and even lightweight knight armoury.

### AVENUE OF THE KNIGHTS ★
*(📖 14/B–C3)*

The Odós Ippotón is the only late medieval residential street in Europe which has remained fully intact. It runs in a perfectly straight line from the hospital of the Order of St John, which now houses the Museum of Archaeology, to the Palace of the Grand Masters. The finest lodgings belonged to the French knights and stand almost in the centre. *Permanently accessible; building interiors cannot be viewed | Odós Ippotón | Old Town*

### INSIDER TIP  TURKISH CEMETERY
*(📖 14/B2)*

It may seem like an unlikely place to relax and unwind, but the city's old Turkish cemetery is a perfect retreat. *Accessible during the day | access from the Platía Koundourióti | New Town*

Relics of antiquity in Lindos

## WHERE TO GO

### LÍNDOS ★

Lindos is like a picture-book village. Sprawling from a bay with lovely sandy beaches, whitewashed houses cover the hillside and the ridge, reaching St Paul's Bay, which is almost completely encircled by rocks. Towering above, there are the formidable fortifications of a ☀️ *crusader castle (Apr–Oct. Sat–Mon 8am–3pm, Tue–Fri 8am–8pm)*. Behind the castle walls, the columns of an ancient Athena temple soar into the sky. *46 km/28 mi from Rhodes City*

### FILÉRIMOS ☀️

On the 267 m high plateau of the Filérimos mountain stood the remains of the acropolis of the ancient city of Ialissós, the ruins of a tiny temple dedicated to the Goddess Athena from the 3rd/2nd centuries BC. The foundations of an early Christian basilica and several chapels have also been preserved. *April–Oct, daily from 8am | 10.5 miles from Rhodes Town*

# TRAVEL TIPS

## ADMISSION

Average admission prices for museums and archaeological sites are 4–6 euros. If an excavation site is part of a museum, you might have to pay for two admissions. Significant excavation sites and museums cost 8–15 euros. Between November and March, tickets are half-price, except for Athens. Schoolchildren and students from EU countries (with national school- or international student's identification cards) pay no admission. Senior citizens aged over 65 pay reduced admission. State museums and all excavation sites charge no admission from November to March on every first Sunday of the month, and on 6 March, 18 April, 18 May, 5 June, 28 October and the last weekend of September.

## BERTHS

### ▶ PIRAEUS (ATHENS)
Cruise ships can dock in Greece's largest port. Athens' city centre is approx. 10 km/6 mi away. Taxis and the metro are available.
### ▶ CORFU
The cruise-ship port of Corfu Town is located on the north of the island. Cruise ships dock in the Old Port. You can walk or take a bus to the town, which is approx. 2.5 km/1.5 mi away.
### ▶ OLYMPIA
Cruise ships are moored in the port of Katakolon, which is 33 km/20 mi away from the historic sights of Olympia. You can either take a taxi or the train (travelling time approx. 45 minutes).
### ▶ MYKONOS
Modern cruise ships dock in the port of Tourlos. There is a shuttle-bus service or the Mykonos SeaBus to the town's port, which is approx. 2 km/1.2 mi away.
### ▶ SANTORINI
Large cruise ships anchor near the coast and tender boats transfer you to the island.
### ▶ IRÁKLIO
Cruise ships dock directly in the port of Iráklion. Depending on the berth, shuttle buses take you to the terminal. From here, a walk to the town takes approx. 15 minutes. Taxis and buses are also available
### ▶ RHODES TOWN
Since the new port of Rhodes is quite close to the historic centre, you can reach the sights on foot.

## EMERGENCY SERVICES

Countrywide for police, ambulance, fire brigade: 112. Your interlocutor may not be able to communicate with you in a foreign language, so rather ask a local person to make the call.

## HEALTH

Basic medical care is available. However, should you have any serious injuries or ailments, it would be best to return home. Greece has social insurance treaties with EU member countries. Should you have a *European Health Insurance Card (EHIC)*, you are entitled to free medical treatment at doctors contracted with the Greek medical aid fund IKA, as well as in state hospitals and health-care centres. If you are willing to pay in cash, you can consult any doctor of your choice. All larger towns have pharmacies; you can get a wide range of medication without a doctor's prescription. Costs might be less than in your home country. Remember to bring your own protection against mosquitoes.

# Greece

Your holiday from start to finish: the most important addresses and information for your trip

All travellers, regardless of nationality and country of origin, should take out adequate travel medical/health insurance well in advance of the cruise.

More info and updates for travellers from the UK, USA, Canada and Australia at:

UK: https://www.gov.uk/browse/abroad/travel-abroad and https://www.gov.uk/foreign-travel-advice/greece/health

USA: https://www.state.gov/travel/ and https://travel.state.gov/content/travel/en/international-travel/before-you-go/travelers-with-special-considerations/cruise-ship-passengers.html

CAN: https://travel.gc.ca/travelling/advisories

AUS: https://smartraveller.gov.au/guide/all-travellers/health/Pages/default.aspx

## INTERNET & WIFI

Many cafes and bars offer free WiFi. City and town municipalities have installed free WiFi zones at central places. If you need a computer, larger cities or towns have internet cafes (though decreasing in number), and they charge an hourly rate of 3 to 5 euros.

## MONEY & PRICES

You can withdraw cash at a minimal rate with your bankcard at any of the numerous cash ATMs of banks. Bank tariffs are much higher if you use your credit card to withdraw cash. Banks and post offices exchange traveller's cheques and foreign exchange. Opening hours of banks are Mon–Thu 8am–2pm, Fri 8am–1.30pm, longer hours sometimes in larger towns or cities and in tourist destinations. Food and other consumables might be somewhat more expensive than in your home country.

## TAXI

Taxis are readily available throughout the country and not expensive. They use taximeters in cities and towns; in smaller towns, the agoraion taxis use tariff schedules, which are publicly available. Small surcharges, not indicated by taximeters, may be charged for trips from airports, ports and stations, as well as for luggage weighing more than 10 kg/22 lb.

## TIME DIFFERENCE

Throughout the year, Greece is one hour in advance of Central European Time (CET) and two hours in advance of Greenwich Mean Time (GMT).

## BUDGETING

| | |
|---|---|
| Taxi | £0.63–£1.11/$0.84–$1.47 per km *city/country tour 5am–12pm* |
| Beach | £4.25–£6.80/$5.60–$9 *umbrella daily rent incl. 2 loungers* |
| Wine | £3/$4 *for a glass of table wine* |
| Fish | £34–£51/$45–$68 *for 1 kg/2 lb in restaurants* |
| Petrol | £1.30–£1.50/$1.70–$1.90 *for 1l regular* |
| Gyros | £2.10/$2.80 *for 1 portion with pita* |

# TURKEY

**A country the size of France and the UK put together, a country full of beauty and juxtapositions.**

Its geographical location between Europe, Asia and the African continent makes its character so distinct yet is also responsible for problems which the country continually has to face. A young and dynamic population, endless debates on modern culture and Islam as well as an ambitious economic upswing characterise this country in the 21st century. For the beach lover there is 4,000 km/2,485 miles of the Aegean and Mediterranean coastline with secluded bays and the cleanest water in southern Europe. Some of the last specimens of the *Caretta sea turtles* hatch on some of the Mediterranean beaches.

# ISTANBUL

**The city (pop. 12 million), built on two continents, is the heart of Turkey and its economic and cultural capital.**

Known as Constantinople, the city was the capital of the Byzantine Empire from the 4th century to 1453. Thereafter the Ottomans ruled and changed its name to *Istanbul*. Today İstanbul is a fascinating city with countless things to see, an immense selection of hotels and restaurants as well as shopping miles with all of the international brand names. Accommodation can be found in the old part of the city Sultanahmet and to the north around the Taksim square.

## From Istanbul to Kuşadası: seaside resorts and the most important sites of antiquity

### SIGHTSEEING

#### SULTANAHMET CAMII (BLUE MOSQUE) ★ (⬚ 16/E4)

The most famous mosque in the city takes its name from the 20,000 amazing blue faience tiles that decorate the walls and minarets. The building was completed in 1616 by the architect of the court, Mehmed Aga. With its six minarets, it is one of the largest mosques of Islam. A mosque can only be visited outside of prayer times (usually daily 8:30am–12:15pm, 2–4:30pm and 5:45–6:30pm). Women have to cover their heads.

#### HAGIA SOPHIA (AYASOFYA) ★ (⬚ 16/E4)

The largest basilica of the Byzantine Empire was inaugurated in 537 AD. The dome is 18 floors high and has a diameter of 30 m /98 ft. Visitors should start on the ground floor and end on the galleries, where there is a magnificent view of the interior. Tue–Sun 9am–7pm (in the winter until 5pm) | admission approx. 30 lira | Sultanahmet

## TOPKAPI SARAYI
### (TOPKAPI PALACE) ★ ☆ (*16/F3*)

Seat of the Ottoman rulers for more than 400 years and the city's landmark. The palace grew gradually from 1460 onwards, behind the extensive walls, resulting in a confusing complex with gates, courtyards and outside pavilions. The precious items on display at Topkapi include jewellery and ceramics, a collection of weaponry and relics of the Prophet Mohammed. From its terrace, you have a view over the whole city. *Palace, harem and the Byzantine church Hagia Irene in the forecourt Wed–Mon mid-April–Oct 9am–6:45pm, Nov–mid-April 9am–4:45pm; counter closes 45 min. before closing | admission approx. 45, harem 20, Hagia Irene 28 lira | www. topkapisarayi.gov.tr*

## YEREBATAN SARNICI
### (SUNKEN PALACE) ★ (*16/E3*)

The Byzantine cistern, which resembles a palace, is supported by 336 Corinthian pillars, most of which are decorated with carvings. Two of them stand on Medusa heads. The cistern was built by Emperor Justinian in 532 in order to resolve the water crisis. Today INSIDER TIP concerts and other events take place here. *Daily 10am–6pm | admission 10 lira | www.yerebatan.com*

## GALATA BRIDGE
### (GALATA KÖPRÜSÜ) (*16/D–E2*)

The Galata Bridge crosses the Golden Horn at its mouth and connects the old town with the modern northern districts. The oldest construction to cross the Golden Horn was built in the 6th century on

The largest basilica of the Byzantine Empire: the Hagia Sophia in Istanbul

the instruction of Emperor Justinian I. In the 19th century, Mahmud II ordered the construction of a pontoon bridge, which lasted until 1912. In the same year, the first modern Galata Bridge was built at today's location, but in 1992, a fire damaged it badly. The bridge, as we know it today, is a reconstruction and its centre span can swing open.

## GKAPALI ÇARŞI
## (GRAND BAZAAR) ★
### (𝄙 16/D3)

A stroll through the largest covered bazaar, or the first "shopping centre" in the world (built 1461), is a must for every visitor to Istanbul: 75 acres, 61 streets and 4,400 shops. There are mainly carpets, leather, jewellery and souvenirs on offer. *Mon–Sat 8:30am–7pm | www.kapalicarsi.org.tr*

## ISTANBUL MUSEUM OF MODERN ART (İSTANBUL MODERN SANAT MÜZESI) ★ (𝄙 16/E1)

An unusual exterior with attractive contents: the private museum of contemporary Turkish art in Istanbul houses outstanding examples of modern Turkish art, ranging from the 19th century to today. A library and a cafe on the quay, overlooking Topkapi, round off the scene. *Info & opening hours at: www.istanbulmodern.org*

## ISTIKLAL STREET
## (İSTIKLAL CADDESI) ★ (𝄙 16/E1)

This 1.4 km/0.9 mi pedestrian avenue, with its nostalgic vintage tram, is the centre of vitality in Istanbul. The splendid historic boulevard runs through the district of Beyoğlu and stretches from the upper station exit of the funicular railway Tünel right up to Taksim Square. It boasts cinemas, bars and cafes, and a cultural side too: there are many lovely stores, antiquarian bookshops and art galleries.

## WHERE TO GO

### PRINCES' ISLANDS ★

In Turkish the islands are simply called Adalar (the islands). During the Byzantine era princes and royalty were exiled here. Today they are popular with locals as a place to escape to when they want a break from Istanbul. It takes about an hour to get to one of the nine islands, five of which are inhabited: Büyükada, Heybeliada, Kınalıada, Burgazada and Sedef. Ferries, motorboats and catamarans (faster) to the traffic-free islands are available from Kabataş (on the European side) and Kadiköy and Bostancı (on the Asian side).

### KADIKÖY

Istanbullus like to call the Asian side Kadıköy, once the ancient Chalcedon. It comprises the south-eastern city district on the Sea of Marmara. Featuring long shopping miles, a wonderful market and fish restaurants, bookshops and boutiques, Kadıköy is a vibrant bastion of middle-class secularism. Apart from mosques, there are also Armenian and Greek churches. More towards the south lies the upmarket district of Moda, offering extensive tea gardens along the seaside.

# KUŞADASI

**The name Kuşadası (Bird Island) derives from the nearby offshore "Pigeon Island" that has been connected to the mainland with a causeway since 1834.**
In the foreground of the castle lies the fishing port, from where the city centre stretches to the yacht harbour towards the north. Beyond the fishing port, next to the bazaar with its covered alleys, you will find the remains of the earlier Ottoman town.

# FOOD & DRINK

**More than just döner and kebabs – a Turkish dinner is a treat for the eyes and the palate.**

**The culinary diversity of Turkish cuisine is on par with that of any other Mediterranean country. The origin of many Turkish dishes can be traced back to the nomadic period of the early Turkish people, such as the various types of breads baked in clay ovens and the yoghurt or lamb dishes.**

A characteristic of Turkish cuisine is that the preparation is complex and time consuming, even for those dishes that seem to be quite simple. Breakfast, on the other hand, is less substantial: some white bread with feta cheese, olives and jam. At lunchtime it is usually a soup and a light vegetable dish. Vegetarians also get their money's worth, as salads and vegetable dishes are an integral part of Turkish menus. Many restaurants cater specially for vegetarian customers. The cold starters include vegetables of all kinds, crabs, mussels, calamari, humus (puréed chickpeas), seasonal salads and puff pastry pies. The Turkish expect a dish to taste of the main ingredient and not to be overpowered by sauces or covered in spices. *Lamb and beef* are usually grilled on a skewer (şiş), sparingly seasoned and served almost always without a sauce. The meat is usually accompanied by a salad and rice, bulgur or potatoes. In coastal towns *fish and seafood* naturally dominate the menu. Turkish *dessert* includes a variety of puff pastries, pies covered in syrup and chocolate puddings and there are also lots of succulent fruits. It is rounded off with a *cup of strong Turkish mocha* (*türk kahvesi*). Turkey's national drink is tea (*çay*).

## LOCAL SPECIALITIES

**Acı** – pastry made from very hot red peppers

**Baklava** – layers of pastry filled with pistachios or walnuts

**Biber dolması** – peppers filled with minced meat and rice

**Çiğ köfte** – hotly spiced finger food

**Helva** – "Turkish honey"

**İskender kebap** – slices of döner on flat bread with yoghurt, doused over with melted butter

**Sigara böreği** – puff pastry rolls, filled with feta cheese and parsley

## SIGHTSEEING

### INSIDER TIP GÜVERCINADA (PIGEON ISLAND)

Along the causeway, which is 350 m/1148 ft in length, you can walk to the Pigeon Island and admire the small 14th-century Genovese fortress. The tower served as an ammunition depot in later years. The peninsula is also home to some lovely and inviting teahouses, where you can spend a relaxing afternoon.

### KALEIÇI MOSQUE

The Grand Vizier Öküz Mehmet Paşa built the mosque in 1618. Renovated in 1830, it features a minaret on its right-hand side. The dome rests on a frame with 16 windows. *In the market area*

## SHOPPING

### BAZAAR 54

The largest and best address for carpets in the region is the town of Çamlık near Selçuk, where the carpet retail chain Bazaar 54 has "its own village". Carpets are not only sold, but also made here. *Daily 8am–8pm | Çamlık Köyü*

### KUŞADASI LEATHER

Since 1993, the company has been manufacturing and selling good leather products. Customers can request tailor-made jackets and other clothing. B*arbaros Hayrettin Pasa Bulvari | Cephane Sok. 2*

## WHERE TO GO

### INSIDER TIP DILEK YARIMADASI MILLI PARKI

The large national park on the Dilek peninsula south of Kuşadası is a wonderful nature reserve around ❄️ Mount Samsun, which offers fabulous views. Rare animals live in the national park, like lynx and wild

horses. *Daily 7am–8pm | admission 2.50 euros*

### EFES (EPHESUS) ⭐

A visit to the remains of the ancient Greek city of Ephesus is a special experience. The Temple of Artemis, dating from the 3rd century BC, was one of the Seven Wonders of the Ancient World. The ruins convey an idea of the splendour of the once monumental buildings. View the theatre, gymnasium, baths, agora (gathering place) and the reconstructed Library of Celsus. *(Info & opening hours at: www.ephesus. us; www.ephesustravelguide.com; wikitravel.org/en/Ephesus; or Turkland Travel: ephesustoursfromkusadasi.com*

Classic antiquity: ruins of Ephesus

# SHOPPING

## If you want to haggle in a Turkish bazaar you will need patience and a sense of humour

Shopping in Turkey requires time and a good eye! Bargaining for a melon or a sunhat in a retail store is just as uncommon here as it is at home as the prices are fixed. However, bazaar traders and souvenir shop owners are usually prepared to bargain, but it is not the done thing to bargain someone down for an item you are not genuinely interested in buying. And another tip: don't name a price first and your offer should never be lower than 30–40 per cent of what the trader suggested. In the more modern shops in the big cities the prices are as marked and not negotiable.

### ANTIQUES

Popular souvenirs to take back from Turkey include copper and brassware, hookahs, silver and gold jewellery, ceramics and antiques. Antiques are understood to be pieces that are more than a hundred years old. Taking antiques out of the country is only possible when they are accompanied by official documentation. Sometimes, after closer inspection, the newly acquired "antique" turns out to be a forgery.

### CARPETS

When buying a carpet, there are a few things to look out for. The first is the more knots the carpet has, the more valuable it is. As proof of quality workmanship, the patterns on the back of the carpet should be just as even as those on the front.

### GOLD & SILVER

Reputable jewellers will have a notice up with the day's current gold price and you should definitely request a certificate of authenticity! Always check for the stamp on the piece of jewellery.

### LEATHER & COTTON

Products made of leather and cotton are also among the classic Turkish souvenirs. The leather should not be stained and should be dyed well. There should also be a leather quality label which will ensure that you are not buying defective goods. You can also purchase cotton items at most markets at reasonable prices.

# TRAVEL TIPS

## Turkey: the most important addresses and information

### BERTHS

#### ▶ İSTANBUL

Cruise ships dock at the district of Galata in Istanbul. A new cruise-ship terminal, Galataport, is under construction. The centre of Istanbul is approx. 3 km/1.8 mi away. You can walk, or take a taxi or tram.

#### ▶ KUŞADASI

Kuşadası's cruise-ship port is located in the city centre, which is accessible on foot.

### INTERNET CAFÉS & WIFI

Turkey offers free wireless Internet and WiFi hotspots almost everywhere. In holiday resorts almost every café has the Internet, and you only have to request the access code. Due to all this public access, it is not recommended to do your bank transactions from your hotel room or from a coffee table! Surfing the net costs about 4.50 lira per hour.

### PHONES & MOBILE PHONES

In Turkey, telecommunication is a state-owned enterprise and phone calls home are expensive! Between 8pm and 6am night rates apply. Prepaid phone cards are available in post offices and in kiosks (telefon karti) for public phone boxes. Cheaper still are the prepaid service cards: you rub away the number on the card and dial via a service number, where you first have to enter your secret code and then your inter-national number. Mobiles are very common in Turkey and there is good reception countrywide. Mobile phones from abroad are subject to roaming charges and these can be expensive.

### TIPPING

A ten per cent tip is commonplace – and expected – in restaurants and hotels. When paying for a taxi ride, you can round up.

### WHEN TO GO

The best time to travel to Turkey is from April to the end of October. Mediterranean summers are very hot, and on the Anatolian highland and in east Turkey the heat is also very dry. Winter, on the other hand, means lots of snow and icy cold. In winter, which can stretch into April, there is also often snow in Istanbul. The weather at the Black Sea is often cloudy and humid.

### BUDGETING

| | | |
|---|---|---|
| Coffee | £1.60/$2.50 | |
| | *for a cup of coffee* | |
| Tour bus | £23.50/$37 | |
| | *from Istanbul to Bodrum* | |
| Snack | £1.20/$1.80 | |
| | *for a kebab* | |
| Hammam | £20/$31 | |
| | *for a visit* | |

# CYPRUS

**Aphrodite, the beautiful goddess of love, is said to have been a Cyprus girl.**

This sunny island in the farthest east of the Mediterranean is truly a proper home for a beauty expert, with its long dream beaches, crystal-clear waters and wild and dramatic coasts. Two striking mountain ranges also offer rural highlights. The historic and cultural legacy includes Gothic cathedrals, Turkish mosques, Byzantine monasteries and crusaders' castles. If it wasn't for this big ugly scar cutting right through the island and its vibrant capital ... a border drawn by force in 1974. While the border is omnipresent in Cypriots' minds and emotions, as a visitor you'll hardly be aware of it. You can spend a relaxing Mediterranean holiday as peacefully as anywhere else.

## LIMASSOL

**This is a genuine harbour town! You can witness winning jackpots and luxury yachts. Limassol (Greek: Lemesós) is home to the wealthy. Living side by side with the 180,000 residents, the city has a wealthy Russian population and well-managed shipping companies. That explains the skyscrapers, luxury marina and elegant lakeside promenade.**

Limassol residents certainly understand their city, where modern life doesn't overrule traditional heritage,

Photo: Against the historical backdrop, life in Limassol's breeze

# Fed up with the city's hustle and bustle? Then you can venture in no time into the mountains, and explore the castles and flora and fauna

but rather includes it. Instead of leaving the old town around the historic marina to the nostalgists, the young crowd has won back this neighbourhood. The run-down quarter around the market hall has become a magnet for partygoers. Old workshops have a new lease of life as cafés and bars. Popular locations are tucked away in tiny sidestreets. The marina is an exclusive district; with its squares, small backstreets and bridges over the water, it has a touch of Venice.

## SIGHTSEEING

**INSIDER TIP** 6X6 CENTRE FOR PHOTOGRAPHY

Three amenities in one: a gallery, photo studio and museum. Historical cameras from the era when "watch the birdie!" was still the phrase are displayed alongside modern exhibitions. Creative input and specialist discussion are top of the agenda here. *Information & opening hours: www. centreforphotography6x6.com*

### CAROB MILL

Factory style. The old *carob mill* (1937) is enjoying a second lease of life as a cultural centre: first, it's time for a freshly brewed beer at the *Draught (daily noon–2pm)*, then for one of the top exhibitions *(www.lanitisfoundation. org)*, followed by the *Carob Museum (daily 10am–8pm | free admission)* and to relax after a fine dinner at the *Karatello Tavern*, next to the floodlit castle. *Vasilissis Street | by the castle*

### CYPRUS LAND ★

Give your inner child free rein! Even adults can enjoy watching archery and jousting. The medieval park is perfectly aligned with Limassol's glorious history, which picked up the pace with King Lionheart. Plus, a 3D model of the island and historical handcraftsmanship – perfect for an entertaining afternoon. *Daily 9am–8pm | admission 14 euros | 12 Andokidou Street | Germasogia | www. cyprusland.com.cy*

## SPORTS & BEACHES

City beach – on the plus side, there are bars and it's right in the centre. On the minus side: the four-lane B1 runs right next to it. A more secluded and shadier spot is at *Dasoudi Beach,* with its own woodland area. The beaches on the west side of the city are amazing, like the long *Lady's Mile Beach* at the salt lake as well as wide *Koúrion Beach. Governor's Beach* is also charming. How about some extras, like freediving *(www.freediving-cyprus.com)* or standup paddling *(www. supclublimassol.com)* on the waves?

## WHERE TO GO

### 'ALASSA ★

A diving station instead of a church! To build the Koúris dam about 14 km/8.7 mi north-west of Limassol, 'Alassa village had to be resettled in 1985. Only the church remained and was flooded. Today, it is an attraction for divers. The church tower is visible again in the dry summers. It's a bizarre sight and great motif for a photo.

### KOLÓSSI

Roaming through this fortified castle, about 12 km/7.5 mi from Limassol, is rather eerie. Everything still looks intact – rough stone walls, small windows, a single chimney for a vast hall. The crusaders must have frozen here! *Kolóssi Castle* once belonged to the order of Saint John crusaders, which had its headquarters here until 1309. *Daily from 8.15am | admission 2.50 euros*

# OH, YOU JUICY MELON!

Bay laurels grow in the park, thyme on the beach and capers by the roadside. Back home, we are familiar with these herbs from the spice rack – in Cyprus, they grow everywhere. Besides, Cypriots are fortunate to supply stock all their fruit and vegetable stores with home-grown fruits from the island. The plants are large and small – bananas from Páfos are small, but sweet, while watermelons can weigh up to 15 kg/33 lbs. Tall pine and cypress trees grow in the Tróodos mountains, whereas in Akámas the wild orchids are miniature.

# FOOD & DRINK

## Cyprus offers tasty local food and relics from colonial days

The style of cuisine on Cyprus is multi-cultural and the product of the many residents who earlier added their own creative dishes. Nowadays, mum's recipes from all around the world and foreign spices are on the Cypriot menu. Pulses are popular both in cold and warm dishes, in salads you can find all kinds of green leaves – from fresh coriander to wild herbs.

A lot of vegetables are also eaten raw or pickled (caper twigs). A *mezé* (pronounced "mee-see") consists of 12 or 20 different dishes served on small plate. The *Cypriot breakfast (www. cyprusbreakfast.eu)* versus the eternal English breakfast with sausages, bacon and eggs is becoming more popular. Venture into the *archaic tavernas* and modern gourmet temples of the local Cypriots. You can enjoy authentic home-style cooking in the former, and discover creations by *young Cypriot chefs*, who combine their skills with traditional, locally sourced ingredients in the latter. The cake shops on Cyprus are *temples of temptation*, which sell oriental sweet pastries, cakes and biscuits as well as crème desserts and mousses ... simply everything! Order a Cypriot *mocha* in a coffeehouse or *Kafeníon* (Turkish *kah-vehani*). You ask for this as a café and explain how you like it: *skétto* (Turkish *sadez*) – without sugar; *métrio* (Turkish *orta*) – with a little sugar; *warígliko* (Turkish *sekerli*) – with a lot of sugar.

### LOCAL SPECIALITIES

**Afélia** – marinated pork, braised in red wine and fairly fatty

**Dolmádes** – vine leaves stuffed with rice and sometimes mincemeat

**Halloumi** – Cypriot cheese made with sheep's and goat's milk

**Kúpes/kupékia** – doughballs made of coarsely ground wheat, stuffed with pork mince, onions and parsley

**Scheftaliá** – well seasoned grilled sausages made of pork mince in a lamb's stomach lining

**Tachíni** – a thick sauce made of sesame, olive oil, garlic, lemon juice

# SHOPPING

## Not off the peg: tailor-made clothing, natural super food and country art.

Boring souvenirs? No, thank you! Those looking for cool and special souvenirs should visit Cyprus's retro and vintage shops.

### LACE

Only available here! If you're thinking of the design of grandma's sewing basket, you're missing out. In Lefkara, exclusive handmade fine lace is produced – it's not available anywhere else in the world. "Lefkaritika" products range from table cloths to decorative patches for home-made clothes. Admitteldly, they're not cheap, but it's worth acquiring a piece of luxury for back home.

### TAILOR-MADE

Why not have a favourite item custom-made? Clothes, bags or shoes – all made to your design. There are tailors in every town and for shoes in particular you should head for *Lydias Shoes* (Limassol) and *Kelpis Shoes* (Páfos). Fabulous bags are made at *Pana's Bag* (Limassol).

### NATURAL COSMETICS

On the island of the goddess of beauty, Aphrodite, beauty products are a must. Cosmetics made with donkey's milk are hugely popular (directly available from the donkey farm in Skarínou). Olive soaps and creams are bestsellers and also available in souvenir shops. Don't forget to try the products made with rose water! The petals are freshly picked and distilled and then made into face water, shampoo and creams.

### SUPERFOOD

Feed your suitcase with lots of delicious food. Cyprus's Mediterranean cuisine has plenty of healthy treats to offer: *carob syrup, soujouko* ("snakes" made from almonds and wine syrup) or *loukoumi* (jelly treats) for sweet-lovers, *halloumi* (cheese for baking) and *pastourma* (sausage preserved in red wine) as savoury snacks and of course the famous *Commandaria*, now the oldest wine in the world.

# TRAVEL TIPS

## Cyprus: the most important addresses and information

### BERTH

▶ **LIMASSOL**

The cruise-ship port of Limassol has a modern terminal featuring, among other things, a variety of shops. The centre is approx. 4 km/2.5 mi away, and taxis, shuttle-bus and public bus services provide transport.

### DRINKING WATER

It is safe to drink the water in the south of the island, but the tap water in northern Cyprus is unsuitable for drinking.

### PHONE & MOBILE PHONE

Cypriot phone numbers have eight digits in the south, seven in the north, and have to be dialled in full even when only making a local call. Phone calls between northern and southern Cyprus are considered international calls. To dial the north from abroad (and from the south), dial *0090* followed by *392* for landline numbers or *533* or *542* for mobile phone numbers. The initial *0* of these numbers (provided in this guide) is then omitted. For landline calls within northern Cyprus, the area code *0392* is omitted. From abroad to the south, the country code is *00357*. Country codes: *UK 0044, Ireland 0353, Canada & US 001.*

## BUDGETING

| Taxi | £0.65/0.75 / $0.85/0.95 |
| | *per km/0.6 mi (day/night)* |
| Mocha | £1.75 / $2.25 |
| | *a cup* |
| Deckchair | £5.30–6.15 / $6.70–7.85 |
| | *a day for two* |
| Wine | from £9 / $11 |
| | *for a bottle in a restaurant* |
| Kebab | £3.10–4 / $3.90–5 |
| | *for one portion in pita bread* |

### TIME DIFFERENCE

The south of Cyprus is two hours ahead of the UK all year round, the north is one hour ahead of the UK in summer and two hours in winter.

### TIPPING

While the bills issued by hotels and restaurants already include a service charge, if you were happy with the service, staff appreciate a tip (5–10 %).

### WHEN TO GO

Cyprus is an all-year-round destination, even though between December and April only hardy folk will want to swim in the sea. Nature lovers appreciate the months of March and April for the spectacular flowers.

# EGYPT

**Celebrate a myriad of unbeatable superlatives: only in the country on the Nile.**
Ancient Egypt, the cradle of civilization, calls for celebration! Here, we revere humankind's oldest administration and government systems. We admire unsurpassed stone-building techniques masterminded by ancient Egyptian architects. We venerate the Step Pyramid of Saqqara, the earliest attestation of their mastery. We marvel at the last remaining Wonder of the Ancient World, the Pyramids of Giza. We gaze at archaeologists' priceless discoveries, notably the relics of ancient scripts, the oldest ever found in the long history of humankind.

Equally important, though, is another eminent superlative: Egypt is the oldest travel destination of the world! For millenniums, the country lured scientists, pilgrims, adventurers and inquisitive minds alike. Still today visitors and explorers are attracted by its temples and pharaohs' tombs, resounding with names like Ramses, Tutankhamun, Nefertiti or Akhenaten; its splendid mosques and churches of one of the oldest Christian communities in the world; its lush gardens along the Nile and its pilgrimage destinations. Against this background, one can logically conclude that Egypt is the birthplace of tourism.

# ALEXANDRIA

**There are hardly any remaining relics of ancient Alexandria, where once the Ptolemaic dynasty ruled and Cleopatra**

Magical culture of the pharaohs, idyllic landscapes and impressive underwater worlds – Egypt offers a lot

committed suicide. **Even though very little is reminiscent of its ancient grandeur, Alexandria has a special atmosphere evocative of a blend of European and Oriental influences.**

It is easy to find one's way in the city, which sprawls over a narrow stretch between the sea and *Lake Mariout*. Near the centre, the Pharos peninsula extends into the sea. One can sense old-world charm by strolling through the European quarter of Alexandria, just south of the Corniche, between the squares of *Midan Saad Zaghloul* and *Midan Orabi*. Especially lovely are walks along the Mediterranean seafront and in the *Montazah Palace Gardens* (admission 1 £E) on the eastern side of the city.

## SIGHTSEEING

INSIDER TIP **ALEXANDRIA NATIONAL MUSEUM**

Spread out across three floors, the former Bassili Pasha Palace exhibition, curated by the Italian Maurizio De Paulo, can be viewed. It covers Greek-Roman, Coptic and Islamic eras. *Daily 9am–4.30pm | admission 40 £E | Tariq Al-Horreya 110*

### BIBLIOTHECA ALEXANDRINA ⭐

Alexandria's historic library burnt down in 49 BC. The architecture of the modern new building is reminiscent of a tilted disc, which measures 160 m/ 525 ft in diameter. Worth seeing are the collections of old manuscripts and historic photos of the city. *Sun–Thu 10am–4pm | admission 60 £E | Al-Shatby | www.bibalex.org*

### INSIDER TIP ELIYAHU HANAVI SYNAGOGUE

Catch a glimpse of Alexandria's cosmopolitan past. Originally built in 1354, the synagogue was rebuilt in 1850. Unfortunately, religious services came to end in 2012. *Daily 10am–5pm | Sharia Nabi Daniel | Visits by appointment: call mobile 0122 7 03 10 31*

### FORT QAITBEY

This 15th-century fortress houses a naval museum and is built on the site of the once famous *Pharos Lighthouse* that was destroyed by an earthquake in the 14th century *(admission 10 £E)*. *Daily 9am–4pm | admission 25 £E | in the Eastern Harbour*

### ABU AL-ABBAS AL-MURSI MOSQUE

Alexandria's most magnificent mosque was rebuilt several times. The present edifice dates from 1943. *South of Fort Qaitbey on the Corniche*

### ROMAN THEATRE ⭐

The ancient theatre was unearthed in 1964; it could seat 800 spectators. Admire the INSIDER TIP mosaic flooring with depictions of birds in the *Villa of the Birds*. *Daily 8am–5pm | admission 15 £E, Villa of the Birds 10 £E | Kom Al-Dikka Sharia Yussif*

## SHOPPING

### ATTARINE DISTRICT

The stores and little shops in the Attarine district are replete with all kinds of jumble and trinkets, as well as antiquarian books. South of the Sharia Al-Mitwalli

Impressive architecture: Alexandria's Abu Al-Abbas Al-Mursi Mosque

# FOOD & DRINK

## Since time immemorial, the fertile Nile valley has been providing food and nourishment

**To a certain extent, Egyptian cuisine stands on two pillars: *fuul* and *ta'ameya*.**

*Fuul* (ful medames) is a dish made of mashed fava beans that require cooking for hours, flavoured with sesame sauce, lemon, spices, oil and sometimes tomato. *Ta'ameya* are crispy fried balls, similar to falafel, but made with a higher content of bean paste (usually crushed fava beans instead of chickpeas). Pita or flatbread is served with all dishes, sauces, soups, stews and meat or pasterma. Many small side dishes, called *mezze*, embellish each meal and include delicious sauces and other cold dishes. The most popular side dishes are *tehina*, an oily sesame-paste, and *hummus*, a chickpea-purée, and *baba ghannoug*, mashed eggplant. You can also sample *mahshi*, dishes made of stuffed vegetables or stuffed cabbage and grapevine leaves. Each meal is complemented with a small plate of *torshi* – salty pickled onions, radishes, carrots and other vegetables.

After a meal, mocha or black tea is served. Tea, called shai, is served with sugar only, or sample *shai bi-nana*, tea with mint leaves. Tea is frequently enjoyed in *coffee shops*. Lovers of freshly pressed fruit juices will find a paradise in Egypt. A selection of reasonably priced juices is offered everywhere, often made with puréed fruit. Especially tasty: INSIDER TIP *fresh mango juice* between July and November.

### LOCAL SPECIALITIES

**Bitingan ma'li bi-toum** – fried eggplant with garlic

**Fatier** – Egyptian variation of pizza, made with crispy puff-pastry, with sweet or spicy toppings or fillings

**Kuszbariyya** – oven-baked fish with tomato sauce

**Mahallabiyya** – dessert made with rice flour

**Shawarma** – the Arabian form of doner kebab

**Wara ainab** – grapevine leaves, stuffed with spicy rice

# CAIRO

**The largest city in Africa sprawls into the Sahara desert like a giant ragged-fringed carpet with a mended and touched-up centre: a gigantic patchwork pattern of civilization.**

Evenly covered with a sand-hued veil, Cairo's residential districts stretch far out towards the horizon, interspersed with mosques, minarets and principal arterial thoroughfares. In the centre, skyscrapers seam the Nile – the vital source of life – as it cuts through the concrete landscape. Without the Nile, Cairo would not be able to exist in the middle of the desert.

## SIGHTSEEING

### MUSEUM OF EGYPTIAN ANTIQUITIES (EGYPTIAN MUSEUM) ★ (*① 17/C2*)

Egypt's most famous museum houses 100,000 objects relating Pharaonic history: statuary, coffins, mummies, wigs, script tablets, fabrics and much more. Many artefacts, however, remain inaccessible to the public, since they are stowed in storerooms. Enthusiasts spend a few days in the museum. Highlights on the top floor are the two mummy rooms (the second one opened in 2006) and funerary items from the tomb of Tutankhamun. Apart from the inside coffin – 225 kg/496 lb of solid gold – and other precious items from the young Pharaoh's last resting place, his funerary mask is the showstopper of the museum. *Daily 9am–6pm | admission 50 £E, Mummy Room 100 £E | Midan Al-Tahrir*

### KHAN EL-KHALILI BAZAAR

In this enormous and bustling maze of winding streets and twisting alleys, there are myriads of little shops, workshops and coffee houses. Seek out the area adjacent to the Hussein Hotel and the alley of *Sikket Al-Badestan* for Oriental souvenirs. Workshops of brass-, copper-, gold- and silversmiths are located in the *Sharia Al-Mu'izz Li-Din Allah*, east of the Sharia El-Muski.

### CAIRO TOWER ⚆ (*① 17/B2*)

On a clear day, when Cairo's haze opens up, you can even see the pyramids from the observation deck of the television tower, which is 187 m/613 ft tall. The cafe and revolving rooftop restaurant of the tower are mediocre.

# RAMADAN

Once a year, for four weeks, the entire rhythm of life in Egypt changes and follows rules other than those that apply during the remainder of the year. During this time, between dawn and sunset, religious Muslims abstain from consuming food and drinking liquids. Less religious Muslims also join the fasting period, maybe for a week or two. Businesses, government offices and companies close three hours ahead of sunset. At the end of every fasting day, after sunset, the daily fast is broken and the post-fast-breaking feast, called Iftar, starts. Then people stay at home and enjoy a festive meal. The pre-fasting meal, or last meal at night, is referred to as Suhoor. Until then, people go out to coffee houses or festive tents, enjoy a shisha (water pipe), tea and coffee. The four-week Ramadan ends with a three-day-long feast to celebrate the breaking of the fast, referred to as *Eid Al-Fitr*.

## ISLAMIC OLD TOWN ⭐

The main road of the old town is the *Sharia Al-Mu'izz Li-Din Allah* and is 1.5 km/1 mi long. Speckled with Unesco world heritage sites, the neighbourhood abounds with market women, mopeds, milk-rice vendors, mosques and madrasas (education centres). The *Al-Hakim* Mosque is located at the Bab Al-Futuh. From there, 300 m/984 ft away, to the left, is the *Darb El-Asfar*, the Yellow Alley. Its heart is the Ottoman merchant house *Beit Al-Suheimi*, dating from the 17th century. Further to the south, you will find the enormous Qalawun Complex, built in 1284. Opposite the *Madrasa al-Nasir Muhammad ibn Qalawun* is the *Textile Museum (daily 9am–4.30pm | admission 30 £E | Sharia Al-Mu'izz Li-Din Allah/Corner Beit al-Qadi)*, adjoining the bazaar of the brass- and goldsmiths and the spice-merchants' market.

## COPTIC QUARTER ⭐

The Greeks called the settlement Babylon; the Romans built a fortress there and retained the name. Today the neighbourhood's name is Old Cairo *(Masr Al-Qadimah)*. It is older than the Islamic city centre; the main inhabitants are Orthodox Christians. Some of Egypt's prettiest and oldest churches stand here. Especially worth a visit: the Hanging Church of *Al-Muallaqah*, more than 1000 years old, with Baroque-evoking towers.

## AL-AZHAR MOSQUE ⭐

Worldwide, about a billion Sunnite Muslims highly revere this institution, also named "The Most Resplendent Congregational Mosque", and consider it the most prestigious theological authority. Shortly after it was built in 971, the mosque was declared a university. You should definitely admire its interior courtyard. For 10 £E, you can climb up to the top of the minaret. *Midan Al-Hussein | www.azhar.edu.eg*

Vibrant activity in Cairo's Old Town

## INSIDER TIP ▶ AL-GHURI MOSQUE

The place of worship is a genuine jewel of Mamluk architecture dating from the 16th century. During the last renovation of the mosque, workers discovered a gilded wall frieze that was hidden behind wood for a hundred years. *Sharia Al-Mu'izz Li-Din Allah/corner of Sharia Al-Azhar*

## MOSQUE OF IBN TULUN ⭐

Experts consider this mosque as one of the most beautiful in the world. Built between 876 and 879, its harmonious and clear forms remained virtually unchanged. At the entrance, the INSIDER TIP *Gayer-Anderson Museum (daily 9am–4pm | admission free)* shows historical domestic living in two Mamluk nobility houses. *Midan Ahmed Ibn Tulun | Sayyida Zeinab*

## MUSEUM OF ISLAMIC ART ⭐

The building dates from 1887 and houses the world's largest, most precious collection of Islamic art and Islamic artisanship. *Daily 9am–5pm | admission 30 £E | Sharia Bur Sa'id*

# SHOPPING

Let your senses indulge in a colourful and noisy feast of bazaars, markets and shop-lined streets

For many travellers, Egypt is a shopping experience, but for others, a nightmare: in bazaars, vendors accost passers-by and expect them to haggle over prices. In the end, shoppers still wonder whether they were taken for a ride or not. Do not let this put you off, since Egyptians are also hagglers. It is, however, not customary to bargain over prices at grocers, supermarkets and in shopping malls.

## ARTISANSHIP

You will find excellent Egyptian artisanship and craftsmanship almost everywhere in Cairo. Head to *Khan El-Khalili*, where metalsmiths buzz along an entire street. Berbers in the Siwa Oasis make the best silver jewellery. The workshop of INSIDER TIP NADIM *(www.nadim.org)* is renowned in the whole country for its splendid woodwork, small tea tables, Koran holders and stands, and picture frames featuring the Oriental *mashrabiyya* design.

## MALLS & BOUTIQUES

The largest mall of the country is the *Ci-*tystars Centre* in Cairo, where two floors are brimming with a variety of stores and shops with souvenirs. The more modern boutiques are also worth visiting: Egypt is famous for its cotton, and the well-made pieces boast an excellent quality.

## SPICES, TEA & PERFUME

Ice-cold *karkadeh*, an Upper-Egyptian hibiscus tea, is an ideal summer refreshment. Most perfumeries maintain honest service principles, although tourists frequently report unpleasant experiences. Therefore, be particularly alert and ensure that you get the exact quantity you requested and that the wrapped-up product you receive contains what you have paid for!

## WATER PIPES (SHISHA)

If you would you like to take a water pipe (shisha) home, you can assemble your own personal design. The tobacco is available in a variety of tastes. It is also considerably cheaper in Egypt than in your home country.

## PYRAMIDS OF GIZA ⭐

Built more than 4500 years ago, and venerated as the last remaining representative of the Seven Wonders of the Ancient World, the pyramids of *Cheops*, *Chephren* and *Mykerinos* predominate on the Giza Plateau, on the outskirts of the greater Cairo/Giza-area. South-west of the pyramids, a hill offers a stunning view of the three monumental structures and the Nile valley, especially in the morning and evening. *Daily from 8am | admission 75 £E, plus Chephren- and Cheops pyramids each 100 £E, all other pyramids from 40 £E, Solar Barge 50 £E.*

## CITADEL ☾

Salah Al-Din, known as Saladin, conquered the Christian Crusaders and built the citadel more than 800 years ago. Today's structure is 150 years old. Crowning the complex, the *Ottoman Mosque of Muhammad Ali (Alabaster Mosque | closed during prayers)* presides majestically over the city. Adjacent to it stands the smaller Al-Nasir Muhammad Mosque. *Daily 9am–4pm | admission 50 £E | between Midan Al-Qal'a and Sharia Salah Salem*

## MOSQUE OF SULTAN HASSAN

The edifice dates from 1372 and resembles a fortress. For many centuries, it featured the tallest minaret of the city. The resplendent interior is awe-inspiring. The well-balanced arrangement of halls enhances a solemn silence, and behind the splendour of the bronze portals stands the Sultan's mausoleum. *Midan Al-Qal'a*

WHERE TO GO

## MEMPHIS AND SAQQARA ⭐

Not much has remained of ancient Memphis. At the open-air museum, a small building *(admission 50 £E)* shelters the colossal statue of Ramses II. The *Alabaster*

The Step Pyramid of Djoser

*Sphinx* stands west of the building, a mere 200 m/650 ft away. Juxtaposed with this site, the ancient Memphis necropolis at *Saqqara* can still be viewed, featuring a host of temples and tombs *(admission 90 £E)*. The *Step Pyramid of Djoser* is considered humankind's first monumental structure made of stone. Catch a sight of the restored *Serapeum*, an immense underground burial place for sacred Apis bulls. *Daily 8am-4pm*

TRAVEL WITH KIDS

### DREAMPARK

The large amusement park close to the capital entices with 47 riding opportunities and daily events in the Rosa Amphitheatre. Great fun for the whole family! *Info & opening hours at: www.dreamparkegypt.com*

# TRAVEL TIPS

## BERTH

▶ **ALEXANDRIA**

Cruise ships dock in the so-called West Harbour. The city centre is approx. 4 km/2 mi away. A large number of taxis in the harbour area provide transport.

## CUSTOMS

When travelling to Egypt, some items for personal use are exempt from duty, for instance, 1l perfume, up to 200 cigarettes or 250g of tobacco and 1l spirits or 2l wine with less than 22 vol % alcohol content, or 4l sparkling wine. Until two days after entering Egypt, you may buy an additional 3l of spirits in duty-free shops. There is a strict ban on the export of antiques/antiquities and of protected animal and plant species.

## HEALTH

Special vaccinations are not prescribed. However, vaccinations against tetanus and poliomyelitis are advisable. For visits to the Nile Delta and oases, malaria prophylaxis is recommended for the period from July to November. In rural areas, there is a risk of hepatitis-A-contagion. Refrain from swimming in still-standing waters and in the Nile, for there is the danger of bilharzia. Only consume fruit and vegetables that have been peeled or thoroughly rinsed. Drink only bottled mineral water. Medical and health services in the tourist destinations and in Cairo are adequate. Should you travel in the desert, it is advisable to take disinfectants and pain medication with you. Most medicines are freely available. You will have to pay medical treatments in cash. Above all, take out travel medical

insurance before you embark on your trip. More info and updates for travellers from the UK, USA, Canada and Australia at:
UK: https://www.gov.uk/browse/abroad/travel-abroad and https://www.gov.uk/foreign-travel-advice/egypt/health
USA: https://www.state.gov/travel/ and https://travel.state.gov/content/travel/en/international-travel/before-you-go/travelers-with-special-considerations/cruise-ship-passengers.html
CAN: https://travel.gc.ca/travelling/advisories
AUS: https://smartraveller.gov.au/guide/all-travellers/health/Pages/default.aspx

## INTERNET & WIFI

For internet surfing, internet cafes charge 2 £E and more per hour. Many cafes and restaurants offer guests free WiFi. Cheap prepaid cards and data sticks for mobile internet access are available at outlets of mobile service providers, like Vodafone, Mobinil and Etisalat.

## LANDMINES

In the deserts and on the coasts of the Red Sea there are still landmines from wars. Never leave roads. Should you do so, ensure that a local guide accompanies you. Take warning signs seriously and do not trespass barriers.

## PHONE & MOBILE PHONE

Calls to other countries are expensive, prices range from 9 £E upwards per minute. When making calls from your own mobile device, the price greatly increases. The dialling code for Egypt is 0020, for the UK 0044, for the USA and Canada 001, and for Australia 0061. Before embarking on your trip, get advice from your mobile phone service provider in your home country. If you use an Egyptian prepaid card, there are no extra costs for incoming calls.

## PHOTOGRAPHY

With the exception of military installations, ports, bridges, train stations and airports you can photograph just about everything. The use of flashlights and tripods is not allowed in museums and pharaoh tombs. In the larger museums, there is a no-photo policy.

## PRICES & CURRENCY

One Egyptian pound (£E or EGP) has 100 piasters (PT). Banks and foreign exchange bureaus take travellers' cheques and exchange currencies. At ATMs, you can withdraw cash with credit or Maestro cards and a PIN. Restaurants, hotels and businesses also accept cards. Take cash when visiting oases. Keep all your foreign-exchange slips. You will need them when changing currency back; you may import/export a maximum of 5000 £E.

## TIME DIFFERENCE

Egypt is located in the Eastern European time zone (EET) and time is calculated according to Coordinated Universal Time (UCT) or Greenwich Mean Time (GMT) + 2 hours. Summer time has been discontinued.

## TIPPING

In restaurants and cafes, it is customary to tip between five and ten percent of the total amount.

## WHEN TO GO

The best time to travel to Egypt is between October and April. Severe afternoon heat conditions prevail during the other months, when temperatures climb to over 40°C/104°F, especially in Upper Egypt.

## WOMEN

Egyptian men frequently accost and woo female tourists. This can be a nuisance but it is generally not dangerous. Avoid everything that could encourage such behaviour: wear a wedding ring, and if need be, borrow one. Tell them about your husband and children. Avoid over-crowded buses because of ubiquitous gropers. Avoid attire that over-emphasises your body, as well as short skirts and off-the-shoulder tops. Short sleeves are acceptable. If you are the victim of harassment, shout loudly so that bystanders can hear you. Women should avoid large gatherings of people at all costs, for instance demonstrations and protest actions, because attacks have occurred in such situations in recent years.

## BUDGETING

| | |
|---|---|
| Tea | from £0.15/$0.20 *per glass* |
| Entrance | about £5.50/$7.40 *for the Pyramids of Giza (excluding Cheops)* |
| Snack | from £0.25/$0.35 *for a falafel sandwich* |

# TUNISIA

An evening scene in the fasting month of Ramadan: fathers and yuppies pushing and shoving through the narrow shop-lined alleyways of the Medina in Tunis; veiled women strolling arm in arm with girls in hipster pants, passing boutiques and surveying window displays.

In the cafes, young couples gather around water pipes; lounge music swirls through the souks. A few steps further, one hears the sound of muffled drums. In Tunisia, tradition and modernism do not constitute opposites; they are rather complementary aspects. For a long time, Tunisia, as a seaside paradise, has made a name for itself. There is still much to discover inland: from Punic places of sacrifice and Roman temples to fortified mosques and Oriental palaces. Culture buffs will be delighted.

## TUNIS

The chirping of thousands of starlings, the hooting of cars in seemingly eternal traffic congestions, and the calls of jasmine sellers all intermingle to create a capital-city-tune. Tunis is loud, but that is only a first impression.

When taking a closer look, this fascinating city reveals concealed charms and quiet corners. It lures with a well-dosed blend of Oriental and Western influences and overwhelms with cascades of exotic fragrances emanating from the glittering world of its souks. It was not for nothing that Unesco added the city's medieval heart, the Medina, to its world heritage list.

Carthaginians and Romans once enjoyed life on the north coast, and today it attracts the world with beaches and holiday resorts

## SIGHTSEEING

### AL-ZAYTOUNA MOSQUE (GREAT MOSQUE/MOSQUE OF THE OLIVE) ★ (*ᗪ 18/B3*)

In the 8th century, a place of worship was first built on this site. Over time, it was restored and converted several times. From the 13th century onwards, Zaytouna and its adjoining education centres (madrasas) proceeded to become the most important university in the country and the third most important one in the Mus-lim world. Non-Muslims are not allowed to enter the interior, but from the courtyard, it is possible to catch a glimpse of the dimly lit prayer room. The quadrila-teral minaret, decorated with stucco and majolica, is an eye-catcher. *Sat–Thu 8am–2pm | 5 TND*

### MUSÉE NATIONAL DU BARDO (BARDO MUSEUM) ★

The archaeological museum in the former Bey's Palace, a historical building, war-rants a visit not only because of its mag-

Absolutely Oriental: Tunisian souks

nificent rooms. The Bardo houses one of the largest collections of Roman mosaics in the world. Among the famous mosaics, there is a depiction of the poet Virgil receiving the verses of the "Aeneid" from two muses (3rd century). The museum also traces the Punic and early Christian eras. April–Sept Tue–Sun 9am–5pm, Oct–March 9.30am–4.30pm | Quartier Bardo

### INSIDER TIP PLACE HALFAOUINE (☐ 18/A1)

The old town quarter surrounding Place Halfaouine is located north of the actual Medina. It became famous because of the film "Halfaouine: Child of the Terraces" (1990) by director Férid Boughedir. Once a kind of demi-world, the neighbourhood is today a relaxed haven, where one can while away the time and enjoy plane-tree-shaded cafes at leisure.

### COMPLEXE DES TROIS MEDERSAS (THREE MADRASAS) (☐ 18/B3)

Close to the Great Mosque, three madrasas dating from the end of the 18th century are tucked away behind high portals. They are the earlier education centres of the Al-Zaytouna Mosque. Today, only the *Medersa du Palmier* (Madrasa of the Palm Tree) still offers Koran studies. The *Medersa Bachia* is currently a training centre for young artisans. *Irregular opening hours | Rue des Libraires*

### SOUKS (☐ 17/B3)

Souk, denoting market, is the name of the inner-city neighbourhood. Its narrow alleys and squares are lined with tiny shops, and straw mats and barrel vaults provide shelter against the heat of the sun. Check out one of the most interesting souks, INSIDER TIP *Souk ech-Chechia*, which offers woollen hats, known as chechias, the pride of every tradition-conscious Tunisian. Moreover, here you will also find one of the most popular cafes of the Medina, the *Café Chaouechin*.

# VEILS

In earlier times, mostly older women and women in rural regions used to wear headscarves to cover their hair, neck and shoulders. Today one sees more and more young girls wearing headscarves. However, many women regard the growing and widespread use of headscarves with concern, for it is considered a token of the re-Islamization of Tunisia. It can be generally assumed that many families once again compel young girls to wear a veil.

# FOOD & DRINK

Exhilarate your senses! Let your eyes, palate and nose feast on spicy herbs and hot harissa

**Are you onshore and suffering from hunger? Then get a taste of the North African culinary adventure. Seize the moment and venture out to a genuine traditional local restaurant that will regale you with typical Tunisian specialities. Savour authentic delights of Tunisian cuisine and its multitude of spices. You will certainly be delighted!**

Yet, as a precaution, rather refrain from consuming raw or under-cooked food, for instance salads or medium- to rare-cooked meat and fish. There is really no need to eat these, since Tunisian cuisine offers many cooked delicacies, including a salad made with fried vegetables, known as salade mechouia.

*Harissa*, a hot red spicy chili-pepper paste, is the most important ingredient used by Tunisian foodies. The paste contains spices and herbs, including curcuma, coriander and caraway seeds, saffron, red chili pepper and mint. Capers and olives are important additions to many dishes, since they enhance the special aromatic flavours. Garlic, paprika and tomatoes are hardly ever absent from dishes. Chickpeas

are a principal side dish. The crown of all meals is *couscous*, the Arabian word for semolina. This versatile dish is served with vegetable or meat sauce, or with fruits of the sea and fish. The preparation of couscous is a protracted process, and restaurants therefore often require advance orders.

## LOCAL SPECIALITIES

baklava – delicate cakes made of phyllo-pastry layers filled with chopped nuts and drizzled with honey or sugar syrup, delicious if steeped in loads of syrup

kebab – a kind of lamb stew, flavoured with lemon and fresh parsley

merguez – tiny hot spicy lamb sausages, flavoured with garlic

tajine – compared to the Moroccan dish of the same name, Tunisian tajine is a well-seasoned oven-baked gratin, made with eggs, meats, vegetables and cheese, and in a way resembles quiche

makroudh – sweet pastry made with semolina, filled with dates and soaked in a honey or sugar syrup

# SHOPPING

## The diverse offerings range from traditional colourful pottery to silver- and gold jewellery

Leather camels, bronze vessels, ceramic vases and silk kaftans – which of these are typical Tunisian? None, actually. If you would like to buy something that is not especially directed at tourists, then bring along some patience and a penchant for browsing. Seek out the back of shops. You will discover lovely and more utilitarian objects that locals usually purchase. For instance, check out the plain brown or glazed-pottery items.

### DECORATIVE CERAMICS

Green and yellow are like the two major Tunisian landscapes: the fertile north and the arid desert. These are the colours of the traditional serving dishes, bowls and platters for couscous, the national dish. Should you like to buy something special, then searching for this might be worthwhile.

### NATURAL COSMETICS

For centuries, Tunisian women have been using vervain, henna, argan oil and other natural products. Today these ancient beauty products are readily and commercially available as ingredients in soaps, lotions and creams, presented in pretty bottles.

### SILVER JEWELLERY

Many Tunisian women show off their silver jewellery in order to ward off the evil eye, disaster and sickness. The hand of Fatima and pendants in the form of a fish or a stylized eye are good-luck symbols with a protective function and are very decorative.

### SPICES

Spices and fragrant essential oils are favourite souvenirs and fit conveniently into luggage. In the spice souks, you will find all kinds of spices, including curcuma, paprika, cardamom, mint, orange and rosewater. All the food shops stock *harissa*, the spicy hot chili-pepper paste, packed in tubes and cans. Note: avoid saffron! It is in most cases not genuine.

# TRAVEL TIPS

## Tunisia: the most important information for your trip

### BERTH

▶ TUNIS

Cruise ships drop anchor in La Goulette. The La Goulette Village Harbour is a modern cruise-ship terminal featuring a tourist information service, a variety of stores and restaurants. The Tunis city centre is approx. 10 km/6 mi away. At the port, there is an adequate supply of taxis offering transport.

### HEALTH

Obtain information on vaccinations well in advance of your trip. Refrain from consuming unpeeled fruit, vegetables and fresh salads. Do not drink tap/faucet water and avoid consuming ice-cubes or uncovered ice cream. Year-round protection against the sun is imperative, and ensure that you have an insect repellent against mosquitoes on hand in summer.

### OPENING HOURS

The shops in the souks are open from mornings until evenings, but most close on Friday afternoons and Sundays. Restaurants in the tourist regions are mostly open from mornings until late at night. Only a few restaurants have weekly closing/resting days or rigid opening hours. Announced times for sightseeing may vary and spontaneous adjustments may occur, depending on circumstances. During Ramadan, government offices and shops are open mornings only, and eateries open in the evenings for the breaking of the daily fast.

### PHOTOGRAPHY

Show consideration and only take photos of people if you have their permission. Photographing/videoing of military installations and bridges is not permitted. Often museums and excavation sites request an extra photo surcharge of 1–2 TND, which is considerably more for video cameras.

### PRICES & CURRENCY

Tunisia is a reasonably priced holiday destination. The cost of beverages, taxis or sightseeing is low. The currency is the Tunisian dinar (TND), comprising 1000 millimes. Banks are usually open from Mondays to Fridays. Cash withdrawals at ATMs can be made in all larger towns and tourist areas.

### BUDGETING

| | | |
|---|---|---|
| Coffee | £0.60/$0.79 | |
| | *for an espresso* | |
| Museum | approx. £2.10/$2.80 | |
| | *for one museum visit* | |
| Beer | £1.70–£2.60/$2.30–$3.40 | |
| | *in a restaurant* | |
| Snack | £1.70/$2.30 | |
| | *for a brik at a stall* | |

# MOROCCO

If you take the boat from Spain to Morocco, it's possible to make out the outline of the city of Tangier well before you get there, a mass of white houses glimmering in the sunlight, picturesquely huddled together on a cliff that drops steeply to the sea.

"Once you've seen the white city once, you'll always long to return", or so the inhabitants of Tangier like to remind us. It might sound a touch sentimental, but it's part of the myth of the city of Tangier, which, prior to Morocco's independence, was an "International Zone": a meeting place for the rich and famous, rogues and artists, and known for its cosmopolitan flair. This "Gateway to Africa" lies barely 14 km/9 miles from the coast of Spain on the

other side of the Strait of Gibraltar. A fascinating and unique part of the world awaits you behind this gateway. The reigning monarch's father, King Hassan II, once described the country as "a tree with its roots in Africa and its branches in Europe", and if you travel to Morocco, you'll find both continents there.

# CASABLANCA

"You must remember this, a kiss is still a kiss...": the classic film starring Ingrid Bergman and Humphrey Bogart certainly brings back memories when thinking of Casablanca (pop. 4 million). But the Casablanca of today

## Here you will find an abundance of sunlight, spectacular scenery, lovely beaches and impressive sights

bears little resemblance to the one portrayed in the film: an industrial and trading megacity of 6 million people that is only worth visiting if you like a city with a vibrant nightlife (there are more clubs and restaurants per square metre here than in Marrakech), luxury shopping (Western style) or want to visit the ★ *Mosquée Hassan II (Sat–Thu 9am, 10am, 11am and 2pm (with guided tour), Fri 9am and 2pm, different opening times during Ramadan | admission 120 dh)*. Since its comple-

tion in 1993, the mosque has become the city's landmark. It is the biggest mosque in the world after Mecca and can hold 100,000 people. Despite the controversy surrounding it, this sacred building impresses every visitor standing on its promontory looking out to the Atlantic Ocean. Contemporary Moroccan art awaits you in the *Musée Villa des Arts*, a member of the Fondation ONA, the country's leading cultural organisation. *30, Boulevard Brahim Roudani | www.fondationona.ma*

# FOOD & DRINK

## An explosion of tastes to tickle your tastebuds: couscous, tajine and more

**The repertoire of Moroccan dishes ranges from boiled goat's head, which is eaten with salt and cumin, to meat kebabs, grilled swordfish to cabbage balls stuffed with minced meat.**

*Salad* can be eaten as a starter or together with the meal. For dessert there might be French fruit tart or simply fruit. The national dishes are tajine and couscous. *Tajine* is a stew cooked in a clay pot with a conical lid, and there are endless varieties of the dish: with fish, lamb or beef, perhaps sweet and salty with prunes, or completely vegetarian. *Couscous* is traditionally served on Fridays. Every week after Friday prayers at the mosque, a plate of couscous is waiting at home. It is customary to eat it using the fingers of the right hand. This requires a good deal of skill and co-ordination, the idea being to scoop up the couscous grains with a bit of meat and vegetable, squash them together and create a *little ball* by tossing it lightly in the cupped hand; finally flicking it into the mouth with the thumb! Moroccan *wines* are very good and fit for any occasion. Especially recommended are Cabernet President Rouge or an ice-cold *Ksar Rosé* for the summer heat. The local beer brands Flag and Storck are very similar to lager. Religious Moroccans drink cola or lemonade with their meals. There is either fizzy mineral water (Oulmes) or the still variety (Sidi Ali and Sidi Harazem). Very important is *thé à la menthe*, which can be drunk either with the meal or on its own in a café.

## LOCAL SPECIALITIES

**Briouats** – Small, crispy pastries stuffed with mince and/or cheese and/or vegetables and/or prawns

**Beghrir** – pancake usually eaten for breakfast with honey, butter or Amlou (mixture of honey, almonds and argan oil)

**Couscous** – durum wheat semolina with seven vegetables, together with either beef, lamb or chicken, or less frequently fish. Sweet couscous is prepared with caramelised onions and raisins, most often with chicken

**Pastilla** – puff-pastry pie filled with chicken, pigeon or mince and sprinkled with icing sugar and cinnamon

# TANGIER

**To this day the "gateway to Africa" still has a somewhat dubious reputation. A century ago, when Tangier was a free-trade zone, it was a haunt of agents, gamblers and drug bosses.**

Then it became a home to numerous emigrés, including Paul Bowles, Truman Capote and André Gide, who made the city famous around the world. Shades of the past are still tangible on the streets of Tangier.

Today Tangier (pop. 715,000) is a modern city. Perhaps the most advanced in the country, as its comprehensive re-modelling has been going on for half a decade now. The construction work in the Marina is still underway. This new and trendy harbour area is Tangier's showcase district and presents itself just the way the city planners want it to: rich, luxurious and up-to-date. But as modern as some of it now looks, in the labyrinth of alleys in the medina time seems to have stood still. From the Kasbah you look out to the green hills with their luxury villas. In no other Moroccan city are social differences so pronounced.

## SIGHTSEEING

### GRAND SOCCO

This is where the heart of Tangier beats. *La Place du 9 Avril 1947*, as the Grand Socco is officially called, marks the gateway to the medina and link to the New Town. This is the location of a large market held on Thursday and Sunday, when farmers from the surrounding area come to sell their produce dressed in their traditional costumes. Take a look inside the *Cinéma Rif (www.cinemathequedetanger.com)*, a small cultural centre with café, exhibitions and a cinema. Take a break just like the locals do: Unwind under shady trees just around the corner in *Parc Mendoubia*. And don't miss out on the halls of the *Marché Central*. It's the largest food market in the city and hence a beehive of activity.

### KASBAH QUARTER

High up, right at the top, sits Tangier's kasbah, the ancient royal residence

# ORIENTAL WELLNESS

The fact that Moroccans like going to public baths to wash up does not mean they have no bathrooms at home. But Moroccans agree that you don't get truly clean there. For that you need the haman. Because there you don't simply wash yourself, you cleanse your soul. The swathes of hot steam soften the skin, which is then easier to scrub while your soul gently floats away.

It is a deep relaxation you can never experience under a shower. Take care, though: before holidays and on Fridays hamams can be filled to bursting point. No chance of deep relaxation, there's enough blabbering and jabbering to make your ears ring. The hamam operators are shrewd enough to guarantee a good customer turnover: on such days they simply turn on the heat. It's the only way to ensure that nobody stays for too long.

Tangier's picturesque alleys

*Les Fils du Detroit (a small donation is appreciated)*, where you can listen to old folks jamming.

### PETIT SOCCO
This square lies in the heart of Tangier's Old City, and like its big brother the *Grand Socco*, which is not far away, it is surrounded by cafés, simple guesthouses and small shops. It's worth staying here for a while to take in the throbbing vibe of the city. Let your gaze wander upwards to marvel at the art nouveau house fronts.

## SHOPPING

For food and everday needs, head for the Sunday market on the Grand Socco. The gallery and its bookshop INSIDER TIP *Les Insolites (Mon–Sat 11am–8pm | Rue Ibn Khalid Oualid | former Rue Velazquez | librairielesinsolites.tanger.over-blog.com)* are definitely worth a visit. Visitors are invited to stroll around the exhibitions (contemporary, photography), and browse through the very interesting collection of books, music and prints. Finish the visit with refreshment in the small café in the museum's courtyard.

## BEACHES

The city has a beautiful, clean white-sand beach; the water is clear, but unfortunately not that clean. The beaches of a ☀ *Cap Malabata*, 14 km/9 miles away, are excellent.

## WHERE TO GO

### ASILAH
Those wanting a relaxing holiday on the Atlantic have discovered just the right place, here approximately 46 km/30 miles southwest of Tangier. The people of

from the 17th century. This is where anyone goes who would like to visit the *Museum (Wed–Mon 9am–4pm | entry 10 DH/0.8 GBP/1.0 USD/)* in the old palace, the old treasury or the ☀ visitors' terrace, from where you have a splendid view of the sea right across to Spain. But the kasbah offers the visitor more than that. Here you can go searching for clues. Go take a look at the *Bab Al Assa*, conspicuous by the beautiful fountain with its decorative mosaic: do you recognise it? This is the famous "Porte de la Casbah" painted by Henri Matisse in 1913. Or can you see the small door next to the arts and crafts shop on the square? This is the home of the band

Asilah (pop 25,000) are friendly and modest, the sand on the beach is white and clean. Asilah's old town is all turquoise, blue and white. Artists have painted the house walls, and everywhere there are nice little outdoor cafés under shady trees. Those who find Essaouira too touristy should definitely visit the much quieter Asilah.

## TETOUAN

Tetouan (pop. 365,000) lies on a plateau at the western edge of the Rif mountains, 40 km/25 miles southeast of Tangier. It doesn't have the best of reputations, particularly with first-time visitors to the country. This isn't surprising because of the comparatively large numbers of hashish dealers, pickpockets and *faux guides* that hang out here. Be that as it may, you still shouldn't miss – the ⭐ *Medina of Tetouan*, which in 1997 was made a Unesco World Heritage Site. White alleyways spanned by brick archways wind their way through the city. You will find many small restaurants around *Place Hassan II.*

# AGADIR

### Agadir (pop. 600,000) attracts with 330 days of sunshine.

This is where most beach tourists tend to arrive and stay. And indeed, Agadir has everything a tourist resort should have: a long sandy beach (it stretches for miles), a glorious hinterland that is perfect for excursions, an excellent tourist infrastructure and, not least, lots of guaranteed days of sun a year. Morocco derives a large proportion of its tourist income from here. The coast is lined with hotels and all visitors' needs or wants are taken care of: there's even a British pub with a good selection of beers and live football! While the rents have been steadily rising, the water table has been sinking because freshwater consumption far outstrips the sustainable supply. Petty crime and rip-offs, rare elsewhere in Morocco, are not at all unusual in Agadir. Everyone finds his own way of profiting from the foreign visitors.

In 1960 Agadir was struck by an earthquake which claimed the lives of 15,000 people. Most of the city's buildings therefore date from after 1962, when reconstruction began. Nevertheless, Agadir is still an attractive place. Away from the main tourist thoroughfares, you'll see other sides to it: a university town with lots of students, a modern town with lively residential districts and a commercial centre with colourful markets and lots of shops and businesses.

# TRAVEL WITH KIDS

### CROCOPARC AGADIR

One of the latest attractions immediately before of the gates of Agadir is the fascinating crocodile park in the little town of Drarga, near the highway. It is laid out like a small zoo, and there are any number of crocodiles living here in large pools. It's not cruelty to animals, because they are being prepared for release into the wild again, and they live here only temporarily. Children like the park, because besides the shivers of excitement there are also play areas and cafeterias. *Info & opening times at: www.crocoparc.com.*

# AGADIR

## SIGHTSEEING

### MEDINA POLIZZI
Roman theatre, medina alleys, mosaics and cedarwood decorations: if this vaguely evokes a Walt Disney feeling, no wonder; at one stage this medina accommodated a small handicraft centre. Today the only thing that makes it worth visiting is the wonderful architecture the Italian Coco Polizzi erected here. There is also a decent café under eucalyptus trees. *Tue–Sun 9am–7pm | Ben Sergao | Entry 60 DH/4.9 GBP/6.3 USD*

### MUSÉE DU PATRIMOINE AMAZIGH
This museum has a small but impressive collection of exhibits devoted to Berber art and culture, in a beautifully designed building near the pedestrian zone of *Ait Souss. Mon–Sat 9.30am–5.30pm | admission 20 dh*

Traditional transport

## SHOPPING

Be sure to visit the *Souk el Had (Sat–Thu from early morning | Av. Abderrahim Bouabib à Rabat | south of the centre)*, one of the country's finest market halls. Here you'll find nearly everything – except alcohol.

## BEACHES

As described, Agadir has its own very long, clean beach; in the southern part you can sometimes even see flamingos. There are other beaches in the vicinity, including the dunes of *Taghazoute* (20 km/13 miles to the north), where the coast has been taken over by surfers.

## WHERE TO GO

### PARC NATIONAL OUED MASSA ★ ✪
At the mouth of the Oued Massa river, 45 km/28 miles south of Agadir, lies Morocco's largest bird sanctuary. It is home to a large variety of birds, including hoopoes, peregrines, Barbary falcons, booted eagles, herons and spoonbills. They share their habitat with jackals, wildcats and weasels, and some interesting reptiles and amphibians. In addition to the beautiful riverscapes, which you can explore on foot, there are some lovely beaches with caves where local fishermen prepare their catches.

### TAROUDANNT
Taroudannt (pop. 57,000) is a pretty town in the middle of the fertile Sous Valley, 80 km/50 miles east of Agadir. Once a busy commercial centre and for a brief period during the 16th century even becoming the Saadian capital, Taroudannt remains a lively place to this day. The bazaar is correspondingly colourful, and of further interest is the perfectly preserved city wall, which dates from the 16th century.

# SHOPPING

## Whether you want argan oil, jewellery or carpets – bargaining is considered good style

The range of products available in the medinas of Moroccan cities is truly overwhelming. There's one shop after another, specializing in typical leather goods, jewellery, ceramics, clothes, lamps and woodwork.

Even if there are increasing numbers of shops, even in the souks, that charge fixed prices, the bargaining tradition is still alive and well and can be nerve-wracking as well as great fun. However, if you don't fancy the cut and thrust of shopping in the bazaars and souks, you can always have a look at the state-owned shops, where all goods are sold at fixed prices.

Each street or district in the old part of the city is usually occupied by a particular trade guild. Besides offering a wider range of handmade products, it is also an enjoyable experience to stroll along the narrow streets. Buy souvenirs in the regions where they have been made, as the goods are usually of a better quality and price.

### CERAMICS

Fès is famous not just for its copperware but also for its ceramics, with their typical blue-and-white glazes. Crockery from Fès – especially the blue and white – also looks very classy.

### CULINARY ITEMS

In every souk there are tempting piles of herbs and spices, such as fresh pepper, cumin or virgin olive oil. Especially recommended: the indigenous INSIDER TIP argan oil, extracted from the argan tree. The tree is endemic to Morocco and lives up to 300 years. This cold-pressed, nutty tasting oil is extracted from the tree's nuts and is used to decorate Moroccan dishes. In Morocco, argan oil is also mixed together with almonds and honey to form a paste to spread on bread (*Amlou*).

### LEATHER

A favourite and beautiful purchase is a pair of traditional backless leather slippers or *babouches* as well as leather bags: there are numerous colours and forms to choose from, best bought in the souks of Fès and Marrakech.

# MARRAKECH

**Marrakech (pop. 1 million) is the most exciting of the four imperial cities, drawing many people as a result.**

Marrakech is a vibrant, trend-setting metropolis and a cosmopolitan city on a par with some of the world's other cosmopolitan destinations. It was founded in the 11th century, and ever since then whoever has managed to conquer Marrakech has gone on to rule the entire country. This reign of power is still reflected in the city's architecture, with its majestic buildings dating from times of the Almoravid, Almohad Caliphate and Saadi dynasties.

Even if Marrakech is no longer the country's most powerful city, the "Red City", as it is commonly known for the colour of its walls, still plays a significant role in Moroccan culture. Marrakech is the capital of the Berbers and, alongside Casablanca, is also the country's economic and financial hub. No other city in Morocco is growing at the same rate (unofficially, between 3 and 4 million people live here). The city is witnessing the spread of new satellite towns and new districts, which are responsible for setting new trends. The city is under renovation and restoration; global summits are held here as well as international festivals: Marrakech tourism is also breaking visitor records year on year! Backpackers, fans of the Orient, package holidaymakers, artists and stars all flock here, attracted by the city's charm.

Marrakech's popularity can be traced back to its origins: the city remained untouched by modern developments for many years. The *Jemaa el Fna* is Marrakech's market place and has been attracting visitors for many centuries, fascinated by its immunity to modernity and Western influences. A change in the law in 1999, entitling foreigners to real estate ownership in the country, saw many of the rich and powerful buy a riad in the medina or a villa on the palmeraie (palm oasis). Stars such as Brad Pitt, Alain Delon and Kate Moss all have a second, third or even fourth residence in Marrakech. Many private individuals, especially French nationals, have succumbed to Marrakech's charm and opened up guesthouses, where many of the city's guests now stay. The city has profited from these changes: old buildings have been preserved and new investors support new innovations.

## SIGHTSEEING

### JEMAA EL FNA ⭐

This square is the absolute highlight of Morocco! For a few years now, the Jemaa el Fna (Square of the Beheaded) has been on Unesco's representative list of the "Intangible Cultural Heritage of Humanity". And indeed: day after day and night after night it continues to attract thousands of Moroccans from far and wide, who come to listen to the storytellers, cheer on the fire-eaters, and believe everything the healers tell them. Acrobats perform here, and there are snake charmers too. Mobile dentists set out their stalls and water sellers allow themselves to be photographed for a hefty fee. Tourists tend to just wander around, many preferring to observe the spectacle from a distance. But whoever wants to immerse themselves in the wild side of Morocco, this is one of the best places to do it, in the bustling heart of Marrakech. Things get going especially in the late afternoon and early evening. And don't worry: it is safe and stressless here, but like everywhere else with lots of tourists, there are also thieves and fraudsters. If

### MADRASA BEN YOUSSEF ⭐

Do you remember the Hollywood flick "Hideous Kinky" staring Kate Winslet? If

Crowd pleaser especially in the evenings: Jemaa el Fna

so, you might recognise the Madrasa Ben Youssef, because this is where the protagonist converts to Islam.

The country's most beautiful madrasa was founded in the 14th century and was last renovated in 2001. However, it obtained its present form under the Saadians in the 16th century. The impressively large and magnificent courtyard with a fountain has floor tiles made of Carrara marble. The walls are immaculately adorned with ornamented tiles and Islamic calligraphy, decorated with stucco capitals and finely engraved cedar arabesques on the first floor. A small prayer room also branches off from the courtyard. It is also worth seeing the studies on the first floor, the Koran school and the old hammam, which is now used

as the toilets (clean and worth seeing!). *Daily 9am–6pm | Place Ben Youssef | admission 20 DH/1.5 GBP/2.5 USD*

### MOSQUÉE KOUTOUBIYA

This mosque, which non-Muslims can view only from the outside, acquired its name from the book market, Kutubia, which once surrounded it. It was built in the 12th century as the new capital's first mosque and was intended to give Marrakech the status of a free city. The minaret is an impressive sight and a good example of traditional Moroccan-Islam architecture. It was completely renovated in 1997. The pulpit *(minbar)*, which was made in Cordoba, is particularly beautiful; today it is housed in the *Palais el Badi*. *Place de Koutoubia*

# MARRAKECH

INSIDER TIP **MUSÉE DE L'EAU AMAN**

With the water museum, officially called the Musée Mohammed VI de la civilisation de l'Eau au Maroc Aman, Morocco entered the postmodern era. It's a truly incredible achievement. Museology at its best. Films, displays, models as well as multimedia shows, and time and again it's information you can touch. In a desert country with water problems, people – especially school-going children and the locals – have to learn the significance of water (aman in Morocco). *Daily 9.30am-7.30pm | Route de Casablanca | Entry 60 DH/4.9 GBP/6.3 USD*

## SOUKS

The souks of Marrakech have been adapted to suit the needs of tourists, so everything the Western heart desires can be found here. But if you go deeper into the maze of alleyways you'll encounter craftsmen who still make their products on the street, hundreds of traditional shoe shops, clothes markets, the wool dying bazaar and much else besides. Typical and not touristy at all: the food markets, e.g. near the Bab Doukkala. If you don't want to buy souvenirs, but just experience the souk, this is the right place.

## SHOPPING

The souk is full of beautiful things and a stroll around the bustling marketplace will surely uncover 1,001 bargain souvenirs. If you are more inclined to shop in European style, you should head to *Gueliz*, the new neighbourhood in Marrakech, with its wide range of chic boutiques and excellent selection of goods.

Oriental-style shopping in the souks of Marrakech

# TRAVEL TIPS

## Morocco: the most important information for your trip

### BERTHS

▶ **CASABLANCA**

In Casablanca the cruise ships moor in the industrial port. The places of interest in the city are about 2-4 km/1½-2½ mi) away; if you'd rather not walk, you can catch a taxi at the port to take you to the city centre.

▶ **TANGIER**

The cruise ship terminal is near the medina, the old town, within walking distance. Taxis are also available at the port.

▶ **AGADIR**

Agadir has no cruise ship terminal; cruise ships moor in the industrial port, some 6 km/3,7 mi) outside the city. Taxis and shuttle buses provide transport to the city centre.

### CLIMATE & WHEN TO GO

It's possible to travel in Morocco all year round – but not everywhere. In the mountains, you can expect snow from October onwards. Even in cities, it can be cold from December to February, and not all hotels have heating. The summer months are more pleasant on the coast, but not suitable for desert tours. The ideal time for beach holidays is from May to September on the Atlantic coast and April to October on the Mediterranean.

### PHONE & MOBILE PHONE

So-called *téléboutiques* are replacing the public telephone booths. You can phone using 1, 2, 5, and sometimes 10 dh coins. International codes: US 001, UK 0044, Morocco 00 212. The mobile network is very well developed in Morocco. If you're going to be in the country for any length of time, it may be worth getting a Moroccan prepaid SIM *(carte jawal)* for your own mobile *(le portable)*; it costs 30 dh plus the credit balance. In Morocco, always dial the 0 with any number; when calling from abroad, the 0 after the national code is omitted.

### TIPPING

Restaurant waiters get around 10 percent (1 dh per drink in cafés); porters 5–15 dh per item of luggage, depending on the hotel. It is usual to give taxi drivers a little more than the amount displayed in the taximeter – from about 2–5 dh, depending on the fare.

## BUDGETING

| | |
|---|---|
| Coffee | from £0.90/$1.20 |
| | *for a glass of coffee* |
| Hamam | from 40 DH |
| | *without massage etc.* |

# USEFUL PHRASES

| ENGLISH | SPANISH |
|---|---|
| **IN BRIEF** | |
| yes/no/maybe | sí/no/quizás |
| please/thank you | por favor/gracias |
| Sorry! | ¡Perdona! |
| Excuse me! | ¡Perdone! |
| May I ...? | ¿Puedo ...? |
| Pardon? | ¿Cómo dice? |
| I would like to ... | Querría ... |
| Have you got ...? | ¿Tiene usted ...? |
| How much is ...? | ¿Cuánto cuesta ...? |
| I (don't) like this. | Esto (no) me gusta. |
| good/bad | bien/mal |
| open/closed | abierto/cerrado |
| **SALUTATION & TRAVEL** | |
| Good morning!/ afternoon! | ¡Buenos días!/ días! |
| Good evening!/night! | ¡Buenas tardes!/noches! |
| Hello!/Goodbye! | ¡Hola!/¡Adiós!! |
| Bye! | ¡Hasta luego! |
| My name is ... | Me llamo ... |
| What's your name? | ¿Cómo se llama usted? |
| I'm from ... | Soy de ... |
| station/harbour | estación/puerto |
| departure/arrival | salida/salida/llegada |
| What time is it? | ¿Qué hora es? |
| It's three o'clock. | Son las tres. |
| today/tomorrow/ yesterday | hoy/mañana/ ayer |
| **FOOD & DRINK** | |
| The menue, please. | ¡El menú, por favor! |
| May I have ...? | ¿Podría traerme ... por favor? |
| knife/fork/ spoon | cuchillo/tenedor/ cuchara |
| salt/pepper/sugar | sal/pimienta/azúcar |
| vinegar/oil | vinagre/aceite |
| milk/cream/lemon | leche/crema/limón |
| with/without ice | con/sin hielo |
| vegetarian | vegetariano |
| May I have the bill, please? | Querría pagar, por favor. |

# Short and sweet

This short list of phrases will help you say the most important words and phrases in the languages listed below:

| FRENCH | ITALIAN | CROATIAN |
|---|---|---|
| oui/non/peut-être | sì/no/forse | da/ne/možda |
| s'il vous plaît/merci | per favore/grazie | molim/hvala |
| Pardon! | Scusa!/ | Oprostite molim! |
| Pardon! | Scusi! | Oprostite molim vas! |
| Puis-je ...? | Posso...? | Smijem li ...? |
| Comment? | Come dice?/Prego? | Molim? |
| Je voudrais ... | Vorrei .../ | Htio bih ... |
| Avez-vous ...? | Avete ...? | Imate li ...? |
| Combien coûte ...? | Quanto costa ...? | Koliko košta ...? |
| Ça (ne) me plaît (pas). | (Non) mi piace. | To mi se (ne) dopada. |
| bon/mauvais | buono/cattivo | dobro/loše |
| ouvert/fermé | aperto/chiuso | otvoreno/zatvoreno |
| | | |
| Bonjour!/ | Buon giorno!/ | Dobro jutro!/ |
| Bonjour! | Buon giorno! | Dobar dan! |
| Bonsoir!/Bonne nuit! | Buona sera!/Buona notte! | Dobra večer!/Laku noć! |
| Salut!/Au revoir!/ | Ciao!/Arrivederci! | Zdravo!/Do viđnja! |
| Salut! | Ciao! | Bok! |
| Je m'appelle ... | Mi chiamo ... | Moje ime je... |
| Quel est votre nom? | Come si chiama?/ | Kako se vi zovete? |
| Je suis de ... | Sono di ... | Dolazim iz ... |
| gare/port | stazione/porto | željeznička stanica/luka |
| départ/départ/arrivée | partenza/partenza/arrivo | odlazak/odletište/doletište |
| Quelle heure est-t-il? | Che ora è? | Koliko je sati? |
| Il est trois heures. | Sono le tre. | Sad je tri sata. |
| aujourd'hui/demain/ | oggi/domani/ | danas/sutra/ |
| hier | ieri | jučer |
| | | |
| La carte, s'il vous plaît. | Il menù, per favore. | Molim donesite jelovnik. |
| Puis-je avoir ... | Potrei avere...per | Mogu li dobiti ...? |
| s'il vous plaît | favore? | |
| couteau/fourchette/ | coltello/forchetta/ | nož/vilicu/ |
| cuillère | cucchiaio | žlicu |
| sel/poivre/sucre | sale/pepe/zucchero | sol/papar/šećer |
| vinaigre/huile | aceto/olio aceto/olio | ocat/ulje |
| lait/crème/citron | latte/panna/limone | mljeko/vrhnje/limun |
| avec/sans glaçons | con/senza ghiaccio | sa/bez Led |
| végétarien(ne) | vegetariano/vegetariana | vegetarijanac(ci) |
| Je voudrais payer, | Vorrei pagare, | Želim platiti, |
| s'il vous plaît. | per favore | molim. |

# USEFUL PHRASES

| ENGLISH | GREEK |
|---------|-------|
| **IN BRIEF** | |
| yes/no/maybe | nä/'ochi/'issos |
| please/thank you | efcharisto/parakalo |
| Sorry! | sig'nomi |
| Excuse me! | mä sig'chorite |
| May I ...? | Äpi'träppäte ...? |
| Pardon? | O'riste? |
| I would like to ... | 'Thälo ... |
| Have you got ...? | 'Ächäte ...? |
| How much is ...? | 'Posso 'kani ...? |
| I (don't) like this. | Af'to (dhän) mu a'rässi. |
| good/bad | ka'llo/kak'ko |
| open/closed | annik'ta/klis'to |

| | |
|---------|-------|
| **SALUTATION & TRAVEL** | |
| Good morning!/ afternoon! | Kalli'mära!/ Kalli'mära! |
| Good evening!/night! | Kalli'spära!/Kalli'nichta! |
| Hello!/Goodbye! | 'Ja (su/sass)!/A'dio! |
| Bye! | Ja (su/sass)! |
| My name is ... | Mä 'läne ... |
| What's your name? | Poss sass 'läne? |
| I'm from ... | érchome apó... |
| station/harbour | stathmós/limani |
| departure/arrival | anachórisi/anachórisi/'afiksi |
| What time is it? | Ti 'ora 'ine? |
| It's three o'clock. | Íne tris i óra |
| today/tomorrow/ yesterday | 'simära/'awrio/ chtess |

| | |
|---------|-------|
| **FOOD & DRINK** | |
| The menue, please. | Tonn ka'taloggo parakal'lo. |
| May I have ...? | Tha 'ithälla na 'ächo ...? |
| knife/fork/ spoon | machéri/piroúni/koutáli aláti/pipéri/sáchari |
| salt/pepper/sugar | xídi/ládi |
| vinegar/oil | gála/santigí/lemóni |
| milk/cream/lemon | mä/cho'ris 'pago/ |
| with/without ice | anthrakik'ko |
| vegetarian | chorto'fagos |
| May I have the bill, please? | 'Thäl'lo na pli'rosso parakal'lo. |

174

# Short and sweet

This short list of phrases will help you say the most important words and phrases in the languages listed below:

| TURKISH | CATALAN |
|---|---|
| evet/hayır/belki | sí/no/potser |
| Lütfen./Teşekkür. | si us plau/gràcies |
| Afedersin! | Perdona! |
| Afedersiniz! | Perdoni! |
| Müsaadenizle...? | Puc ...? |
| Pardon? | Com diu (Sie)? Com dius (Du)? |
| ... istiyorum | Voldria ... |
| ... var mı? | Té ...? |
| ... ne kadar? Fiyatı ne? | Quant val ...? |
| Beğendim./Beğenmedim. | (No) m'agrada. |
| iyi/kötü | bé/malament |
| açık/kapalı | obert/tancat |
| | |
| Günaydın!/ | Bon dia! |
| İyi Günler! | |
| İyi Akşamlar!/İyi Geceler! | Bona tarda!/Bona nit! |
| Merhaba!/Allaha ısmarladık! | Hola!/Passi-ho bé! |
| Hoşçakal (Plural: Hoşçakalın)/Bye bye! | Adéu! |
| Adım ... oder İsmim ... | Em dic ... |
| Sizin adınız ne?/Sizin isminiz ne? | Com es diu? |
| ... den/dan geliyorum. | Sóc de ... |
| istasyon/liman | estació/port |
| kalkış/kalkış/varış | sortida/sortida del vol/arribada |
| Saat kaç? | Quina hora és? |
| Saat üç. | Són les tres. |
| bugün/yarın/ | avui/demà/ |
| dün | ahir |
| | |
| Menü lütfen. | La carta, si us plau. |
| ... alabilir miyim lütfen? | Podria portar-me ...? |
| | |
| bıçak/çatal/kaşık | ganivet/forquilla/cullera |
| tuz/karabiber/şeker | sal/pebre/sucre |
| sirke/zeytinyağı | vinagre/oli |
| süt/kaymak/limon | llet/nata/llimona |
| buzlu/buzsuz | amb/sense gel/ |
| su/soda | gas |
| vejetaryan | vegetarià/vegetariana |
| Hesap lütfen. | El compte, si us plau. |

# HOW TO CRUISE

## EMBARKING

On arrival at the cruise terminal, you hand over your baggage. Remember to put important items you will need after you have gone aboard in your hand luggage, as it may take quite a while before the suitcases are brought to the relevant cabins. At the check-in point you will get your boarding pass and a security check. If you are lucky, you can go on board immediately, but it is also possible that you may have to stay in the waiting hall a little longer before it's your turn.

## DISEMBARKING

Put your bags outside the cabin door the evening before disembarking. Once again: Keep anything you will need the next morning with your hand luggage.

## EMERGENCY DRILL

All passengers must take part in the emergency drill, which usually takes place on the day of embarkation. You will find a life jacket in your cabin which you must put on for the drill. You will be informed of the drill on the PA system; proceed to your allocated master station, which is a place near the lifeboats. This is where the actual practice is done.

## LIFEBOATS

The number of lifeboats is prescribed by international law and exceeds the maximum passenger capacity by 125 per cent.

Finally on board!

# Tips & tricks for your cruise

**Is this your first big cruise? We have collected some info and concepts for you about life on the high seas.**

"Women and children first" does not apply to emergencies; for handicapped persons there are boats adapted to their special needs.

## MEDICAL CARE

Cruise ships have medical personnel on board; on the larger ships, there is even a hospital. Any serious case of sickness is transferred to a hospital on land. Find out to what extent your medical insurance covers any medical treatment for which you initially have to pay yourself. In case of doubt, take out appropriate international health insurance.

## SEASICKNESS

On the Atlantic, the weather can sometimes change and turn stormy, which will make the going a bit rougher. The stabilisers of modern ships suppress most of the rolling, but in severe cases they cannot completely eliminate it. To be on the safe side, you can buy medication against seasickness at a pharmacy.

## BERTHING TIMES

Before going ashore, you will be informed how much time you have available. You must show your boarding pass when leaving and returning to the ship. Note: Allow enough time for your return to the ship. Even though ships wait a while for delayed passengers, sooner or later they have to leave, as extended stays in port incur costs for the shipping line. Once it has left, you've got a problem.

The gangway leads into the ship

## SHORE EXCURSIONS

You can book shore excursions, including shuttle buses, on board and join sightseeing trips, for example. But you can also organise your on-shore activities yourself. If you want to go off on our own, you will find taxis in most ports; sometimes you're lucky and can reach the city centre on foot.

## ROADSTEAD

Many ports are too small for large cruise ships to enter. In such cases the ships anchor outside; they ride at anchor "in the roadstead".

## TENDER BOAT

Passengers are carried ashore from ships lying in a roadstead by smaller boats, called tenders or tender boats, for their excursions.

## DRESS

Although dress rules have become less strict nowadays because of the greater variety of cruise ships, you should enquire what dress code is required on board your ship. As a general rule: the more stars a ship has, the more formal the dress. The dress code for dinner is usually indicated on the board programme for the day. Many shipping lines also publish information on the proper dress style on their website.

## TIPPING

Many cruise lines charge a flat rate at the end of the trip that is allocated to the crew. Other lines leave it up to you how much you want to tip whom. If uncertain, enquire at your line what their customs are.

## ICEBREAKERS

Cruises are also very popular with people travelling alone. For these passengers the lines arrange appropriate evenings where one can get to know other passengers travelling alone. Don't worry, these evenings are not dating occasions!

## ON-BOARD ACCOUNT

All purchases made on board are cashless transactions. When you embark, you Index your credit card or pay a deposit. Dollars and euros are the most common cruise currencies. Note that in the case of dollars, conversion fees are charged to the credit card account. You receive your cruise account before you disembark. What you pay afterwards is charged separately.

## ON-BOARD PROGRAM AND BUSINESS

On cruise ships, entertainment is provided at appropriate (evening) events. Shops and boutiques are provided for shopping.

# CABIN INFORMATION

On cruise ships, there are normally four classes of cabins that differ quite a bit as regards furnishings and price.
▶ **Inside cabins:** These are the cheapest type, without a view of the sea and with rather limited space.
▶ **Outside cabins:** Here the porthole allows you to see the sea, but the cabins are usually not noticeably larger than inside cabins.
▶ **Balcony cabins:** These have their own balcony, which can be an advantage if the weather is fine.
▶ **Suites:** the most expensive category, with better furnishings, more space and additional service.

# ABC OF SHIPPING

**Aft** – rear part of the ship (stern, poop)

**Anchor** – keeps the ship in place; cruise ships have several

**Bearing** – direction of travel of a ship, course

**Bell(s)** – nautical indication of time in half hours

**Bow** – front part of a ship

**Bridge** – place from where the captain steers the ship

**Bunker** – fuel store (tanks) on a ship

**Captain** – person in command of a ship

**Companionway** – narrow stairway inside a ship

**Dock** – part of a port where a ship moors

**Fathom** – nautical measure of length; a fathom equals six feet

**Flagship** – best ship of a shipping line, often also the largest and newest

**Galley** – ship's kitchen

**Gangway** – stair or bridge whereby the passengers embark

**Heave to** – slowing down and changing direction of a ship

**Hull** – body of a ship, without superstructure

**Keel** – part of a ship running continuously from stem to stern of a ship and mostly submerged

**Knot** – nautical unit of speed; 1 knot = 1 nautical mile per hour

**Lee** – the downwind side of a ship

**Luff** – the upwind (windward) side of a ship

**Maiden voyage** – first voyage of a ship with passengers

**Master stations** – waiting areas at the lifeboats in emergencies

**Mayday** – international call for help on sea

**Nautical mile** – nautical unit of measurement, equal to 1852 m / 1.1508 mi

**Pier** – mooring place for ships (also called a quay)

**Pilot** – steers the ship through tricky waters

**Pitching** – Lengthwise up-and-down movement of a ship

**Port fee** – is calculated in each port on the basis of a ship's size

**Porthole** – round window

**Port side** – left side of a ship (looking forward)

**Purser** – ship's officer who keeps the accounts

**Rolling** – lateral swinging of a ship

**Set sail** – to depart from a port on a course

**Sextant** – nautical measuring instrument for determining position

**Sister ships** – ships with the same construction and belonging to the same line

**SOS** – international distress code

**Starboard side** – right-hand side of a ship (looking forward)

**Stern** – rear part of the ship *(see* Aft)

**Swell** – movement of water caused by wind

**Tide** – daily rise and fall of the sea level (ebb and flow)

**Wake** – water trail dragged along by a ship while sailing

**Watch** – on-duty time of the crew

**Waterline** – height of the water level measured on the ship's hull

**Weighing anchor** – raising the anchor before the ship sails

**Yawing** – not steering a straight course

# INDEX

This index lists selected places of interest and worth seeing that are mentioned in this tour guide.

# INDEX

## PICTURE CREDITS

Cover: Mykonos (Getty Images/iStockphoto)
Photos: Getty Images/iStockphoto (1); © iStock.com: AtanasBozhikovNasko (2 top, 42/43), HHakim (3 bottom, 130/131), brunette (3 top, 144/145), Olena_Znak (4), Roxiller (21), dvoevnore (22), Gargolas (26), Hakat (28), jotily (35), Selitbul (37), margouillatphotos (47), gianliguori (48), Madzia71 (50), PocholoCalapre (51), cavalla-pazza (53), eugenesergeev (54), bluejayphoto (58/59), canbedone (63), fotografiche (65), swisshippo (67), eu-genesergeev (68), bluejayphoto (71), ultraforma (73), Okssi68 (74), SeanPavonePhoto (78), davidionut (81), Konstantin Aksenov (92), WitR (94/95), iascic (97), zeleno (98), xbrchx (99), Mawardibahar (102), emicristea (106/107), sugar0607 (116), ivanmateev (118), GWMB (120), excentric_01 (123), muharremz (132), hayatikay-han (134), Kuzenkova Yuliya (135), Nikada (136), Kirillm (138/139), DronG (141), InnaFelker (142), efesenko (146), tbralnina (147), urf (149), sergio_kumer (150), Meinzahn (151), ejwhite (157), Eduardo1961 (160/161), Naeblys (164), AlxeyPnferov (166), kasto80 (167), ugurhan (169), oversnap (170), apomares (178); © fotolia.com: vul-canus (2 bottom, 14/15), Harris Shiffman (6/7), Orhan Çam (12), vulcanus (14/15), Ingo Bartussek (31), e55e-vu (77), ushuaia2001 (83), javarman (88/89), dudlajzov (90), digitalsignal (91), cge2010 (100), pillerss (109), Kavalenkava (110), entrechat (113), Magrig (114), Jürgen Reitz (122), gatsi (125), lubos K (127), Dasha Petren-ko (158), tbralnina (162); © mauritius Images: Hackenberg-Photo-Cologne/Alamy (5), Magdalena Dral/Alamy (8/9), Pawel Kazmierczak/Alamy (10/11), Digital-Fotofusion Gallery/Alamy (24), travelstock44/Alamy (39), age fotostock/José Fuste Raga (154/155), age fotostock/Lucas Vallecillos (156), Juan SiLVA/Alamy (176), Jochen Tack/Alamy (177); © Michael Scheuring (16, 18, 33, 45, 60, 75, 84)

# WRITE TO US

e-mail: info@marcopologuides.co.uk

Did you have a great holiday? Is there something on your mind? Whatever it is, let us know! Whether you want to praise, alert us to errors or give us a personal tip – MARCO POLO would be pleased to hear from you.
We do everything we can to provide the very latest information for your trip. Nevertheless, despite all of our authors' thorough research, errors can creep in. MARCO POLO does not accept any liability for this. Please contact us by e-mail or post.

MARCO POLO Travel Publishing Ltd
Pinewood, Chineham Business Park
Crockford Lane, Chineham
Basingstoke, Hampshire RG24 8AL
United Kingdom

**1st edition 2020**
Worldwide Distribution: Marco Polo Travel Publishing Ltd, Pinewood, Chineham Business Park, Crockford Lane, Basingstoke, Hampshire RG24 8AL, United Kingdom. Email: sales@marcopolouk.com

© MAIRDUMONT GmbH & Co. KG , Ostfildern

Chief editor: Stefanie Penck

Authors: Andreas Drouve, Martin Dahms, Petra Rossbach, Jördis Kimpfler, Muriel Kiefel, Peter Bausch, Gabriele Kalmbach, Barbara Markert, Bettina Dürr, Christiane Büld Campetti, Hans Bausenhardt, Klaus Bötig, Daniela Schetar, Gunnar Köhne, Dilek Zaptçıoğlu, Jürgen Gottschlich, Jürgen Stryjak, Friedrich Köthe, Muriel Brunswig-Ibrahim; Coauthors: Jürgen Gottschlich, Dilek Zaptçıoğlu, Laura Schmid, Michael Allhoff, Lothar Schmid, Brigitte Kramer, Tom Gebhardt, Marcel Brunnthaler, Annika Joeres, Dorothea Schmidt, Hilke Maunder, Stefanie Buommino, Stefanie Claus, Sabine Oberpriller, Friederike Anz, Peter Höh, Timo Lutz, Peter Peter, Nina Cancar, Christina Sternberg

Cartography and pull-out maps: © MAIRDUMONT, Ostfildern

Translated from German by Elfriede du Preez, Andrea Scheuer, Birgitt Lederer, Christopher Wynne, Frauke Watson, Jane Rieste, Jennifer Walcoff Neuheiser , John Sykes, Jozef van der Voort, Kathleen Becker, Lindsay Chalmers-Gerbracht, Mo Croasdale, Nicole Meyer, Robert McInnes , Rotkel Textwerkstatt, Berlin, Samantha Riffle, Sarah Trenker, Susan Jones, Suzanne Kirkbright, Tony Halliday, Wendy Barrow

Pre-press: trans texas publishing services GmbH, Cologne

MIX
Paper from
responsible sources
FSC® C124385
www.fsc.org

# DOS AND DON'TS ☝

**Details you should know**

## DISREGARD LAWS: ANTIQUES OR ANTIQUITIES

As a rule, nobody may export antiquities, old icons and similar historical treasures, unless special approval has been obtained. As in Greece, it is punishable to pick up stones or to dig at places of antiquity. In Turkey, guileless and unsuspecting tourists who have appropriated or "pocketed" any lovely stone(s) may be charged or indicted with criminal offences and could face court trials and very stiff fines.

## INAPPROPRIATE ATTIRE

In the holiday destinations and tourist regions, local people are generally used to light summer attire. Especially in Turkey and the North African countries, women should dress modestly when leaving the tourist areas in order to protect themselves from unwelcome advances.

## DISRESPECTFUL IN CHURCHES AND MOSQUES

In Mediterranean countries, the Catholic and/or Muslim religions are widely observed and religious faith is an important component of most people's lives. When visiting churches, mosques, and any place of religious worship, you should always show respect towards worshippers and people engaged in prayers. Refrain from photographing and talking. Do not wear open-shoulder attire, shorts and minis. Do not disturb any religious service; rather wait until the end before entering. You have to take off your shoes before entering a mosque.

## PHOTOGRAPHING EVERYTHING

Everybody will appreciate your wish to capture as many travel memories as possible on photos and videos. Nevertheless, you should be considerate and first request people's permission if you wish to take a photo/video of them. A friendly smile is often very helpful! Always accept and heed a no-answer. Photographing/videoing of military installations is strictly forbidden.

## BE ROBBED

In places where many crowds throng and bustle, you should always have an eye on your valuables. In cities, you should be particularly alert and take care to protect your valuables. When browsing or strolling, you should wear your handbag and camera to the side of the buildings, never towards the street side. Chest pockets, belt bags or fanny packs are more secure for stowing your cash, credit cards, passports and identity documents.

## BUYING EXOTIC SOUVENIRS

Do not get involved in any tortoise/turtle-shell products, as offered in Malta for instance. Countries that adhere to the Convention on International Trade in Endangered Species of Wild Fauna and Flora (Cites) ban the import of such products, including ivory, taxidermy, stuffed reptiles, amphibians, fish and birds. Currently, more than 180 countries are contracting parties to Cites, including Tunisia, Morocco, Egypt, Malta, the USA, Canada, the UK and Australia (www.cites.org).